INTELLIGENT MARKETING for

EMPLOYMENT LAWYERS

How to Boost your Profits in a Recession

DANIEL BARNETT and EUGENIE VERNEY

ELS Publishing
Employment Law Services Ltd
Chequers Farm
Chequers Lane
Watford
Herts W07 7BH
Company no.: 4067549

ISBN 9780955388613

A Cataloguing-in-Publication (CIP) catalogue record for this book
is available from the British Library.

Typeset in 12pt Sabon by Troubador Publishing Ltd, Leicester, UK

Printed in Great Britain by the MPG Books Group, Bodmin and King's Lynn

Contents

Acknowledgements

We first and foremost thank all those who so generously gave up their time to be interviewed for the profiles we feature in this book. In alphabetical order: Alain Cohen, Mark Ellis, Robin Fawsett, Ronnie Fox, Darren Maw, Dean Morris, Mirella Sikorski, and Tom Walker. Their contributions have ensured that this book is informed by what's happening in the real world and their insight has been enlightening and invaluable.

Some other individuals need special mention. Doug Armstrong of Domeweb helped make search engine optimisation accessible to mere mortals like us. The team at Blue Planet Internet deserve huge plaudits for their fabulous web design. British marketing guru Chris Cardell, as well as US internet marketing geniuses Alex Mandossian, Rick Raddatz, and Armand Morin, were the initial inspiration for us to write this book —we believe the first in the UK—which turns away from traditional methods of marketing and focuses on innovative and modern techniques.

Eugenie Verney would like to thank Alison Stenhouse for highlighting one or two dispensable flights of fancy; Rod Caird for always saying the right things at the right times; Jude and Steve Barker for their unwavering lifetime's support; Sir Tim Berners-Lee for gifting us all the world wide web; and above all Claire Buchan for being an extraordinarily patient, generous and understanding daughter.

Daniel Barnett would like to thank his friend and business partner, barrister Tim Kevan, as well as Garry Wright, James Arney, Neil Russell, Marc Jones, Tracey Cowell, Grace Bays and Jo Pye. A massive thank you to the clerks and fellow barristers at 1 Temple Gardens who put up with my shameless self-promotion with tolerance and good humour. Thank you to my parents for their love and support. Finally, and most importantly, my love and gratitude go, as always, to my wife Miranda and children Tabitha, Cressida and Rufus.

Introduction

The challenges of a double whammy

You would need to have been on secondment to another planet not to know that the UK's legal profession is at a challenging crossroads. Not only are there the uncharted waters of the Legal Services Act 2007 to navigate, but we're now in the middle of a full-blown recession. This double whammy will inevitably leave casualties in its wake.

The good news, however, is that while employment law is a prime alternative business structures target, as a source of income it's significantly less likely to be a major casualty of a recession than some others. Indeed, there is scope for fresh work as businesses consolidate, merge and restructure to accommodate the new economic climate. They may cut back in some areas of their spending with you, but they will have no option but to be properly advised in others. So while the next few years are unlikely to be easy for anyone—and many law firms are already downsizing—those prepared to spend time consolidating existing income streams, identifying new markets, breaking with tradition and standing out from the crowd will be the ones most likely to emerge in good shape.

The Chartered Institute of Marketing defines marketing as "the management process responsible for identifying, anticipating and satisfying customer/client requirements profitably". Throughout this book, you'll find out how to keep your existing clients while attracting new ones by putting in place a cost-effective, imaginative marketing strategy that involves both traditional and cutting-edge elements and focuses on building fruitful relationships. Mindful that you may have to fight hard to hang on to your marketing budget, we'll highlight low-investment marketing tools particularly suited to a tough economic climate.

To add perspective and context, we'll reveal what some of the UK's most innovative employment law specialists are doing to meet the coming challenges, profiling seven firms: Ashby Cohen, Colemans-ctts, Ellis Whittam, Fox Lawyers, Lewis Silkin, Morris Legal, and Vista. We'll also give you the view from across the Atlantic with a profile of leading Florida practice Shutts & Bowen LLP. You'll find all eight profiles at the start of Part 1, and you'll also find tips from all these firms on what has (and hasn't) worked for them punctuating the book.

This book is not all theory—wherever you see an Action heading in the text, you'll get the chance to test our ideas and apply them immediately in very straightforward and practical ways, to give your firm's marketing an instant kick-start. To get the maximum benefit, we suggest you make a firm commitment to completing the exercises in Chapters 1–5 sequentially. Thereafter, while it's not absolutely crucial that you finish one before tackling another—or indeed complete them all—you will get a great deal more out of this book if you do!

An extensive Resources section is linked chronologically to each chapter. It provides details of the sources we reference in the main text, and a wealth of other information and ideas. A PDF of the Resources section is available on the book's website, from where you can click straight through to the online resources we recommend:

www.intelligentmarketingforemploymentlawyers.co.uk/resources.pdf

Our role in this book is to show you what is possible. We obviously can't guarantee you success. However, we are confident that if you adopt all— or even some—of our marketing ideas, not only will you be in a much stronger position to take on the new ABS opposition in 2011, you will also have the tools to help get your employment law practice profitably through the recession in the short term, and to lay the groundwork for solid, dependable growth in the long term.

Daniel Barnett and Eugenie Verney

Firm profiles

Standing out from the crowd: what makes our firms different

How do some of the UK's most innovative employment law firms take their message to their clients? And who are those customers—which niches do they fill? Here we explore what drives seven highly successful businesses and what sets them apart. We also cross the Atlantic for the view from inside a leading US labour and employment law attorney's office. The firms are profiled in alphabetical order.

Ashby Cohen, London

"Somebody who wants an employment lawyer is going to Google for one".

The seeds of solicitor Alain Cohen's niche practice were sown in 1999 when he was kicking his heels after selling a successful manufacturing business and moving to London from his native Manchester. "I had nothing to do and was bored for a few months, and then I saw a newspaper article saying that the limits for compensation for employment tribunals had been increased from £12,000 to £50,000. I thought, 'Ah ha! There could be something here'." London solicitor Paul Samuel agreed and together they set up employment law specialist Ashby Cohen. "Because personal injury had developed on a basic no-win, no-fee deal arrangement, we thought, 'Why not copy that in the employment field?'" said Cohen. "The 'Ashby' was made up", he added. "It just balanced well with Cohen."

They spent a year in Victoria before moving to their present offices in the heart of London's West End. The team has now grown to seven—five solicitors there and one apiece in London's St Paul's and Manchester. These offices opened in the last 18 months and are located within another law firm. "We share premises and act as their employment department", said Cohen, who is pioneering this business model. "They get a contribution towards their overheads, a profit share in the joint venture, and they've got a specialised department that's cost them peanuts to set up." Another office in Leeds is in the pipeline, and if Cohen had unlimited funds he'd open up across the country. Why? "Because our business is very much location-based. I'd say around 85 per cent of our clients come from within a mile of the office."

Cohen's vision of a nationwide network seems at first glance somewhat counter-intuitive, given that virtually all his business is now driven through the internet. But the statistics don't lie. Cohen is a past master at monitoring exactly what work is coming from where, testing different marketing tools, and ditching those that don't work. His business is almost all one-offs, and the practice therefore needs a constant flow of new work. "Here you're dealing with a firm that has no clients", he says. "Our business is 90 per cent individuals, 10 per cent small companies, and our main clients are senior executives—middle-management upwards."

And they find him online. "In February 2006, I switched all our marketing emphasis onto internet marketing. Google was really going places by then, and I thought, 'Somebody who wants an employment solicitor is going to Google for one, so that's what we've got to do'." Cohen has become an expert in the use of AdWords. Google "employment solicitor" and Ashby Cohen will consistently come up near the top in the right hand column. In the last year he hired a specialist to boost his left-hand side position through search engine optimisation. "I couldn't work out how to do it— we weren't even on the horizon. Now we're often on the second page, sometimes the first." His website's overriding function is to prompt visitors to phone, and he actively discourages email inquiries. "We find it far more time-consuming to deal with an email than a quick phone call— and you can judge the person better."

Cohen—who logs the source of every call—is constantly vigilant, and aware that his website needs regularly refreshing. "Our original concept was to keep it simple and just give them enough information to make that call, but it may be that people now want more." He has already seen more than once how what appears to be a winning formula can lose its punch. "When we started, all our business came from ads in the *Evening Standard*. We'd get 35 to 40 calls per advert and pick up one or two cases. Then it started diminishing and by the time we stopped advertising in 2003, we were getting ten to twelve calls and picking up nothing." His experience with poster advertising was similar: "We used posters at Underground stations and at Liverpool Street railway station. They were very effective for the first twelve months, less effective for the second year, and non-effective the third."

A key marketing tool is a free initial telephone consultation. "I haven't seen many do that", says Cohen. He also aims to make the firm accessible for prospective clients. "We're open to arrangements that make sense to the client. Funnily enough, we do very little no-win, no-fee now—our business has moved on." And he's careful to discourage anyone without legal cover who clearly will struggle to pay. "We tell them we're going to be too expensive for them. Even if they want to pay, we decline."

Ashby Cohen gets some work through referrals, mainly from other law firms and primarily from big City practices with a corporate client base. "If one of their companies is getting rid of an executive, they'll say, 'these guys will look after you'."

For Cohen, the Legal Services Act presents an opportunity, not a threat. "It means you can bring in outside investors, and that would allow us to expand with capital which I suspect the banks won't be prepared to hand over easily in the coming period", he says, before comparing the 21st century marketplace to how it was when he qualified in 1973. "I set up on my own as a sole practitioner and my 'marketing tool' was to make the gold lettering on my windows a little bigger than normal. I got a letter from the local Law Society telling me to go back to the normal size as this was unfair competition. Then a year later, I began opening on Saturday mornings and got another letter telling me this was unfair competition. I wrote back, saying I came in on Saturdays because it was the only time a lot of my clients could see me—and I was minded to open on Sunday too. I never heard from the Law Society again.

"For lawyers of my age, there was no marketing—your gold lettering and a little brass plaque was the extent of it. You weren't allowed to market – you'd be struck off."

His stint in industry was an eye-opener. "There were no restrictions, no Law Society breathing down your neck telling you you're a bad boy, and so you tended to have wider vision." And this broader understanding of commerce underpins how Cohen runs his business today. As he puts it: "We're a quality employment law firm, but ours is a business entirely driven by marketing."

Colemans-ctts, Kingston upon Thames

"The real sign of success is when you're in with the operations director".

Solicitor Tom Walker chose employment law for one main reason: "We deal with people and their disputes—our commodity is people. But the really great thing is that you're not just stuck with Mrs Jones's problems at 33 Acacia Avenue. You're in the big commercial world as well—a foot in both camps."

Walker joined Holborn firm Manches as head of employment law at the end of 2008 after building up a successful practice group in the same role at Colemans-ctts (the name derives from a series of mergers), which has 255 staff based in offices across the south-east, in Walsall, and in Manchester. Before that he was with another south-east firm, Brachers, and very early in his career was seconded to a team based in Paris, but litigating at the International Court of Justice at The Hague. This was while he was working for Frere Cholmeley, and the case—heard in 1994—arose from a conflict between Iran and the US. "Our primary sources were newspapers and journals from the time. It was what law should be."

During his time at Colemans-ctts, Walker was based in Kingston, Surrey. "I was in the commercial block—commercial law, civil litigation, debt collection, employment. There are very strong roots in the firm—it's one of the leaders in the field in insurance law and has been expanding commercially in the last five years. I inherited a small insurance employment law practice and built it up into a commercial one." The work generally flowed first to him and he would then delegate it to his colleagues in Manchester and Kingston, one of whom, Lorna Valcin, has now taken over as department head. Two types of client dominate, and the split is roughly 50–50. "One is the traditional client I inherited, the insurance firm where Colemans-ctts is on their panel. There are several of those, and my team managed to expand and grow that area. Then there is the quality commercial client—and they're important for two reasons. First, you get the quality work from them, and second it's the word of mouth thing. If you do good work for big names in your geographical area, your reputation spreads."

Walker believes strongly in word of mouth. Indeed, for him, it is the most important marketing tool. "Most commercial clients come to me that way, through referrals. I don't know the exact proportion, but it's the majority. A typical phone call is, 'Hi, do you know Jane Smith at XYZ Ltd? I'm an old friend of hers and I'm the financial director of ABC Ltd'." While he was with Colemans-ctts, around 70 per cent of Walker's work was commercial. "It's the non-contentious side I greatly enjoy, the advising. If an operations or financial director comes up to me and says, 'Tom, this is what we need to do', I'm still surprised by how many lawyers will reply, 'Ooh, that's illegal—you can't do this, you can't do that'. I say, 'Yes, you can do it—this is how we do it'. I'll always be positive. To me the real sign of success is when you're not just in with the HR director, but you're also in with the operations director. Then it shows the movers and shakers are with you."

And it's this attitude Walker believes will be necessary to address the changes flowing from ABS. "It is a challenge. Everything has to adapt, and you could go back thirty years when everyone sat in oak-panelled rooms, never left the office and just billed clients without explaining why." The firm's greatest competition currently comes from other solicitor practices. "If five or six around Kingston closed down, Colemans-ctts would double their income. If another five or six opened next door, the firm would have to fight. In the long term though it is HR insurance-based companies, for example Peninsula—that is the challenge that's coming. At Colemans-ctts, they're not putting up any artificial barriers on the basis of 'We can't do that because...', and I still believe that high-quality accessible legal advice will carry you through."

It's this that Walker believes Colemans-ctts has got right. "While they do a lot of insurance work, they're high quality. It's not just a case of, 'Ooh, I'd better phone a barrister—I don't know what that means'."

Colemans-ctts has a small in-house marketing team, but for Walker personally the key has always been personal relationships, and the seminar is his favoured way of growing business. While he was with Colemans-ctts, he would also host one or two lectures a year. "These were to update people on hot topics and offer guidance, but I prefer seminars. With existing clients or potential clients you can say, 'Can I come to your offices, sit around the table with your HR team and your managers?' That way they don't have to put any effort into it—just turn up and sit down. And there's feedback, whereas there often isn't any at lectures."

He ran two types of seminar: one packaged for the HR team—"TUPE is a classic example"— and the other more focused on training and directed at line management. He agrees that this type of non-contentious work straddles the border between employment law and HR. "Yes it does, but it's basically standing up as a lawyer and saying, 'This is the law but this is what you do'.

He also runs equal opportunities training: "I quite enjoy the laddish attitude that sometimes comes back. 'They all find it funny'—well, do they? 'If you find it funny, well great, but try saying that in the witness box. Are you sure the tribunal will find it funny as well?'"

Walker never actively sought feedback from his Colemans-ctts clients. "I'd like to think my relationships were so good that I'd hear about any blips or pluses immediately. I do not need a form. Maybe that's arrogance, but the whole style I've built up doesn't need a formal structure."

The firm's website echoes this emphasis on the personal, featuring branding that declares "We're people too." Walker remains a fan. "I'm a lawyer who enjoys my subject, so I like to meet clients and say, 'Wow, look at this!' I'm not teaching them, but discussing it with them and that's really how I operate. Too many lawyers had—and still have—this reputation for high and mighty arrogance. At the end of the day, we're approachable, accessible human beings. If I'm dealing with a client on a tight, tight deadline and I've got to go and pick up my daughter, sometimes I'll just say that and they'll say, 'Oh, my daughter's three—where's yours? At nursery?' And then suddenly two humans start talking, rather than lawyer and client."

Ellis Whittam, Chester

> *"I'm more willing to take risks and more naturally inclined to try doing things differently".*

For Mark Ellis, the traditional solicitor partnership structure was simply the wrong model for success. "I had a drive to be my own boss and create a tangible asset, which I couldn't do in a law firm. I think one of the problems that hold many of them back in terms of their business development and marketing is the model itself—a partnership." So Ellis turned his back on a successful career as an equity partner at Chester firm Aaron and Partners—where he had set up the ten-strong employment team he led for eight years—and started all over again.

That was five years ago and he has since proved his point. He describes Ellis Whittam as a regulatory consultancy, a limited company providing employment law support services to employers—and only employers—across the UK. Ellis is the majority shareholder, the CEO and very much the boss. (The "Whittam" half of the name derives from former managing director Chris Whittam, who has since moved on.) "We have getting on for a thousand active clients. The rate of growth is high and increasing—between 50 per cent and 65 per cent year on year—which is much higher than a traditional law firm." Among his clients are a cathedral, a City of London gentlemen's club, a Premier Division football club, and some of the business interests of two of the dragons from BBC2's Dragon's Den. "It's a very wide and interesting mix", says Ellis, who directly employs 60 people at his offices in a converted country house near Chester. Of his client advisors, 80 per cent are non-practising solicitors. "The niche Ellis Whittam has tried to fill is to provide a fixed-fee service that matches or betters the quality of service provided by a leading firm of commercial lawyers but which takes the entrepreneurial facets and bells and whistles of the likes of Peninsula. Each of our clients has a dedicated advisor—there's no call centre—and that person builds rapport in the same way they would in private practice."

That Ellis has followed this route is perhaps not entirely surprising: before taking his law finals, he completed the Chartered Institute of Marketing post-graduate course and spent two years working for a marketing consultancy. "It was a really great way to learn about how business works and how to develop and grow a business." He followed this with starting a cosmetics business with two friends, while he was a trainee. "I'd pop from the law firm to the rented office across the road, and that was fascinating—for a trainee solicitor to be literally looking after the cash flow of a business, selling the products, going to exhibitions. A great learning curve. I suppose it means I'm more willing to take risks and more naturally inclined to try to do things differently. It's just raw exposure to the difficulties of running a business, which of course most solicitors don't have and most marketing people working for solicitors don't have."

Around the same time, he had chosen employment law as his niche. "I decided to specialise early on, during my training, as I thought it was interesting and fast-moving and earthy and profitable. And it didn't send me to sleep, whereas sitting doing conveyancing did. Employment law was real people and real problems and was much more appealing."

With Ellis Whittam, he has further honed his niche, offering employers a fixed-fee, insurance-backed employment law, HR and health and safety support service. "We are an outsourcing solution. We say to employers, 'Why go to a traditional law firm for your employment law and HR support? Why not come to us instead, and for a fixed fee?'" Central to the model is behind-the-scenes legal expenses insurance which makes it possible for Ellis to tell prospective clients that should they lose a tribunal claim they will not have to pay legal fees or any award made against them.

The firm has clients right across the UK—from Scotland to Cornwall—with the biggest clusters in the Midlands and south-east. "That's where we've been more active and perhaps more effective", says Ellis. He uses a very traditional marketing approach, with a team comprising 15 telesales executives (he calls them business development executives) who work on a ratio of two to one business manager. "The job of the business development executive is to put an appointment in the diary of the business manager, and the job of the business manager is to go out and write new business. We cover the whole of the UK—there is no area they don't reach. And it works. If I was the CEO of a traditional practice, I would be saying—and despite the cries of horror and shame from my partners—we should look at this model."

Ellis Whittam's main competitors are the big regulatory consultancies like Peninsula and Croner, but they're not the only ones. "You've also got your local firm of solicitors in every town in the country that's been looking after the business of ABC Ltd for the past five years. Each of our business managers knows how to distinguish our USPs [unique selling propositions] as compared to a regulatory consultancy competitor or a solicitor competitor."

Among those USPs is a solid commitment to quality service and customer care". It's too easy in this business to put up barriers. We recognise that we will only be successful if we offer clients solutions, so we have to take a bit of a risk sometimes. We can't just say 'no' or 'don't dismiss', we have to be practical and pragmatic. And we have a full-time accounts manager whose role is to call all our clients three times a year to check our database is up to date, to make sure they're happy. Our business managers see every client at least once a year for a face-to-face to pick up on grumbles or gain referrals."

Ellis is already developing the business beyond the original core services, and offers clients an online absence management and office control package. He is working with other providers to supply further add-ons, including recruitment and talent management, flexible benefits, occupational health support, and commercial legal services. As part of all packages, clients get a steady flow of information and updates, and full access, via the Ellis Whittam website, to all their documents. "They can look right into our server and see their client file."

The recession is opening new doors. "We see it as an opportunity to win more work from the traditional business sector", says Ellis. "I anticipate a significant increase in income, and we're recruiting hard at the moment—in fact, I'm looking for employment lawyers right now."

Fox Lawyers, London

"I've got a bit of a problem—only 24 hours in the day!"

When *The Times* described Ronnie Fox as "the doyen of employment lawyers" in an item about bankers' bonuses, he speculated rhetorically: "How much would it cost to get *The Times* to say that?" And then added: "Well, actually you couldn't buy it." Fox—principal of the boutique City employment and partnership law practice bearing his name—has over a long and distinguished career made friends with the media and understands better than most how to generate positive PR.

Fox spent the first 20 years of his career as a corporate transactional lawyer before going it alone. He and Tina Williams formed Fox Williams in 1989 and Fox switched his professional focus. "To manage the firm effectively required a time commitment. I couldn't also set aside four or six weeks for one deal, as you have to on a big merger or acquisition", he said. "So I thought I'd develop my sideline in golden handshake work, and that sideline grew to be a big employment practice." He and Williams parted company more than 15 years later, leaving Fox at a crossroads. "Am I going to retire? Should I join another firm? Am I going to do something completely different? Why, when I enjoy what I do? Then I asked myself, 'What was the most fun I've had in my career?' The first few years after setting up Fox Williams was the most enjoyable time. So I thought, 'I could do that again!'"

And so he did, taking with him key Fox Williams' legal and support staff colleagues, and he opened for business as Fox from offices in Cornhill in May 2006. It was at this point that Fox called in the PR professionals. "Fox Williams had declined to change their name, and I needed people to know that I was no longer there. To do that quickly, I needed professional help." He has been working with Lehmann Communications ever since—they were, for example, responsible for generating *The Times* item. "We toss ideas back and forth. They come to me, and I go to them." Not that Fox is ever short of attention-grabbing ideas: following a chance conversation he found himself test-driving a Sherman tank in his capacity as motoring correspondent of *City Solicitor*, the City of London Solicitors' Company newsletter. The story, with photo, was picked up by the *Law Society Gazette* and then by *The Times*. "I discovered that almost nobody had heard of the Tank Museum. I told them, 'You need to raise your profile', and said I'd write an article if I could test-drive a tank."

Great publicity for Fox, great publicity for his business, but there's more to it than that: "Look carefully at those stories—they're about the museum, not just about me", said Fox, who has since joined the museum's appeal board. "You've got to assume we're only going to have one life and during that life, you have to add something to the community, make a living and have some fun."

This ethos has for years underwritten much of what Fox does outside office hours. Attending International Bar Association annual meetings is a particular highlight. "You can genuinely be friends with people you see three days a year—and I have also come back with work. Once from somebody I shared a taxi with, and another time from a guy I met at a cocktail party. We swapped Christmas cards, and seven years later, his brother rang me and said, 'You met my brother and he's mentioned your name....'"

Fox is currently chair of the IBA Senior Lawyers Committee. He also wears the City of London Solicitors' Company award for distinguished service, and is particularly proud of his role in the multidiscipline Association of Partnership Practitioners (APP), which he founded in 1998. "Before the APP, partnership was hardly recognised as an area of expertise. I think I helped secure recognition."

Fox's high personal profile and professional track record explain why his practice has achieved so much so quickly—he has recently expanded both his legal complement and his office space—and he deliberately focuses his marketing attention on precisely this: reputation and what he calls "the comfort factor". He compares the process to choosing a restaurant. First you ask a friend for a recommendation, then seek a second opinion, then visit the website. "So someone will ask, 'You were sacked and you went to Ronnie Fox. How did you get on?' Then they'll get comfort from the fact that the guides say very nice things about us, and that the vast majority of clients say positive things too." The next stage he likens to the doctrine of precedent. "That's part of the way we sell ourselves. You tell me you've just had a row with the head of the hedge fund who says you haven't been performing, and I tell you, 'Well, actually, I've got three other cases on my book just like that'. That's partly comfort factor, but mainly the fact that I've got the relevant experience and expertise."

At any one time, Fox has around 50 clients on his books, 60 to 70 per cent of them one-offs. Of these, a minority are companies and most are very senior City employees. "We only take people whose compensation is in excess of six figures—preferably well in excess, because otherwise our overhead structure makes it very difficult to work cost-effectively." Right at the outset, Fox is upfront about his fees and how he works. "I do this before I've done any work because that's what I would want if I was a client. I test whether their objectives are realistic and how much it would cost to achieve them." And in response to feedback, he goes further and discusses third party funding, after-the-event insurance, and conditional fees. "That's because clients have said, 'Well, I wish I'd known about this'. So I now make a point of discussing it at that initial meeting."

Problems caused by the recession are keeping Fox busy. "My practice is counter-cyclical. The economy is in for a rough ride, the country is in for a rough ride, and that will create more work for me. My target is a new job every working day—I achieved that for a number of years at Fox Williams and I'm achieving it now."

And at an age when many might contemplate slowing down, Fox is as focused and busy as ever—in the office, and out of it. "I've got a bit of a problem", he said. "Only 24 hours in the day! It's one of the ways in which we're all equal—we all have 24 hours. The difference is in what we do with them."

Lewis Silkin, London

"Everyone's energy is focused on HR rather than the next major transaction".

Employment work brings in more than a third of high-profile London practice Lewis Silkin's business and is accordingly the focus of a significant marketing effort. "In many big firms, employment would only be a small part of the business, but here it's a significant part of the business", says Mirella Sikorski, who supports the employment practice on a range of business development and marketing initiatives.

Sikorski has been with Lewis Silkin since early 2007 after working first as a fashion industry merchandiser and then in business development and communications at KPMG. Next came three years at an international investment bank where she brought together different marketing strands under one umbrella, followed by several years within other legal firms. Her main area of responsibility is marketing Lewis Silkin's extensive employment law portfolio—that takes up 90 per cent of her time— together with the sports group, a multidisciplinary team of lawyers focusing on the sports industry. And there is significant cross-fertilisation: "Our good credentials within the sports sector is in part due to the employment law work we do with sports clients."

Lewis Silkin has a novel marketing approach. "We are much more creative than a lot of legal firm marketing departments, and we think it sets us apart. We have a strategy that focuses on three areas: mediascape, landscape, and peoplescape, which is anything to do with people, including employment law. Landscape covers property, construction, the housing sector, and mediascape anything to do with the creative industries—advertising, media and so on."

Unusually for a firm of its stature, 20 per cent of Lewis Silkin's employment business comes from employees. "We believe this makes us better lawyers as we see both sides of the fence," Sikorski says.

The department is big. "There are 57 employment lawyers, and the team is growing. We really do have strength in breadth, strength in depth, and we're able to serve a client at all levels. We have people with 30 years' qualified experience and people with three. We have people who, for example, specialise in trade unions, specialist immigration lawyers, specialist incentive lawyers, TUPE specialists. Discrimination law is a particular strength— particularly age discrimination. We'll give each client a team, but if there was an issue involving High Court litigation, say, then we have a specialist we can bring in."

One key sector specialism is work from other law firms: "We are the lawyers' lawyer—we have a really good portfolio of law firms where we do their HR work for them and advise on partnership issues." The team won *The Lawyer* Employment Team of the Year award in 2008, in part for successfully defending solicitors Freshfields against former partner Peter Bloxham's age discrimination claim.

What particularly distinguishes Lewis Silkin from the Magic Circle firms is the employment/corporate law ratio. "They all have big corporate departments and the role of their employment teams is to support them. We do corporate support work but it's not the main driver of our business. Everyone's energy is focused on HR issues and providing the HR teams with a comprehensive service rather than supporting the next major transaction." From this flows a commitment to simple communications. "We really don't speak legalese", says Sikorski. "And we don't sit on the fence—from the team's experience, we can say, 'You should do this because...' Our biggest audience is HR people and in-house employment lawyers, plus financial directors and managing directors...." She adds: "When we talk to a potential client, we make sure we really understand their business and anticipate their needs."

The firm is a member of the international Ius Laboris alliance, the only UK firm represented apart from pension law specialist Sacker and Partners. "We believe this is the leading alliance that concentrates on employment law and our membership of it is increasingly attracting international new business." Membership gives Lewis Silkin the edge over Magic Circle firms, even those with a large overseas presence, says Sikorski. "Although they may have offices all around the world, do they necessarily have the best employment lawyers in those offices? They might have one or two employment lawyers in an office while we know that Ius Laboris member firms have leading employment law practices in their country. Our alliance partners also have large teams like us, so there is strength across the board. It allows us to have one project manager in the lead country supported by a team of lawyers with excellent reputations in every jurisdiction. We see that as a real selling point."

The firm's main competition comes from other practitioners, says Sikorski, "mainly London-based and international". She and her colleagues carefully monitor these rivals. "The people who know most about what the competitors are doing are the lawyers themselves who either have friends at these firms or come into contact with them on cases. From a marketing communications point of view, we monitor the competition through desk research. I also have a good network of friends in many major law firms so we get to know a little bit about what each other is up to."

She adds: "We aim to be the best through the strength of the team. For example, we feel we are most effective face-to-face and one-to-one and can demonstrate this best through the proposal process. When we talk to a potential client, unlike some firms, we make sure we're focused on their issues rather than trying to sell them the latest 'hot product'."

Sikorski and her colleagues use an array of marketing methods, both online and offline, but there's one that consistently stands out. "The most effective marketing tool for both existing and prospective clients is simply picking up the phone and speaking to them. Most lawyers prefer email, but that's second best. Sending someone an email and expecting them to click on it and respond is less effective than speaking to them. With email, you just have to hope they haven't got that much in their inbox that day!"

Following directly from that, if she could wave a magic wand she would buy her lawyer colleagues extra hours in the day. "The one thing I'd like most costs time, not money. I'd like to see our teams spend more time building relationships and building on personal contacts. Ideally we should always focus time on doing more of what we already do so well."

Morris Legal, West Midlands

"The need to have your client sat in front of your big desk has just gone".

Sole practitioner Dean Morris is the man behind the website with arguably the most memorable branding in the online employment law marketplace, **www.got-the-boot.com**. And his clients and competitors generally agree. "I am often told by clients and other solicitors, 'What a great name!'", he says. "It's novel and unique. It immediately explains what the site is about without any need to read any further." This, and the innovative website design that underpins it, drives Morris's business, which—as the name suggests—is focused almost exclusively on claimant work. It was the obvious route for him to take when he decided to go it alone: he has been specialising in contentious employment law since 1996 after gaining general post-qualification experience in civil litigation. "Contentious employment law seemed a natural specialisation from a civil litigation base."

Morris has been trading as Morris Legal since May 2006, re-launching **www.got-the-boot.com** at the outset and adding a PI site—**www.not-my-fault.com**—in 2008. He chose the online route coupled with a no-win, no-fee contingency fee model to give him a good work/life balance that accommodates his young family. "Today the vast majority of people have access to the internet. This allows the website to be a source of information to them day or night, and therefore a source of potential clients 24/7. Modern communications such as email, scanning and video conferencing limit the need to meet the client to the rare complex cases. And 70 per cent of cases settle in any event."

Morris has also reduced his overheads hugely. "I have an office at home and a virtual office half a mile down the road, so if I do need to see any clients I see them there. All the calls are handled by an answering service. It's a very economical way of achieving the end result."

One of Morris's key selling points is providing a service that extends far beyond his West Midlands base, and no one area brings in significantly more work than another. "The full geographical coverage offered on the website is largely because I'm prepared to cover an area from Aberdeen to Southampton, over to Cardiff and Belfast. Sometimes I can be in Kent, or in Bristol, Nottingham, Leicester or Glasgow." He also works with other solicitor practices, sharing around 5 per cent of work the site generates that does not match his business model or brings with it an excessive workload. "These other firms are not necessarily located where the clients are, but they are also prepared to travel." And just as there is no geographical bias among his clients, neither is there an age bias, perhaps surprisingly given that they overwhelmingly arrive via the web. "They're an absolutely broad spread, right up to retirement age, and I think that says a lot about the acceleration of broadband and everything else online." Nor is there a typical got-the-boot.com claimant: "We've had £200,000-a-year execs and completely the opposite end. Probably more blue-collar claimants than white-collar—if you look across the board, there's probably a 60/40 split. But I don't think that's to do with the site—the captive audience is out there in that proportion."

The got-the-boot.com website generates about ten inquiries a day. "If I convert a couple of those, as a minimum, I'm quite happy. The weekends can generate more", Morris says. Prospective clients complete a detailed online form designed to capture key information. "Most people fill it in fairly fully, and they can attach documents to it. As soon as a form comes through, I will try to go through it. If I can be on the phone within 15 minutes or sooner after they've sent it saying I've read it, they'll say to me, 'My God, that was quick!' That creates a very good first impression. Once you've captured them at the very beginning, then you have every chance of successfully converting them into a client."

Morris drives traffic to his website through optimising his website (Google "employment law solicitors" and got-the-boot.com routinely comes up in second place on page one) and using Yahoo! pay per click (more about this in Chapter 15). He monitors his PPC traffic but not, so far, traffic generated organically. "I don't have the software, and that's something I'm almost certainly going to get." Unlike many competitors, he offers visitors an array of very detailed guidance. "If anything, I give them too much, so that they go, 'Oh my God! This is really potentially more complicated than I thought—maybe we do need a lawyer'. Experience tells me that people do actually look at it. Are we more likely to get the client to make an inquiry having given them all that information? Who knows?"

Competition comes from small to mid-tier solicitor practices and from non-solicitor employment law advisors, whom Morris in general gives short shrift. "They are largely unqualified and unregulated, save for the minimal requirements imposed by the Claims Management Regulations. I don't believe they generally offer the public the quality of expertise they deserve and they should be subject to much tighter regulation or barred from representing claimants in tribunal proceedings."

He monitors all his competitors closely—"I have found that some have taken parts of my website and used it with little or no alteration"—and now sees a new trend emerging. "The waters—as it was with PI—are becoming infested with the claims management companies jumping in. They only have a market because the legal profession's general back-seat approach to proactive marketing means they'd rather pay a claims management company a cut of their profit costs or a fee than actually deal with the cutting-edge, lead-gathering methods and marketing themselves. Claims management companies are generally wide boys—they're only after one thing and that's not necessarily in the potential client's best interests in terms of the choice of lawyer who ultimately ends up acting for them."

Morris is, however, confident that the niche he has carved out for got-the-boot.com will continue to remain highly competitive, and that not-my-fault.com will also begin to produce a steady income stream. "It works differently from got-the-boot only in that I don't do any of the work—that's passed on, and it's purely a lead generation tool. If I get three referrals a month, or even a couple of referrals, by having something slightly different from the big players, it pays for itself. I'm prepared to let it sit there for the next year or so and let it make its way up through the search engine rankings."

And for Morris, there is no argument: he is completely persuaded that online law is the future. "The need to have your client sat in front of your big desk has just gone."

Shutts & Bowen LLP, Orlando, Florida

"Our job is to be there for clients and to help them, to make things easy for them".

Orlando attorney Charles Robinson—Robin—Fawsett is one of Florida's employment law big hitters. A senior partner with full-service commercial firm Shutts & Bowen LLP, he jointly heads a ten-strong practice group that numbers among its clients some of the State's largest employers, including, according to court records, Disney. "I've always represented employers—private sector and public sector", he says. "I've never represented an employee and I've never represented a labour union—and I never will. It's unheard of for any reputable lawyer in America to represent unions and management."

For Fawsett, though, this goes beyond a pragmatic professional choice: "To represent management effectively you do have to be somewhat conservative. You have to understand that management creates the jobs, takes the risk, spends the money, takes the loss if the business doesn't work out." On an ideological level, therefore, he views with concern Barack Obama's commitment to strengthen union rights through the Employee Free Choice Act, despite the likely commercial benefits. "I am very much against it, even though it would obviously greatly expand our practice. It would be a horrible disservice to American business and to the American people, a disaster for our country."

His clear convictions date from his student days at the University of Florida College of Law, from where he graduated in 1964. He read an article by journalist Victor Reisel who had some years earlier been blinded after acid was thrown at his face, allegedly by the Teamsters Union. "But he kept on writing and he wrote this very inspiring column about how the labour movement was one of the most interesting things about America, how the whole labour scene was fascinating because it had to do with human behaviour. That inspired me, and I thought, 'Oh well, I'll become a labour lawyer'. And I knew I'd be a management labour lawyer."

Fawsett drew further inspiration from the 1957 anti-communist classic, *Atlas Shrugged*, by Russian émigré Ayn Rand. "If I had to start listing the 20 best books I've ever read, it would be up there."

Fawsett's first job was with the National Labor Relations Board, the agency regulating US workplace relations. Employment law was in its infancy then. Title VII of the Civil Rights Act of 1964 protecting against discrimination based on race, colour, religion, sex or national origin had only just reached the statute book, and the Age Discrimination in Employment Act of 1967 was yet to be passed. Nonetheless, the experience was invaluable. "I was a trial attorney there for two years and learned the most that I use in my practice now of anywhere I've been."

From there Fawsett went into private commercial practice, focusing fully on employment law from 1981 and joining Shutts & Bowen as a partner in 1985. The firm is one of Florida's oldest, founded in 1910 in Miami—where Fawsett's practice group co-chair Sheila Cesarano is based—employing more than 200 lawyers, and now with offices across the State, including in the capital, Tallahassee. "That's a lobbying office, with a Republican emphasis", Fawsett explains. The firm has a significant international practice and has at times also been represented in London and Switzerland, retaining a European presence now in Amsterdam. "This is otherwise an exclusively Florida firm. We have made an iron-clad decision not to have offices in other States. We get plenty of referrals from big cities—we don't need to have offices there, and I can do anything in the management–labour law area that somebody from New York or Atlanta can do."

The employment group represents about 5 per cent of the firm's business and covers the whole of Florida, with four lawyers based in Miami, four in Orlando, and a further two who also cover complementary practice areas. Fawsett heads up the Orlando team. "Eighty-five to ninety per cent is our work reacting to situations. That's not the way it should be—the really highest and best use of someone like me would be to prevent problems from happening before they happen. But that's just the way

American industry works." His team spends a maximum of 15 per cent of their time writing employee handbooks, shaping policies, and delivering training on core issues such as workplace harassment. "Over the years, I have spent extensive time training employers how to avoid being organised by unions. I haven't done much of that lately, but I think that's going to change." About half his time is taken up with litigation in federal and state courts. "In Florida, mediation is mandatory and most cases settle."

The majority of his clients are Florida-based, but he also represents multinationals with large Florida workforces. His favourite employers are locally-owned businesses with between 200 and 400 employees. "They listen to your advice. They don't have in-house people who think they know more than they really do. You have more direct access to the top management, and your advice doesn't have to be filtered through a lot of people."

Much of Fawsett's work comes through word of mouth and he does little active marketing himself. "Almost all of my clients heard of me from other clients. Some of them are referred by attorneys in other firms who know me and in many cases have referred to me before." He takes enormous pride in how he responds to his clients. "One thing many lawyers, including very successful ones, simply don't understand is you're providing a service at a very high rate and you can afford to be responsive, prompt, understanding of the client's problems. Our job is to be there for clients and to help them, to make things easy for them. With a new client, at the beginning of the transaction I tell them what my hourly rate is, I tell them whether any other people will be working on their matter. I assure them that once their matter is undertaken, it will not be transferred around—they won't be paying for anyone's learning curve."

Fawsett was recently named as a "Florida Super Lawyer". "It was done by peer review. I don't talk to newspapers, I don't go out of my way to promote myself, so it's kind of an honour." He has also been included in the 2009 *Best Lawyers in America* legal talent guide, further recognition of a distinguished career. Although 70 in December 2009 and the oldest Shutts & Bowen partner, he has no plans to stop working—and has no need to as the firm has no mandatory retirement age. "I'm pretty strong and active, and I'll be around for some years to come," he says, adding: "One reason I don't have to do a lot of marketing is because I don't lose clients. They keep inviting us back to the party."

Vista, Stockport

"We had to take off the pinstripes, put down the fountain pen and pick up a Biro".

Vista was set up in September 2005 by barrister Darren Maw, employment law advisor Tim Cross, and solicitor Abayomi Alemoru, who all worked together at the Engineering Employers' Federation. Their aim is to operate in innovative ways that break with tradition and, they argue, deliver greater value to their clients.

Maw, Vista's managing director, says: "The infrastructure of most small and medium-sized—and indeed bigger—commercial practices did not lend itself to what we were trying to achieve. The direct access method would not have worked properly either as you can't get involved in the 'noise' coming from HR. Most solicitor practices, and the Bar, are predicated on a reactive model and that requires the client to identify the issue on which they perceive they need advice and for them to have attached enough value to the issue to justify the cost. Here you have two clear barriers to service delivery."

Maw and his partners focus instead on what he calls "usage", working so closely with their clients that 90 per cent of their time is spent out of the office and on site with the HR teams they support. "Unlike some of our competitors we can genuinely say we understand how our clients' businesses work. That's a cliché every lawyer will try to trot out, but wherever you've got these two barriers to legal intervention you don't get involved in the 'noise'—the day-to-day issues you wouldn't dream of talking to a lawyer about unless they were sitting next to you and you were just having a coffee and saying, 'What do you think about this?', or 'You know Charlie, the site manager? You'll never guess what he's done now....' We're involved in that kind of conversation. Many of our competitors fail, I believe, because they structure a hierarchy of legal issues in the way lawyers have always done. Such as 'this is worthy of a partner', 'this is worthy of instructing counsel', 'this is a five-year PQE issue'. We move all that to one side."

Vista uses a subscription model, with no transactional cost per intervention. "The client has unlimited advice and support, but this should not be confused with a helpline—we could not do what we do from the end of a phone. I can go to a client and speak to their HR director. I know what's happening in their team—sometimes better than they do."

The Vista subscription model differs from many, however. Because the client base comprises only businesses employing 350 or more, what is of prime concern to a smaller enterprise becomes irrelevant and there is no tie-in. "If you're an SME, you may be concerned about significant liability and legal fees. One big case could put you into all sorts of financial difficulty. None of our clients are that vulnerable and once you take away that vulnerability, you take away the value of peace of mind. Our clients don't want peace of mind—they want value for money, a return on investment."

The Vista client list includes major employers such as Airbus, Colgate, Muller, and Vauxhall. "We're not interested in anything smaller because our client is the HR department and we need one that's sufficiently resourced for us to be able to add value", says Maw. "We have turned down a significant amount of work because it does not fit our client profile."

The Vista model means that the distinction between advising on legal matters and advising on managing can be difficult to define. "There is no clear dividing line. I think a good employment lawyer is part HR practitioner, and a good HR practitioner is part employment lawyer. In that grey area we are both within our area of competency, but possibly outside our comfort zone. Something that sets us apart is that we don't claim to be able to deliver answers all the time. We can deliver the legal analysis, but that isn't always the answer. So it becomes a collaborative process, an intelligent conversation between two people who haven't got the answers individually but can work out the best solution proactively." Vista does not have any direct competition, says Maw. "Nobody does what we do, but it doesn't have to be done our way. So we compete against substitutes rather than competitors, and these are established City mid- to top-tier legal practices that have blue-chip credibility. They try to appeal to our market by trying to fit their working methodology into what their client requires. We work backwards from what the client wants; they work towards it. The value is always defined by the client, not the lawyer—that's what it comes down to, whatever the market.

"Lawyers do not like innovation, but we do. When we'd just started we were at a beauty competition and the client said that our competitor had been established since 1920-odd and what did we say to that? I replied: 'How did they get around that disadvantage? Clearly they're going to be set in their ways, they'll have a lot of baggage, they're unlikely to be innovative, and they're focused on how they've always done it rather than what you do. So did they manage to persuade you notwithstanding all that that they could still do a good job?' We got the contract!

"We are absolutely not set in our ways and we don't believe we have got this right—and even if we have got it right today, it's probably going to be wrong tomorrow anyway. We're constantly looking for new ways of doing it—and because we've freed ourselves from the traditional law practice shackles we can move faster and more innovatively than any of our competitors in a market where innovation is only reluctantly accepted rather than extolled.

"Trying to fit our methodology into an existing organisation just would not have worked, which is why we set up on our own. We had to do it from scratch and that required us to take off the pinstripes, put down the fountain pen and pick up a Biro. Not all lawyers are very good at that."

What would you do if we gave you a magic wand?

We asked all our featured firms this question: "If you had a magic wand and could spend as much as you wanted on one marketing initiative, what would it be?"

Here are their replies.

"I'd open more offices."
Alain Cohen, Ashby Cohen

"I'd organise a really, really focused lecture for the business community, with other members of the firm and maybe local politicians and business groups."
Tom Walker, now with Manches but head of employment law at Colemans-ctts at the time of our interview

"A complete and accurate database of all directors and business owners with UK businesses of more than 25 employees."
Mark Ellis, Ellis Whittam

"I'd spend it on image advertising—selling the brand Fox, rather than anything specific."
Ronnie Fox, Fox Lawyers

"I'd like to see our teams spend more time building relationships and building on personal contacts."
Mirella Sikorski, Lewis Silkin

"Raising the got-the-boot.com brand profile through a concerted TV advertising campaign to get the name into the wider public domain as synonymous with being dismissed."
Dean Morris, Morris Legal

"It would be to have clients to be able to see through the advertising and hype, and tell the difference between good legal services and good lawyers and the not so good."
Robin Fawsett, Shutts & Bowen

"It would be finding somebody suitable to join us. Another lawyer to add depth to our business—I can't think of any reason to spend it any other way."
Darren Maw, Vista

PART ONE
Getting to grips with the basics

1

Why this is exactly the right time to focus on marketing

"May you live in interesting times."

This well-known phrase is reputed to be a curse of ancient Chinese origin (although in reality it's more likely to be of recent and Western origin). Certainly at the moment few would argue that as a profession we are now in decidedly choppy waters after a decade or more of stability, continued growth and an expanding marketplace.

Let's start by looking in more detail at what this and the Legal Services Act 2007—drawn up in part in response to public consultation identifying public dissatisfaction with the profession—means for lawyers, and employment lawyers in particular.

The Act breaks open the market in England and Wales, and for the first time allows non-lawyers to provide currently reserved services. (Similar legislation is to follow in Scotland.) This does not of course apply directly to employment law, but is likely to have knock-on effects right across the profession once what has been dubbed Tesco Law becomes a reality. It's a given that employment law lends itself to ABS—the evidence is out there now, and this niche has been steadily growing for at least ten years. A wide variety of organisations are already offering a mix of employment law, health and safety and HR support, either direct to the public or business-to-business (B2B), through various combinations of helplines, advice lines, online, and hands-on support, including tribunal representation. A few of the services are free; most (and almost all the B2Bs) are paid for, usually through subscription. Some are provided by legally-qualified practitioners; many are not; some teams are a mix.

If you haven't done so recently, try Googling "employment law advisor" or "employment law advice" and see just how many hits you get that are not conventional law practices. Thus far these advisors are largely independent, or loosely affiliated to other professionals such as brokers, but that is likely to change in 2011 when the market opens up. At the moment, it wouldn't be worthwhile for the likes of Tesco and, say, Direct Line, to run employment law advice services, but they well could be bundled as part of a much broader legal package.

This, then, is a glimpse into the future: potentially a lot more competition from a lot more sources. How you market your employment law practice—and how well you do it—may be central to defending your employment law fee income in what could quickly become an increasingly crowded sector. None of us can of course predict the full impact of ABS or, crucially, how deeply the economic downturn will curtail new players' plans to expand into this sector. Some will no doubt have their blueprints in place, but a lot can happen between now and 2011.

A lot can also happen in the existing marketplace between now and 2011, and although you are much better placed in a contracting economy than, say, your colleagues in conveyancing, the pressure is still on. Some clients have no doubt already scaled back, for example using fewer of your proactive services, taking work in-house, or exploring the subscription services offered by existing ABS employment law advisors, and you may already be looking for your own savings in the face of rising costs.

In many practices, the odds are that marketing will feature high on the list of expendable expenditure—possibly right near the top.

If that's your own business, congratulations! By buying and reading this book, you've taken the first step towards avoiding falling into a trap that may bring short-term savings but only at the expense of long-term profits. This is because whatever the size of your business, wherever you are located, whoever your clients are, and whatever your own role, the message is the same: drastic cuts to marketing budgets in a recession are a big mistake.

There is plenty of historical evidence to support this—indeed, there is plenty of evidence to support spending *more* on marketing during a recession. As one example, a survey by McGraw-Hill Research of B2B firms that maintained or increased their advertising spend during the 1981–1982 US recession found that their sales growth was significantly higher than for competitors who stopped advertising, or cut right back. And the effect continued once the economy had picked up again. By 1985, the first group had increased their revenue more than 2.5 times faster than the second group. Similar research results for a range of marketing methods have been recorded since 1949 during numerous downturns and subsequent upturns, including the 1991–1992 recession.

But why? It appears completely counter-intuitive, but it isn't if you think it through. If your usual rivals are hunkering down and you are not, you immediately have less competition and you can capitalise by raising your profile and seeking out the clients they are no longer directly addressing. To take just a few more traditional marketing tools as an example, it will be your advertisement these potential clients see (and it will have cost you less to place), it will be media coverage about you they'll read, and it will be your email newsletter they look at first as there will be far fewer flowing into their inboxes. As veteran American marketer Dan Kennedy says, an economic downturn, even a recession, merely presents a set of new circumstances. "There is always 'a set of circumstances' and there are always winners and losers. To complain about there being circumstances or changing circumstances is to complain about there being weather. You have to see the need for change as an exciting opportunity, not as a burden."

And you need to start seeing it right now, even if your instinct is to interject with a "But…" or an "Easier said than done…". Before you leave that Google search you made earlier, take a look at the number of solicitor practices in among the hits, including the paid for listings. These are lawyers who have recognised the power of the internet as something more than a passive shop window and are already harnessing online marketing. Theirs may not be exactly the right blueprint for you, but you ignore at your peril the seismic changes in how products and services—including yours—are increasingly perceived and purchased by those who understand how the World Wide Web has changed the rules.

The bottom line is that marketing—in all its forms—is something no lawyer can afford not to take seriously, and firms who still believe they can rely on the mantra that "we've always done it this way" are in for a nasty surprise. As with many aspects of business development, it's important to look at what's happening in the US, and there the concept of lawyer as entrepreneur is already coming of age. The marketing principle of "return on investment", the idea that lawyers from different disciplines work together as a focused team to target a prospective client (something dubbed a "wolf pack" by a leading American legal marketer, Larry Bodine), the concept of fee earners allocating a certain number of hours a week exclusively to marketing—all these and more are now widely accepted practices across the Atlantic. And that applies even in larger firms employing dedicated marketing professionals: it's increasingly just part of the job description.

Are you thinking: "Yes, but that's America—it won't happen here"? We're prepared to bet that you're wrong. Whether you're a sole practitioner with a modest practice or you work for a magic circle big hitter, how you conduct your employment law business will change in the next decade, perhaps beyond recognition.

To stay one step ahead, you first need to overcome any residual resistance you may have to marketing, in particular that anyone in your business is too important, too skilled, too expensive, too qualified to get involved in selling your services. Ultimately there are only three ways to build your business:

1.   Grow your client base.

2.   Work for them more often.

3.   Charge them more.

Our aim is show you the most effective ways of achieving these in the current climate, while at the same time addressing your concerns with practical advice so that you in turn are better equipped to make the marketing case to your colleagues. We make no apologies for including a lot of ideas from the US, as we've found that American business people in general, including American lawyers, have more to teach us than anyone else.

We also recognise that not everything will be appropriate for you and your business, and for this reason we do not go into forensic detail. Instead, there's an online Resources section (www.intelligentmarketing-foremploymentlawers.co.uk/resources.pdf), where you'll find our recommendations for further research. We ask only that you consider all the options. Please keep an open mind!

Action

Before you go any further, we suggest you make a SWOT analysis of your current marketing activities. First, use the template in the Resources for this chapter to analyse the overall position of your employment law business. Consider the following points:

*   **Strengths**
    What do you offer your existing clients that no one else does? Focus on what currently underpins your employment law service and the services you're confident you do better than— or at least as well as—your competition.

*   **Weaknesses**
    What can you improve? What does your competition do for

their clients that you don't? Focus on anything that detracts from what you can offer clients, both existing and prospective.

- **Opportunities**
  What developments in employment law can you benefit from? Where do you see the biggest opportunities opening up in the short, medium and longer term? Which clients do you consider will provide you with the highest income?

- **Threats**
  What current external challenges does your employment law practice face? Consider who poses your main competition, now and in the short, medium and longer term. What other future challenges can you identify? (The economic downturn and ABS are obvious answers.) What are your direct competitors doing to address these challenges?

Then (and without skimming through this book first!) note down strategies for…

- using your **strengths**

- minimising your **weaknesses**

- harnessing your **opportunities**

- eliminating your **threats**.

Next, use the template to evaluate each tool in your current marketing plan in turn. This could include (and these are given just as examples) newspaper advertising, public relations, direct mail, online marketing (through your website or emailings) and hosting seminars.

The aim is to identify the tools you consider are giving you the greatest advantage or opportunity and those which are least effective, as well as getting you to focus on what your competitors are doing:

- **Strengths**

  How effective is each tool in generating employment law work? Focus on what currently works best, first with existing clients and then with prospective clients. Wherever possible, quantify by matching a tool to a specific outcome—how many clients were attracted, how much business won? What makes your approach more successful than those of your competition?

- **Weaknesses**

  Which marketing tool that you currently use is working least well? Does your competition use this tool more effectively? If so, how?

- **Opportunities**

  Are there marketing tools you have used in the past that could be used again? What new approaches do you think would best generate new business? How do you see these working in the short, medium and longer term?

- **Threats**

  Is your competition using any marketing methods that might take work away from you? If so, how many competitors are involved and how many separate methods?

Then (and again without consulting this book!) note down strategies for…

- using your **strengths**

- minimising your **weaknesses**

- harnessing your **opportunities**

- eliminating your **threats**.

When you've finished reading this book, look again at this SWOT analysis. It should offer a valuable insight into how much you already knew and were getting right, and how much you now want to change.

Throughout the book we'll be asking our profiled firms for their views on the issues we discuss.

We asked the UK-based firms what impact they believe ABS will have on their businesses.

"I see it as an opportunity because it means you can bring in outside investors and you can expand. Our belief is that an employment practice is required in the locality. The people who phone do so within a certain radius of the office and therefore if I had unlimited funds I would open an Ashby Cohen in every city centre in the country because the internet, by virtue of its nature, will bring in to that locality the relevant business—with a little additional local marketing. To me, having outside investors would allow us to expand with capital which I suspect banks won't be prepared to lend easily over the coming period."
Alain Cohen, Ashby Cohen

"I think it is a challenge. Everything has to adapt and you could go back thirty years when everyone sat in oak-panelled rooms, never left the office and just billed clients without explaining why. People want fixed fees, which is coming in more and more. You don't have to lose money on fixed fees; you just need to fix them right."
Tom Walker, former head of employment law at Colemans-ctts, now in the same role at Manches

"I'm in no way worried about it. I think it presents very few challenges for us, and some opportunities in that it will perhaps mean we can go down that route of positioning ourselves on a more level playing field with some of our solicitor competitors. The fact that those traditional firms

from which we pinch work can go into partnership with non-lawyers won't really make a blind bit of difference to us. They're still going to be run by the partners and other non-law partners. I think there's a reasonable amount of hot air about all this. I don't really see any challenges as far as our niche is concerned and what's important to the corporate sector."
Mark Ellis, CEO, Ellis Whittam

"The opportunity is in terms of advising firms and individual partners on agreements with external partners, or advising individual partners who have been managed out by aggressive private equity investors. And advising investors who are taking stakes in law firms. For ourselves, we are a tiny operation. I don't see any great advantage in inward investment into the firm."
Ronnie Fox, Fox Lawyers

"Tesco Law is likely to be slightly larger than me! But are they really going to be interested in an area that is notoriously not mega-buck value? Your average tribunal claim may be £5,000—is that something they're going to want to bother with? With the internet, they still only have the same technology as the rest of us—the only place where they can clearly beat the rest of us is by traditional TV advertising."
Dean Morris, Morris Legal

"It'll make no difference at all. If anything, it'll bring more ill-qualified players into the market and that will give a good point of comparison for us. One of our strengths is that we don't do what we're not good at, and I think lawyers are really bad at that—the Jack of all trades thing. It's too tempting for organisations to think, 'that might work, we'll do it' without

recognising the detrimental impact from a client perception point of view on your core offering."
Darren Maw, Vista

We also asked all eight firms how the recession is affecting them.

"We have seen a significant increase in numbers, with traffic to our website up 20 per cent from January 2008 to January 2009, and visitor numbers up 40 per cent."
Alain Cohen, Ashby Cohen

"It's increasing the work, both from employers and from employees. Employers who might previously have tolerated a situation no longer will. And it isn't always pleasant. In boom times when you're on the employer's side in dismissals, you know everyone's going to get jobs, but here we're getting some quite unpleasant stories from employees. When I began as a lawyer, the 1990s recession was ending and it was coming into the boom time of the mid to late '90s, but there were one or two similar situations. Maybe this is my own subconscious bias, but the family breadwinner who's out of a job with a mortgage to pay to me is perhaps always more troublesome than the 22-year-old who's footloose. In the longer term you have to be aware that you're part of a larger commercial practice and we all want a healthy economy, but in the short term this area is not under threat."
Tom Walker, former head of employment law at Colemans-ctts, now in the same role at Manches

"It's having an impact in that we're extremely busy. We recognised from day one that employment law is relatively

recession-proof in that in hard times it's as much in demand as in the good times. We see the recession as an opportunity and we're responding by marketing ourselves as an essential service. So we are saying to prospects, 'If you were to downsize, why spend five or ten grand on a traditional solicitor with no certainty of outcome at a tribunal when we can see you through the downsizing process with total security in terms of outcome?' So we see it as an opportunity to win more business from the traditional business sector."
Mark Ellis, CEO, Ellis Whittam

"The work I do is counter-cyclical. People are losing their jobs at banks and other financial institutions. We are advising a number of highly-paid individuals who are victims of the credit crunch. One of the ways in which the current recession is different from those in the recent past is that professional firms are also having to institute redundancy programmes. We are advising a couple of law firms which have asked partners, associates and professional staff to leave for economic reasons. We're also acting for several partners who have been asked to leave."
Ronnie Fox, Fox Lawyers

"We are busier than ever."
Mirella Sikorski, senior marketing executive, Lewis Silkin

"There is a downturn—not huge, but nonetheless a downturn. The only rationale I can put on it is that the recession provides employers with a very good way of clearing the decks of all the chaff they don't really want, conveniently under a guise of redundancy that's virtually unchallengeable in the prevailing economic climate. So we're not getting a mass of redundancy claims through because I think people are acknowledging that

what can they do? There's clearly a redundancy situation because there's no work, and if you're redundant that's just unlucky. I can't see any reason at all why my business should increase in this economic climate."
Dean Morris, Morris Legal

"We are adding new people with existing practices and clients to our practice group. Our business is always busy, but in this particular economy it is growing and will continue to grow for several years. Former employees will be after trying to collect money in any way they can. Hundreds of thousands of people around the country are getting laid off, and some of them are filing discrimination charges. Some are just angry, and they go around to lawyers looking for ways to sue."
Robin Fawsett, co-chair of employment and labour law, Shutts & Bowen LLP, Orlando

2
Stay focused and keep it simple!

All marketing is about building relationships, regardless of the size and main focus of your business. There are three key questions you need to ask yourself:

1.   Who are my clients?

2.   What do they want?

3.   How do they want me to provide it?

Now go a step further and strip down to the bare bones the communications that underpin these questions. To quote a remarkable—and remarkably successful—American internet marketer called Frank Kern (who was in turn paraphrasing a top copywriter called John Carlton), you're left with these statements:

1.   Here's who I am.

2.   Here's what I've got.

3.   Here's what it'll do for you.

4.   Here's what I want you to do next.

All a deliberate over-simplification of course, but it beautifully illustrates the importance of keeping it simple and staying focused. You should aim to use it as your starting point and then return to it every time you're in danger of losing sight of what you're aiming to achieve.

To build on this base, here are the next essentials of marketing:

- Give your clients what they want, not what you *think* they want.

- Stick to a single theme in each marketing exercise.

- Test and measure everything you do.

Again, this may appear blindingly obvious, but it's remarkably easy to fall into the trap of designing a service nobody actually needs, bombarding clients with an assortment of messages, and—as an example—running advertisements without ever establishing how much work they bring in. Lack of focus can show up in other common traps that can easily undermine your business. Take a look at anything you're assuming (consciously or unconsciously) about your relationship with your clients. American legal marketing consultant Trey Rider has identified a series of what he calls "deadly assumptions" that law firms often make. Here are a few examples:

1. My clients (existing and prospective) know what services I offer.

2. When a client has a question, they'll call me.

3. My clients understand that I'm busy and don't mind if I'm slow getting back to them.

4. My clients understand legal jargon because they're in business.

By making assumptions—these or any other—about your clients' expectations, you're doing them and yourself a huge disservice. To take as an example the first of Rider's "deadly assumptions", your clients are not clairvoyant. If you don't tell them exactly what your employment law service offers them there's a real risk they will go to somebody who does. Assumptions 2 and 3 are linked and this is one of the areas where intelligent marketing and effective client relationship management overlap. Your client will not necessarily call you when they have a question, and is significantly less likely to unless they know their call or email is welcome, which links straight to assumption 3. Clients invariably will mind if you don't get back to them promptly and this can impact disproportionately on their overall confidence and trust in you and your firm. Inviting your clients to ask you questions helps build up trust, but this only works when you respond swiftly. If you can't provide an immediate reply, let them know upfront and then get back to them later—it's leaving the impression that you care that's important. Dan Hull, American litigation attorney and founder of the What About Clients? website (see Resources), says: "Let your clients know that you are totally accessible—no client worth keeping will abuse the privilege—and then show them. In order for most of us to be competitive, we have to get into the habit of 'being there'— good clients deserve this." (It's worth noting that in the US, poor communication is the single most common reason why clients file grievances with state bars. This data is not currently made public anywhere in the UK.)

The fourth of Rider's deadly assumptions should be obvious: why should anyone who isn't a lawyer be expected to speak legalese? That doesn't stop a lot of lawyers using it, particularly when they're writing. And while some of your clients may be able—and even willing—to follow an argument couched in jargon, most won't. It's one easy way of annoying, intimidating and alienating a client, no matter how successful or powerful they are in their own field. So whether it's face-to-face or in writing, just explain it in plain English. In other words, keep it simple!

What do our featured firms think about legalese?

"Plain English is the language of choice at Lewis Silkin. We really don't speak legalese. Our biggest audience is HR people and in-house employment lawyers, plus FDs and MDs."
Mirella Sikorski, senior marketing executive, Lewis Silkin

"I will not tolerate legalese. There's a well-known quote: 'The sign of a bad lawyer is one who hides his ignorance behind his language.' That has never, ever proved itself wrong. If we get a letter with legalese in it, that just says to me: 'Tom, you're going to win'."
Tom Walker, former head of employment law at Colemans-ctts, now in the same role at Manches

We will look in detail at how to build on your relationships with existing clients in the next chapter, but you may first find it useful to get clear in your own mind exactly who you are already doing business with—and whether any assumptions you are making show up.

Action

In Chapter 1, you did an overall SWOT analysis. Now use this as a starting point to analyse in more detail your existing employment law clients and how you service them. Use sub-categories depending, for example, on the number and types of employment law work you offer, how many clients you have, how many fee earners, and so on. How forensic you want to be about this is up to you—this exercise is about marketing, not detailed business development—but aim to use criteria that work for you. A very basic but effective model could include...

- fees received over the past year

- the nature of the working relationship (how easy—or difficult—a client is to deal with)

- regularity of contact

- their participation in your events

- number of referrals they have made

- their feedback about your service.

Assess each client in turn against your criteria. The aim is to allow you to identify which of your current clients are most valuable to you, not just in terms of the income they bring in, but in all aspects of your working relationship with them—their overall worth. The easiest way to do this is by using a matrix as in Table 1.

From this very simple matrix we can see that the client bringing in the highest income also scores highest against the other criteria, which we could have predicted. However, the working relationship with the client bringing in the next highest income clearly leaves something to be desired: contact is less regular, there's no uptake on using the firm's events, such

Table 1 Client analysis matrix

Client	Fees received	Working relationship	Regularity of contact	Participation in events	Client referrals	Client feedback
Client A	£12,000	6/10	6/10	2/10	2	8/10
Client B	£19,000	8/10	8/10	6/10	7	7/10
Client C	£8,000	5/10	4/10	0/10	1	none
Client D	£27,000	9/10	8/10	8/10	9	9/10
Client E	£6,000	6/10	4/10	2/10	1	none
Client F	£21,000	8/10	6/10	0/10	3	6/10
Client G	£15,000	8/10	6/10	6/10	8	8/10

as seminars, only three referrals have been made, and the feedback score is mediocre. The relationship with the client generating the lowest fees is better, but there's no feedback, so the firm will be unaware of how it is rated. What is revealed here are gaps and inconsistencies in how the firm manages, communicates with, and measures how it works with its clients. By doing this exercise, you're aiming for a similar general overview of your working relationships, and once again identifying your strengths and weaknesses.

3

Clients, referrals and testimonials

Of all your possible sources of new business, one offers more opportunities than the rest put together: your existing clients. And with a weaker economy and tighter budgets all round, it clearly makes sense to make them the starting point for your marketing strategy, not least because much of what we suggest will cost you little more than your time.

In Chapter 1 we said that there are only three ways to generate more income:

1.   Grow your client base.

2.   Work for them more often.

3.   Charge them more.

It's the clients you're working with now who can best help you achieve any of these objectives—and if you're baulking at the third, don't. Very few people buy anything based solely on price, and that will include your clients. There are complex forces at work in all our buying decisions. Pricing is a borderline marketing activity, but we'll look at it in a little more depth as it interrelates so closely with activities that definitely are. (For a fascinating exploration of what motivates us to buy, read Robert Cialdini's classic, *Influence: The Psychology of Persuasion*, more details of which are in the Resources.)

3.1   Is the price right?

When you're setting your fees, always keep this in mind: you can spend weeks analysing how your competitors price their employment law services and accurately pinpointing your desired profitability threshold, or you can pull a figure from thin air, but ultimately the only people who know what you should be charging are your clients. So what should you do?

Consider these assumptions (yes, more assumptions!):

1.   If I charge less than my competitors I'll get more business.

2.   My existing clients will go elsewhere if I charge them more.

3.   Other firms are reducing their charges so I must to stay competitive.

Now let's take them one by one.

If I charge less than my competitors I'll get more business

The majority of your clients are not going to choose you over a competitor simply because you charge less. Indeed, if you just focus on price many may question why you're charging less before finding out anything more about you. Is it because you'll do less for them? Or perhaps you'll cut corners. Or just generally offer a poorer service. This tactic can only ever work in a retailing context, when you're selling as cheaply as possible and relying on high volume for profits. You, in contrast, are offering a complex professional service, and diving for the lowest common denominator is not the way to go—with one caveat.

If you're genuinely able to make a profit on offering a *better* service for less than the competition, you focus your marketing not on price but on value, and you use it primarily to assess the state of the market, then it's worth considering. Select one element to test, re-price it and see what happens, but you must measure the response carefully. There's absolutely no point in testing anything if you don't put in place the means to find out whether it works. (There's more about testing in Chapter 21.)

My existing clients will go elsewhere if I charge them more

This depends hugely on your relationships with your clients, and many law firms—particularly smaller ones—do consistently under charge because they are afraid of losing custom. In a stronger economic climate, your clients will almost certainly be prepared to pay you more than they do now for an excellent service. In the present circumstances, however, charging your clients more when at least some are already feeling the pinch can only work if you also offer more. It would be risky just to increase your fees without providing anything extra in return. However, the intelligent and imaginative use in this context of "upselling"—improving or adding to a service you are already providing—gives you the justification to charge more, and gives your client more perceived value for money (such as offering free participation in mock tribunals, or visiting a client's offices for a half-day complimentary file review, something which costs you a few hours' billing but which can cement client loyalty like nothing else). Doing it this way also allows you both more room for manoeuvre: if a client you would not want to lose does strongly resist paying you more, you can always maintain the status quo without compromising the relationship. Or quietly begin enhancing your service anyway. Your clients will appreciate your efforts and you are then well placed to increase your fees when the market is ready.

Is there a cut-off point beyond which you should not raise your prices? British legal marketing consultant Nick Jervis says it comes when 80 per cent of your potential clients say you are too expensive. Whether you would want to push it that far, and how quickly you get there, depends of course on how much you are already charging. But remember that the only people who know how much you should charge are your clients. You may be pleasantly surprised, so pay close attention to what they say!

Other firms are reducing their charges so I must to stay competitive

The probability of you confronting this dilemma will depend on what type of environment you are practising in. Larger firms with major corporate clients are a great deal less likely to be susceptible to this kind of direct market pressure than smaller practices dealing mainly with SMEs or directly with the public.

Whatever your client base, the answer is the same: don't do it! Start by asking yourself why your competitors are. Are they losing clients—to you, perhaps? Have they lost a key player to a rival? Have they bought into the pile-'em-high psychology? Or are they just panicking because they think they're about to take a hit as clients—existing and potential—tighten their belts? Whatever their motivation, the fact is that if you follow suit and your clients, including any you might attract on this new level playing field, become accustomed to lower fees, not only will you be losing income now but you will find it extremely difficult to restore your previous tariff level once the economy picks up. The fact that your competitors will as well is beside the point: you all lose in the long term. A much wiser approach is to again upsell. Offer enhancements to your service and pay attention to your customer relations management so that you're perceived as better value than your competitors, even though you charge more.

3.2   What do your clients think about you?

3.2.1   The importance of staying in touch

It's anything up to ten times easier to do more business with existing clients than it is to acquire new ones. It's your existing clients who are going to give you referrals, your existing clients who will provide testimonials, your existing clients who are most likely to try new services, and your existing clients who will be most interested in entering into joint ventures with you. And at a time when client loyalty is being tested by constraints outside your control, it's really essential that you grasp the importance of building and maintaining strong relationships—not just because it makes obvious economic sense, but as the foundation of your wider marketing strategy.

What follows may seem simplistic, but it's anything but. Something like 80 per cent of your income is likely to come from around 20 per cent of your clients, almost certainly the 20 per cent with whom you have the strongest relationships. (There's more about identifying your ideal client in Chapter 4; more about the 80–20 rule in Resources.)

So how often do you speak to these key people? Do you visit them? How easily can they get hold of you? You should already have at least an overview of the frequency of your contact from the exercise you did at the end of Chapter 2 (page 18), but you now need to consider this in more detail. We're not just talking about the usual communications that arise in the context of a specific instruction, but the contact you make to find out how they are and what's new with their business—personal (not automated) emails you send just to ask them if there's anything you can do for them, any updates they need, how you interact face-to-face, by visits you make to their place of business or meetings you organise on their premises and yours, for a catch-up coffee or lunch.

If you're not doing any of this, you not only risk undermining your relationship, but you are without question missing out on the best possible source of information about how you are performing. Similarly, if you're only seeking feedback at the end of transactions or on a scheduled basis, and this is through a form, you are also missing out. Structured appraisals of your service remain vital, particularly for single transaction clients, but they will only give you summarised answers to specific questions. Good for amassing statistics and teasing out trends, but the devil is in the detail. Forms provide no scope for expanding or elaborating, exploring ideas, or "by the way..." moments, and it's through these exchanges with your established clientele that you will discover the minutiae of what works and what doesn't. And what works well for one client may be less successful with another. The key to establishing lasting and fruitful relationships is putting in place—and using—flexible communication channels that allow you to tease out the little things that matter to each client as an individual.

This is another cross-over between areas variously labelled CRM, business development and marketing, but there are no absolute demarcation lines—excellent relationships bring you satisfied and trusting clients whose candid feedback will help you improve your services. In turn this feeds into how you market your services, making it easier to focus on your message and communicate with confidence.

The Boston-based BTI Consulting group—the leading US provider of "strategic market research to law firms"—found in its 2008 survey of more than 250 in-house lawyers at Fortune 1000 and other major companies that three major factors account for 80 per cent of the "superior customer service" delivered by the law firms and attorneys named as the year's BTI Client Service All-Stars. These are…

1.   client focus

2.   understanding the client's business

3.   delivering results.

Client focus, which in 2008 comprised 60.5 per cent of the satisfaction quotient, has been the number 1 factor for the past seven years. Legal skills, by contrast, score only 21 per cent.

The survey report says:

"Client focus is a remarkable quality in the eyes of clients and proves a leading differentiator in the quest to deliver superior client service.

Examples of client focus include...

1. being highly responsive to the client's individual goals

2. providing strategic-level advice wrapped in the context of client-specific issues

3. going above and beyond the call of duty."

The 2007 *Legal Week* FTSE/AIM client satisfaction survey found that reality still lags behind customer expectations of UK firms. Here the main emphasis is also on how legal advice is delivered, although other factors—such as the commercial relevance of advice—come out ahead of responsiveness and accessibility.

Sources
*The BTI 2008 Client Service All Stars, BTI, Boston, 2008; **www.bticonsulting.com** (See Resources for 2009 results) FTSE/AIM Client Satisfaction Survey 2007, Legal Week, November 2007 for 2009 and 2008 results respectively)*

3.2.2 Ways to forge your relationships

Does this all sound too time-consuming and difficult to maintain? Well, we're not alone in urging you to make relationship-building a top priority, especially now.

American law marketer Tom Kane stresses the importance of doing this, particularly in a tight market. Here are his top three marketing tips (from his top ten):

1. Visit your clients.

2. Entertain your clients.

3. Seek feedback more often.

Visit your clients
Taking these in turn, Kane argues that "the single most effective marketing technique which leads to immediate business in the vast majority of cases

is to visit your client at their place of business". Fellow American Larry Bodine says: "Marketing is a contact sport and lawyers must get out and visit clients in person. The higher the personal touch, the more effective the marketing." And he adds: "Lawyers are trained not to ask questions they don't know the answer to. You have to overcome this."

The point of the exercise is obviously to underpin your relationship, but also to find out how their business works, to listen to what your contact client's colleagues are saying, and to get a general feel for the organisation. US attorney Dan Hull says: "Take time out to learn the stock price, industry, day-to-day culture, players and overall goals of your client. Learn about your client—and keep learning." Once you have a sense of context, it will be much easier for you to solve your client's problems and highlight potential flashpoints they may not have spotted. This will in turn reinforce your relationship. Let's be clear, though—you are not billing your client for the time you spend doing this. It's an investment, not a source of immediate income.

How do our profiled firms approach visiting clients?

"I definitely visit clients more than they visit me—I'm out of the office at least once a week."
Tom Walker, former head of employment law at Colemans-ctts, now in the same role at Manches

At Vista employment law and HR consultancy, where clients pay through subscription, the team extends "getting out of the office" to cover almost all the work they do with their clients:

"Ninety per cent of our work is done on our clients' premises and it's important that we can control contact with clients. We need to manage our clients well or they'll become unprofitable. One way of doing that is to say: 'Next Thursday,

I'm going to come on site—bring out your dead.' The HR
directors think it's great because they know we'll be back in a
month and we can review it then."
Darren Maw, Vista

Entertain your clients

Entertaining clients is something of anathema to many lawyers. However, instead of viewing it as the setting for a sales pitch you'd never want to make, just look upon it as semi-formal, fairly relaxed socialising over a coffee or lunch. Again, this is not something you can charge for! It's another investment, and another important way for you to consolidate your relationship and find out what's on your client's mind.

Seek feedback more often

Your first move, though, is to ask each client what is *their* preferred way of maintaining contact with you. How often would they appreciate hearing from you during what Kane calls "lulls in the client relationship"? In addition to the methods discussed above, specific ideas for staying in touch include...

- sending newspaper or magazine articles

- emailing links to online articles or news items

- emailing details of judgments of particular relevance to a client's industry or profession

- letting them know about events that might offer them networking opportunities.

3.2.2.1 Formal feedback

Clients generally welcome the chance to provide formal feedback, and their comments are generally favourable. If they're not, it is, as Kane says, better to find out through a candid appraisal than when they take their business elsewhere, particularly if there's a problem that can easily be addressed.

If you're not already doing so, you must put in place mechanisms for eliciting feedback. For single transaction clients this should be at the end of business, and for your regular clients it should be at regular intervals—annually, for example, or every two years. Whenever you make changes to the way you do business or add to your portfolio of services, seek feedback, say within six months of their introduction. This does not need to be from all your clients; a sample will do.

It's by no means the only way, but the most common method of seeking formal feedback is through a form which gives you data in an easily manageable format. We're not going to give you a template, as the priorities for each business are different—information about your premises may be crucial for some firms, for example, but of minimal interest to others. Here are some of the general questions you could include for commercial clients:

Are you currently using our firm's employment law services?

- If no, when was the last time you did?

- If yes, which service(s) are you currently using?

- Are you using any of our firm's other services?

- If yes, which ones?

- What is the nature of your business?

- How many employees do you have?

- Where did you hear about this firm?

- Why did you choose this firm?

- Would you use us again (*for single-transaction clients*)?

You're looking for detailed feedback on your relationship, so ask questions that will help you identify strengths and weaknesses. The tense of the questions will depend on whether they are asked in the context of a single-transaction form or of your regular clients.

You could use a 1–5 scoring method (with 1 being the lowest and 5 the highest) to ask these kinds of sample questions:

- Is your solicitor generally helpful?

- Does your solicitor return your phone calls promptly?

- Does your solicitor reply promptly to a) letters and b) emails?

- Is it easy to get an appointment with your solicitor?

- Was the matter resolved quickly (*for single-transaction forms*)?

- Do you understand everything your solicitor tells you?

- Have you visited our website?

You could also consider using the "Do you agree with this statement?" approach with some of your questions.

Staying with customer care, you could ask clients to consider why they first chose your firm or continue to use your services. Use a 1–10 system (matched to however many questions you include), with 1 being the most important and 10 (or the highest number) the least. Here are some suggestions:

- A recommendation.

- We have used your services before.

- We have clients in common.

- Your employment law service has a good reputation.

- Your firm is large and can offer a range of legal services.

- Your firm is small and friendly.

- The quality of your specialist employment law team.

- The quality of your support staff.

- You offer good value.

- Your website was easy to navigate and informative.

- The initial consultation was free.

Always—for reasons which will become clear later — include an "any other comments" section.

For the information you gather through formal feedback to be of any use, you obviously have to establish a proper system for collating it, analysing it, and looking for recurring themes. That done, you then need to act on it! If you don't pay heed to what your clients are telling you, you may as well not bother asking them. And don't forget to thank them—a phone call, an email, a card, or even a small gift will let them know that you appreciate the effort they have made.

How do our profiled firms seek formal feedback?

Tom Walker, head of employment law at Manches, used two different approaches when he headed the team at Colemans-ctts:

"At the end of a case for individuals, the firm gives out a questionnaire. They are returned in all insurance cases. The feedback I personally seek is getting into Chambers—you give names of certain people who are happy to be approached."

"We have a detailed CRM programme in place and each one of our advisors is prompted to phone every four weeks if there's been activity on the client account. So we'll be calling clients, being proactive, to see how they are and if we can help them—which obviously builds rapport, builds the relationship."
Mark Ellis, CEO, Ellis Whittam

"Questionnaires are work for the client, so we don't use them. Every month we will talk about how far along the track we are. Are we two-thirds of the way along the track? Are we one-third along the way of the budget? Result—happy client. Or are we two-thirds of the way into the budget and only one-third towards achieving our objective? And the client will say, 'I thought we'd be further by now', or 'if you hadn't been sleeping on the job…' or 'I wasn't very pleased with the way you negotiated that item'… But I try and have this review on a monthly basis and of course it leads to a monthly billing."
Ronnie Fox, principal, Fox Lawyers

"Teams are encouraged to get feedback from clients, but this is tailored rather than through a blanket form. We also use an external team for general surveys of the firm's performance. We do this for transparency. The interviews are carried out on the phone and face to face, with thirty done at a time. Through these, we noticed that some of the team were not as good at communicating with clients as others. Clients want good responsiveness and availability and to feel that everything is

tailored for them, so we are now focusing even more strongly on that."
Mirella Sikorski, senior marketing executive, Lewis Silkin

Dean Morris of Morris Legal is directing clients towards **http://solicitor.info** to leave their feedback once business is complete. The full URL is: **http://solicitor.info/solicitors/ solicitor.php?id=1022&name=Morris%20Legal%20(Solicit ors)%20Ltd** (or you can use **http://tinyurl.com/caqgw9**).

Vista employment law and HR consultancy managing director Darren Maw does not use feedback forms to gauge his company's performance. He instead prefers to seek feedback from his clients through regular, but focused, phone calls:

"I call in my capacity as managing director and I phone them regularly. If it's a client who I'm predominantly dealing with myself, I don't tag it on to a service conversation. I make a specific call on a different day to say, 'I'm not calling you to do with X, Y, or Z, just to say how are we doing? Have you got any gripes? Anything we can improve? Anything we can change?' Because we genuinely work differently with every client, that has to be fluid. The service model looks different for every client."

3.2.3 Referrals—probably the best clients in the world

Paying close attention to what your clients think about you—through regular contact and feedback—will make it significantly easier to ask them for referrals. And referrals are, without question, the best possible way of acquiring new clients. Referrals arrive carrying an already favourable impression of your business from whoever referred them, and there's already an element of trust in place. And some may arrive at your door without any specific effort at all on your part—just as an act of goodwill on the part of an existing client, made without any prompting.

The easiest way to get a referral from an existing client is just to ask, and this is clearly going to be easier if the foundations of your relationships are strong. Look for more tenuous leads from clients as well. These are contacts they think might be interested in your services rather than direct referrals. And always remember two things:

1.   Your clients won't know you're looking for referrals or leads unless you ask, so ask!

2.   Your business clients no doubt do the same with their clients, so they will generally be happy to help.

Remember to say thanks for every referral, whether or not anything comes of it. As with seeking feedback, a simple call, email, card or small gift will show that you're not taking your client for granted and will encourage more referrals.

If yours is a larger firm spanning many areas of practice, which tends to become compartmentalised, it's important that all fee earners get into the habit of cross-referring clients. Today's acquisitions and mergers client may well need TUPE advice tomorrow, so make sure the right introductions are made in good time and you're working as a team—as Larry Bodine's "wolf pack".

Seeking referrals from outside your client base and colleagues is also important. Look to your friends, for example. It would obviously be inappropriate to pitch them for their own business, but Larry Bodine has found that if you ask them how you can reach people just like them—over a meal, for example—they are usually more than happy to give you good advice.

Of course there's no use building up a portfolio of referrals and leads if you only pay attention to the ones who arrive on your doorstep with immediate needs. You need to start building on what you have been given—more about this in the next chapter.

Putting in place a sound referrals system and ensuring that everyone knows what's expected of them is important, but there's one key element you must not overlook. What's one of the first things you do if somebody recommends something to you? The odds are that you'll Google it—to find out more from the website, get a feel for the business, establish its credibility. It is, therefore, essential that you have a first-rate online shop window, and one that potential clients can find easily. (More about websites that work in Chapters 11, 13–15.)

Do our profiled firms get clients through referrals?

"Our main referrals are from other law firms—mainly big City firms—either because there's a conflict of interest or because they tend to be our opponents and they know we're OK. So if one of their clients is getting rid of an executive, they'll say, 'these guys will look after you'."
Alain Cohen, director, Ashby Cohen

"The majority of clients come through word of mouth, referrals. I don't know what the proportion is, but it's the majority."
Tom Walker, former head of employment law at Coleman-ctts, now in the same role at Manches

"We get a small percentage of clients through referrals, but it's growing. We do actively ask existing clients for referrals, and we incentivise them—we give the managing director or CEO of a business a crate of champagne for a referral who signs up."
Mark Ellis, CEO, Ellis Whittam

"There's a subtle way that I do it if I've got a client who tells me that he's happy with what we've done. I say:

'Occasionally I get asked by a potential client if they can speak to someone for whom I've acted in similar circumstances. Can I give your name?' Now that is a slightly more subtle way of saying, 'I'm keen to get more work'. And nearly always the people of whom I ask that question end up referring clients to me."
Ronnie Fox, principal, Fox Lawyers

"We get a lot of business through referrals and word of mouth. We ask clients what they think of us and also ask if they feel the same about our competitors. At all our marketing events we ask whether participants would recommend that colleagues take part in the next one and we provide feedback forms asking for the names of two other people who might want to take part. We get a lot of spontaneous recommendations."
Mirella Sikorski, senior marketing executive, Lewis Silkin

"Our clients are largely one-offs, but former clients will refer their friends, and I get referrals via accountants and other solicitors. I do use a referral marketing firm which refers some work to me—that represents five per cent of my work; it's just another income stream."
Dean Morris, principal, Morris Legal

3.2.3.1 You scratch my back—referrals from other professionals

Another valuable—and often under-exploited—source of referrals is from non-competitor professionals: connector clients. If you don't already have one, you are aiming to establish a network of, say, accountants, bankers, brokers and management consultants who recommend you as their employment lawyer of choice. For smaller firms with no in-house employment law specialists, this can also include other solicitors—an insolvency lawyer, for example. The principle is one of reciprocity—they refer clients to you, you refer clients to them. It may take a while to establish and require some intelligent networking on your part—particularly if you are working at blue-chip level—but it's an effective low-cost way to grow your business and widen your circle of influence.

Once in place, the benefits are obvious. Look at it from the standpoint of the client, whether one of yours or one of your connector client's. How appealing to have a ready-made network of professional advisors available to work on your behalf as a multi-discipline team. (There's more about networking in Chapters 7 and 9.)

Action

Whether or not you have a network already in place, this is a useful exercise. Draw up a matrix based on Table 2 and analyse potential (and/or existing) connector clients.

3.2.4 "A pleasure to do business"—the value of testimonials

There's an obvious link between seeking feedback, looking for referrals and asking for testimonials—they all involve you seeking support from your existing clients. And as with feedback and referrals, you are more likely than not to get a favourable response, for two reasons:

1.	The majority of your clients are now likely to be asking their own customers for testimonials.

2.	Being publicly associated with your firm gives your clients added credibility.

Acquiring the material to encapsulate testimonials is not difficult. If your clients are satisfied with your service, your feedback procedures should provide all you need, topped up with any compliments that arrive unsolicited. The "any other comments" sections on feedback forms are

Table 2   Matrix of connector clients

Name	Profession	Client type	Strengths	Weaknesses	Contact?	Already networking?
A & Co	Insurance broker	Mainly SMEs	Large; loyal client base; good reputation	Too focused on SMEs; slow to respond to market changes	None	With C Consulting
B Ltd	Accountant	SMEs; some larger Ltds and a few Plcs	Wide range of clients; strong reputation; business growing	Could be at risk of over-stretch; high turnover of staff at entry/junior level	Brian A (through Chris in A & Co)	With C Consulting and D Bank
C Consulting	Management consultant	Mainly Plcs; some FTSE	Quality client base; business growing; charismatic MD	Heavy emphasis on founder/MD; not much depth of talent	Jane B (but check she's not left!)	With A & Co and B Ltd
D Bank	Bank	From SME to Plc	Long-established; UK/international; excellent reputation; huge client base	Size makes it difficult to build up personal relationship; hard to focus on ideal clients to target	None	With B Ltd

a particularly rich source of material, but don't overlook positive comments from clients during your catch-up meetings and phone calls. Once you establish in your mind the importance of feedback, your ear will become attuned to picking out positive remarks worthy of a wider audience.

No matter how the testimonial arrives, however, it is essential that you get your client's direct consent for you to use it to market your business, and as with referrals and feedback, make sure you say thank you.

3.2.4.1 Using testimonials wisely

It will not have escaped your attention that testimonials now appear everywhere—in advertising, in printed marketing material like leaflets and brochures, and particularly on websites where Web 2.0 audio and video testimony has now joined the written word. So is this particular currency beginning to get devalued by indiscriminate over-use and cynical manipulation? Yes and no: it depends on how it's used.

Let's look first at the traditional role of testimonials. Their prime function has always been to provide credibility and social proof—through what is said and who is saying it—and they have served this purpose well for a long time. Now, though, many consumers—and remember that all your business clients are consumers too—are suffering testimonial fatigue, and the power of praise is sadly diminishing in some contexts. And this is not just because there is so much of it. For any business offering a professional, regulated service, it would be dangerously counter-productive to use manipulated testimonials, but that unfortunately doesn't extend to every corner of commerce, and a lot of online tributes may be short on basic authenticity. (If you're looking for evidence of this, visit **http://forums.digitalpoint.com** and delve around....)

The secret, then, is to use testimonials intelligently. What has clearly lost its impact is the "I think you are brilliant" testimony from retail customers found within B2C advertising and websites. The views of Joe and Jane Public (genuine or ersatz) are now littered so liberally across cyberspace in so many formats that they rarely hold your attention. In the B2C marketplace, independent customer satisfaction ratings (of the kind found on Amazon, eBay, review and social networking sites) are now afforded a great deal more value than the testimonials found on sellers' sites. (And if you think this approach could not extend to the legal profession, think again! See Section 3.2.4.2 below. For more—much more—on the significance and role of the "social web", see Chapter 8.) US online marketing researcher Flint McGlaughlin of Marketing Experiments says that to continue to work, testimonials must have "authority and authenticity". In the context of your website, "plugging a list of quotes from random customers into a page is not likely to produce a significant gain", he says. "You need to get more powerful, specific, authoritative testimonials and use them strategically."

To promote your employment law practice effectively, the testimonials you use need to provide credibility by matching one—and preferably both—of the following criteria:

1.   The testimony is from a prestigious client.

2.   The testimony is directly relevant to a *benefit* you are offering.

Context is everything in how you evaluate the prestige of your existing clients because it's what's relevant to your potential clients that's important. So a blue-chip client's testimonial is a valuable marketing tool for a practice targeting other blue-chip clients, but could possible prove a positive turn-off for a smaller firm with a mainly local B2B or B2C audience. Here, testimony from a respected SME would work significantly better.

With prestige testimonials, you can get away with an element of "I think you are brilliant" content, but wherever possible aim to link it to something specific. "Thank you for your team's recent support when we were restructuring", no matter who is saying it, has much less scope as a marketing device than, for example: "Your employment team's support was invaluable during our recent restructuring exercise. We had to make a number of redundancies and your team made sure we followed all the correct procedures and were always available to give us advice and guidance."

You may have seen how we have used testimonials in order to promote the sale of this book (**www.marketingforemploymentlawyers.co.uk**). And one of the co-authors uses testimonials extremely heavily on his website (**www.danielbarnett.co.uk**), largely because SMEs gain reassurance from the knowledge that their barrister is used regularly by FTSE-100 and similar clients, which provides credibility through association.

Be imaginative in how you use testimonials and go beyond their usual contexts. Quality evidence of your ability to deliver is an invaluable tool in face-to-face conversations, either to cement interest among existing clients in more of your services, or to help bring new clients on board. They can be used too in seminars you organise, at speaking engagements, or during networking events. (We'll discuss this more in Chapter 17.)

How do our profiled firms use testimonials?

"We get unprompted testimonials. I keep them on file. I feel, why do you need to publicise that Mrs Bloggs thinks you're a great lawyer? It's embarrassing—I'd rather not. If it was absolutely necessary for a marketing campaign, I'd do it, but I'd have to be convinced."
Alain Cohen, director, Ashby Cohen

"I always find testimonials on a website can look a bit cheesy, but that's a subjective view. If someone said: 'This law firm is fantastic and we got the result we wanted—Fred Smith, HR Director, Shell', I think that would count. Otherwise it's the language—'I found them friendly…'. You read that a hundred times over!"
Tom Walker, former head of employment at Colemans-ctts, now in the same role at Manches

"We solicit testimonials through the account management process. So our account manager seeks them, and our business manager seeks them at annual visits. And if we are

presenting seminars and events, we solicit them then as well. We do get unsolicited testimonials, but it's an indictment of modern times that people pay a fee and forget to say thank you! It's a minority—the majority are solicited. They're used in face-to-face business development meetings. We also encourage prospects to call clients, to speak to them."
Mark Ellis, CEO, Ellis Whittam

"We ask clients for authority to give their names as referees to potential clients, and to the guides."
Ronnie Fox, principal, Fox Lawyers

"We use testimonials in our pitches, and on the website. When we've had feedback, we ask whether we can use the testimonial in this way—usually the lead partner involved will do this."
Mirella Sikorski, senior marketing executive, Lewis Silkin

"I get thank yous. I haven't put them on the website up till now, but it's probably a very valid thing to do. The way I'd do it is to scan in the letters and cards, and blank out the name—or ask the client's consent to use it. That has a great deal more bite than the usual."
Dean Morris, principal, Morris Legal

"We use testimonials as a way of transferring the credibility of the brands of our clients onto us. It's not really what's said. We use our client base in our conversations—here's our client base, here's what we do. But because we don't really use direct forms of marketing, who's going to go to our website and look at our testimonials? Very few, very, very few."
Darren Maw, Vista

3.2.4.2 The client's revenge!

You'll be well acquainted with the star ratings afforded books, music, electrical equipment, hotels, airlines and a host of other consumer goods and services across a range of retailing, review and social networking sites. No doubt you make use of them yourself. Has it, though, ever crossed your mind that you might one day be on the receiving end? If not, you'd better get used to the idea!

The site **http://solicitor.info** is small but contains (what appears to be) genuine feedback from clients—mostly good, but a few not so good. More disturbing is the **www.solicitorsfromhell.co.uk** website, which seems to consist of anonymous defamatory comments about firms of solicitors and individuals at those firms. A random example, relating to a well-known national firm of claimant employment solicitors, is:

> "This company despite being in the City are useless, they are not to be trusted!! They fail to respond to Telephone calls, emails and correspondance [sic], once they've taken your money you are forgotten and treated with contempt like a piece of dog crap on the bottom of their heels, DO NOT TRUST!!!!"

This entry has received over 1,000 hits; presumably from people searching on the internet for information about the firm.

The US website Avvo (**www.avvo.com**) (from the Italian for lawyer, *avvocato*) is far more established than the equivalent UK sites, and heralds what we are likely to see in the next couple of years. It is a free one-stop service where members of the public can access an impressive range of information about individual American lawyers, who are awarded overall marks out of ten. While the featured lawyers can control their profiles and photos, their entries can also include any professional disciplinary sanctions taken against them (similar to those listed by the Solicitors Regulation Authority for England and Wales), a star rating from their peers, and—crucially—the views of their clients. And some of it does not make for pretty reading!

One New York employment law specialist has this attached to his Avvo entry (this is an edited version!):

> **Customer review:** The lawyer never filed the court for my costs. However he did put in for his own fees. He told me he was going to pad the bill… While I was pulling the exhibits he was working on another case… On a weekend during the trial, he told me to meet him at his office. I waited for 3 hours and he never showed up. His clerk left my exhibits at the defendant's lawyers and when they came back they were missing and mixed up. He was not prepared for the trial. He lost on my case on the district court level and wanted me to pay him to do an appeal. During the trial he told me to revise an exhibit, which he had in his possession for months. He was sanctioned by the court because he did not turn over material and told me to lie about it.

Needless to say this client awarded his employment law specialist *nil points*!

It matters little whether all or any of this is true—it's next to the lawyer's name on a website getting a very substantial number of hits a day from prospective clients. And thus far the US courts have not shown any interest in upholding complaints. Two Seattle lawyers who sued Avvo over the scores they were awarded were sent on their way on the grounds that the website ratings were clearly not an objective opinion, and accordingly protected free speech.

4
Where are you going and who are you talking to?

'Would you tell me, please, which way I ought to go from here?'
'That depends a good deal on where you want to get to,' said the Cat.
'I don't much care where,' said Alice.
'Then it doesn't matter which way you go,' said the Cat.
Lewis Carroll: Chapter VI, *Alice's Adventures in Wonderland*

We have looked at how your existing clients can help build your business; now we turn to the ones you have yet to meet. Approaching them successfully rests on the three factors identified in Chapter 2:

1.   Who are my clients?

2.   What do they want?

3.   How do they want me to provide it?

How you define 1 impacts directly on numbers 2 and 3. It's therefore essential that you and all your colleagues have a very clear understanding of exactly who you are addressing when you market your services. If you are poised to turn the page on the grounds that this is obvious, and anyway a luxury in a difficult market, please stop! The overall premise may be simple, but defining it properly is not. Do it well, however, and you may find you have exactly the tools you need to attract new business more easily and cost-effectively, recession or no recession.

We accept that this is not an ideal world and few of us can pick and choose all of our work, but the fact is that lawyers—like everybody else—are happiest and most effective when they are doing work they enjoy for clients they enjoy working for. Chuck Newton—a Texan "Third Wave" (i.e. office-free, internet-based) lawyer—puts it fairly bluntly: "When you are wrestling with those skanky cases you really do not want, except for a little spending money, you could be hitting the pavement, meeting people, and soliciting the cases you really want. When your efforts and your attention get diverted you will not do as well. It is really a self-fulfilling prophesy. You chase the other cases and clients because you are worried about not succeeding with the cases and clients you want, and as a result you do not succeed because you have diverted your attention and divided your efforts."

Newton is of course both exaggerating and over-simplifying, but his views are echoed by fellow US lawyer-marketers Larry Bodine, Tom Kane and Dan Hull, who observes: "Practising law the right way and with enthusiasm is hard enough. And as a lawyer, you owe some of the highest personal, professional and business duties imaginable to your clients. If you don't like him, her or it, you should chuck him, her or it as soon as you ethically and practically can."

Another American—legal writer and marketing consultant Janet Ellen Raasch—looks at the process more from a marketplace perspective. Only the very largest firms can aim to be the best across the board, she says: "For the rest, this goal can be accomplished by limiting the number of services you offer (and market), or by limiting the categories of clients to whom you market your services—or a logical combination of the two." She adds: "Each individual lawyer, whether with a law firm or operating solo, should spend some time coming up with 'the product that is me' and taking it to market."

UK marketing consultant Chris Cardell comes at this from a different, and much more diffuse, direction. He asks his own clients, at the start of the consultation process, the simple question: "What drives you?" He is looking for the reason they first began doing what they do, over and above the need to make a decent income. His focus is more general, and he points to the uber-successful such as Bill Gates or Richard Branson when he says: "Here's what really drives all these people. At some level, it is a deep desire to make a real difference in the lives of the people they reach. Don't get me wrong—Gates and Branson and Co love money. They love profits, but they're also smart enough to know that it was their passion for making a difference that brought in those profits in the first place."

So what drove you to choose this profession and then to specialise in employment law?

4.1   Identifying your ideal clients

You may be in the enviable position of already seeing dream clients comprise the lion's share of your business, or your corner of your firm's business. Perhaps you've long ago carved out a clearly demarcated segment of the employment law market and you're just looking for the best ways to generate business from it. Or you may still be spending at least some of your time wrestling with Chuck Newton's "skanky cases".

Either way, your ultimate goal is to confidently dominate a niche and position yourself as the best player within it—or at least a major player. Completing the following exercise is a key stage on that journey.

Action

Let's imagine, just for the duration of this exercise, that this is an entirely ideal world!

First, you—and all your colleagues—need to identify who you'd really like as clients and what it is they do. Write this down. For example, if your speciality is trade union law, then you have two clear types of client to target: trade unions or the organisations employing their members. If you particularly enjoy TUPE transfers, then you need to look for clients who specialise in acquiring larger businesses as going concerns. Perhaps you enjoy the arguments to be made in discrimination cases relying on EU law as their fundamental source, so seek out clients whose workplaces traditionally generate the highest number of claims, such as under-staffed SMEs, or local authorities and NHS trusts, as well the unions who bring the cases.

Are you still struggling to identify this ideal client? Then do it in reverse. Define the types of client whose business you know you definitely *don't* want and narrow it down that way. You can do this by categorising the sectors they're in, the scope of the work they're likely to bring to the table, the types of people you know you don't work well with (a pushy entrepreneur, perhaps, a self-important CEO, or over-zealous union official), and so on. (Be honest, even though you are likely to find some of them within your existing client base.)

When you've pinpointed the type of client you really want to work for and start attracting to your practice, inject some reality into the exercise. Identify and list actual businesses and organisations that match your criteria, and then use your research skills and resources to build up a fuller picture of them, including the names of the people you'll need to meet. The more detailed you can be the better, as the clearer the picture you have the easier it will be to move to the next stage.

Since Vista employment law and HR consultancy was launched in 2005, its founders have remained crystal clear about the type of client they want.

"We're not interested in any organisation that employs less than 350 people because our client is the HR department and we need an HR department that's resourced enough for us to

be able to add value. We have turned down a significant amount of work in the last three years because it does not fit our client profile. Of course the customer may grow and come back in a year and a half's time and say: 'We've now got 1,000 people and can we have another conversation?'"
Managing director, Darren Maw, Vista

Before you approach your ideal client, you need to find out who is currently competing with you for their business. Return to the SWOT analysis you did in Chapter 1 and build on it using more focus:

- What can you learn from the competition?

- Are they mainly traditional law firms, or are there ABS advisors in the mix as well?

- Go through their websites in forensic detail. Are the designs professional?

- How do they position themselves? How do they promote their services?

- How are they rated by, for example, Chambers & Partners?

- Look at the fee earners' biographies. Do you know any of them, or do you know anyone who does?

- Find out about their fees structure.

- Do they have a marketing section?

- What professional organisations do they belong to?

Again, this may all seem obvious, but when was the la
you did it? There's a matrix in the Resources section—
entitled "Assessing the competition"—which you might find
useful, but please view it as your starting point and not an
ultimate destination.

4.2   What do your ideal clients want?

Now you have your ideal client in your sights you need to clarify what
they want. One of the most pervasive and dangerous mistakes you can
make is to conflate your clients' needs with what *you* do and who *you* are.
You have to separate out *features*—something factual about you or your
business—from *benefits*, what you are offering to your client. For
example, the type of metal used to build a car is a *feature*, while its ability
to withstand the impact of an accident is a *benefit*.

There'll be more about this shortly. First you need to distance yourself
from the equation and step into your client's shoes.

Action

Imagine you are your target client. Make as detailed and as exhaustive a
list as you can of all the possible reasons why you (as this client) would
need the type of employment law service that you (as yourself) want to
make your specialist niche. If you have any existing clients who fit the
bill—or come fairly close—then use them as your starting point, but
approach the exercise from their perspective, not yours.

This isn't easy, and it's not one for which there's a ready-made template,
but, as with identifying your target in the first place, it's one you need to
complete to ensure you continue heading in the right direction.

4.3   How do you meet their expectations?

At this point, look back at any recent client feedback you have collected, and ask yourself these questions:

- What emerges as your strengths and as your weaknesses?

- How can you build on your strengths?

- Are there ways you can hone them to more accurately match the expectations you've identified your ideal client as having?

- What else do you need to do?

- What *benefits* do you offer?

- What do your competitors offer?

- How do they say they meet their clients' needs and their clients' "What's in it for me?" response?

- Who is illustrating benefits more clearly—you or a competitor?

Action

Identify the following:

1.   three benefits your competitors are offering your target client.

2.   how you would make these benefits more interesting.

3.   three key benefits you can offer that your competitors are not.

4.   how you could make these benefits even more interesting.

5.   from stages 1–4, which three benefits are the most compelling.

This done, you now need to single out your unique selling proposition (the USP much loved by the advertising and marketing world!). It may have hackneyed resonances, but it remains the most commonly used way to distil what is going to make you stand out.

Pull together all the work you have done to identify your ideal client, their needs, and how you can match them. Then rank the three benefits you identified above in order of their importance—the benefit occupying the top spot is your USP. Be mindful, though, that this should not be set in stone. What is your USP today may morph into something subtly—or even radically—different in the months and years ahead. You may also need to identify more than one USP, depending on how narrowly you have defined your market niche and target client, and whether you're doing this alone or as part of a team.

Here are some of our profiled firms' thoughts about their USPs

"We give a free initial consultation, and I haven't seen many do that. We're also of a certain age, most of us, and that is useful in this business. And we're quite flexible in the way we deal with the clients."
Alain Cohen, director, Ashby Cohen

For *Tom Walker, now head of employment law at Manches*, two factors stand out—now and when he was in the same role at Colemans-ctts:

"Being accessible and commercial. There's no point being a counsellor if you're not accessible. So accessibility is really a subset of commercial, and with that you thrive and without it you die, in my view."

"Our niche is to provide the quality of service you'd get from a traditional commercial practice but with the other additional benefits. And really having it built into our culture that the service we seek to offer is practical and pragmatic. By caring for the people who work in the business as much as we do, we have as a result high morale and I think that also makes us more successful."
Mark Ellis, CEO, Ellis Whittam

"I try to put myself in the position of the client. I act for a lot of lawyers and one of the questions I ask is: 'Have you been a client before?' And they'll say, 'Now you say that...', or 'When I got my divorce—and that was even more unhappy than this situation', or 'when I bought a house', which is a completely different situation. But then I try and gauge what the client is looking for and spend more time discussing their objectives. That's one of the ways I try to distinguish myself, and what I say is: 'My colleague here has a magic wand. She keeps it up her left sleeve, she waves it and all clients' wishes come true. If she had such a wand, what would be your wish? You would like to keep your job? After what you've told me, I'm sorry... You threw a book at the managing director, I'm afraid....' If you want to buy apples and I've got pears, I'm sorry but it's not going to work out."
Ronnie Fox, principal, Fox Lawyers

"One way in which we are different from other firms is that we do eighty per cent employer work and twenty per cent employee work. We are also the lawyers' lawyer—we have a really good portfolio of other law firms for whom we do HR work."
Mirella Sikorski, senior marketing executive, Lewis Silkin

"What sets us apart is talent, results and responsiveness—in

no particular order. A lot of times clients are really stressed out about employment problems, and part of our job is to make them feel like they're going to be taken care of, and that requires being responsive and sensitive, and not doing or saying anything to create additional stress."
Robin Fawsett, co-chair employment and labour law, Shutts & Bowen, Orlando

For *Darren Maw, managing director of Vista*, it's the firm's people that are its key selling point: "The only people who really admire really good lawyers are lawyers, not clients, because a legal service delivery presupposes legal competence, so you don't compete on it. Our people recognise that and recognise that our job is to work hard to deliver value to our clients' organisations using what we know, not proving what we know. Our people are differentiated on that basis. You may find people like that littered around other organisations, but they stand alone or are in a minority, whereas we are exclusively of that mindset."

4.4   Defining and refining your message

In Chapter 2, we gave you internet marketer Frank Kern's succinct summary of the basics of marketing communications:

1.   Here's who I am.

2.   Here's what I've got.

3.   Here's what it'll do for you.

4.   Here's what I want you to do next.

We're going to discuss copywriting—which underpins almost every aspect of how you communicate your message—in the next chapter, but there's one more step to take first.

Action

Before you can start getting your message across, you need to refine and define it, clearly and succinctly. This exercise is about *you*, not your client: You need to put your USP and your other benefits into words, and you need to sum up who you are.

This shouldn't take long and it shouldn't be difficult. All you are doing is writing a summary. It's purely an exercise in clarification, and definitely not for publication.

You could use the following points to help you define your message:

1.   Our USP is ...

2.   Our second main benefit is...

3.   Our third main benefit is...

4.   Our firm...

5.   Our team...

Here is an example of a completed summary:

1.   Our USP is representing West Midlands SME employers in sex discrimination claims.

2.   Our second benefit is specialising in employment law services tailored for SMEs.

3.   Our third benefit is specialising in all areas of discrimination law.

4.   Our firm only handles employment law work and primarily represents SME clients from the West Midlands; our firm was established in 1999.

5.   Our team comprises 10 solicitors with 80 years' joint experience in discrimination law. Our HQ is in central Birmingham; we have a sub-office in Wolverhampton.

5

Copywriting is not a gift

To get your message across, you need to be able to translate it into something your audience will respond to. All that stands between you are words, so you need to be clear and you need to be consistent. You need to tell the same story whether it's on your website, in a blog, through advertising, at a seminar, in an email, in a letter, or face-to-face with your client. To do this effectively, you need to know how to write good copy.

Happily—as the chapter title says—copywriting is not a gift. It is a learned skill. And while there are elite, full-time copywriters (particularly those producing direct sales ads and particularly in the US) who quite literally earn millions from their words, the fact remains that what they do is not anything innate. They may be exceptionally good, but their ability to communicate so well has largely been honed by trial, error, hard work and experience—it has nothing to do with creative genius or literature. This is good news because it means we can also become competent copywriters as long as we stick to some pretty straightforward rules. (If you're about to move on to the next chapter because you employ someone else to write your copy, we urge you not to! You can't assess how effective their writing is unless you know what it should—and should not—be doing.)

By now you'll have a clear idea of who you're addressing and what you want to say to them—and you'll say the same thing across all your marketing materials.

Your next job is to put your message into words, always holding the thought that, as we said in Chapter 2, effective marketing flows from keeping it simple and staying focused. So let's once again remind ourselves of Frank Kern's spin on John Carlton's 1-2-3-4 of basic marketing communications:

- Here's who I am.

- Here's what I've got.

- Here's what it'll do for you.

- Here's what I want you to do next.

Clearly, as we've already noted, this is an intentional and gross over-simplification. There are not many contexts in which this approach would work without significant clarification and finessing, and marketing employment law is certainly not one of them. The reason we're repeating it here is just to help you stay on track.

Another device to help you remain focused is to keep in mind the long-established yardstick of effective advertising copywriting centred on the operatic acronym AIDA:

- **Attention**
- Interest
- Desire
- Action.

Translated into the writing process, this is:

- grab your reader's **attention**, usually with a compelling headline

- hold your reader's **interest** by offering something relevant to their needs

- create your reader's **desire** to find out more

- get your reader to take **action**.

And you need to do all this using plain English. Too many lawyers have a fear of simple language, as though it will somehow devalue their status as professionals and reduce their credibility with clients, particularly other professionals. If this was ever a legitimate concern—which is doubtful—it certainly isn't in 21st century Britain. We are now bombarded with information from more sources than we would have thought possible even ten years ago, and as a result we all have a diminished attention span and lower boredom threshold. The ability to quickly engage your audience's attention has therefore never been more important. If you are still using stilted, convoluted English littered with jargon and legalese—identified in Chapter 2 as a particular turn-off for clients—now is the time to stop.

5.1   It's not about you!

We warned in Chapter 4 of the risks of confusing your clients' needs with who you are and what you do. When you're producing copy, the biggest single mistake you can make is to write about yourself and not your client. You will by now have noticed that throughout this book we are addressing you, the reader, directly. Why are we doing this?

Look again at those two sentences:

> The biggest single mistake you can make is to write about yourself and not your client. You will by now have noticed that throughout this book we are addressing you, the reader, directly.

Now let's translate this into the type of language that you may have become accustomed to using, first while you were training and now in your communications with clients and colleagues:

The biggest single mistake that can be made by a copywriter is to write about themselves instead of about their client. The reader of this book will by now have noticed that he or she is being addressed directly by the authors throughout.

Which works better? Which engages you most immediately and swiftly? Which most efficiently *gets the message across*? (Incidentally, the first example is also shorter—by 10 words—and in copywriting brevity is a virtue!)

By talking straight to your client, and not from one level removed, you begin a conversation. That it is at this point a one-way conversation does not matter. You have caught your reader's attention and you can now begin building on that. So this is **copywriting rule number 1**:

- *You* and *yours*—in almost every context, address your client as "you" and not as a disembodied third person.

And this is **copywriting rule number 2**:

- Focus on *benefits* and not on *features*.

5.1.1   The three obstacles of indifference

When you're on the receiving end of somebody else's bid for your attention, you may well do this yourself. You'll be handed a leaflet, land on a website or open an email and after a rudimentary scan you'll move swiftly on after muttering—to yourself or out loud—something along the lines of:

1.   Who cares?

2.   So what?

3.   What's in it for me?

For your own words to work, you have to get past these three obstacles of indifference by learning how to focus on *benefits*.

Let's show how this translates into marketing a service by getting you to imagine you're on a solicitors' website. You're looking for information about handling redundancies and on your screen is their answer, presented with the focus on *features*:

> The team at Bloggs can help when a business has to restructure and reduce its workforce. Our employment lawyers, led by our senior partner, John Bloggs, have many years' experience in handling redundancies and complying with the relevant legislation, and with their thorough knowledge of the law ensure the correct procedures are always followed.

Well, yes, you would hope so. But what do the team at Bloggs actually *do*? How would it *feel*? They tell us they consider themselves experienced and knowledgeable—*features*—but nothing about how this translates into their service—the *benefits*—for you, the client.

Would they clear the three obstacles with this? Who cares if they can help "a business"? Whose business? Any old business? So what if they've got years of experience? All solicitors say that. It all sounds a bit pompous, vague and impersonal. What's in it for me? Does this grab my attention? Or hold my interest? Does it create any desire to find out more? What am I supposed to do next? In short, why should I hire them?

Now here's the same message with the emphasis on *benefits*:

> If you're restructuring your business and have to cut your workforce, we can guide you through the whole process. We'll help you follow the correct redundancy procedures and make sure all your staff understand what's happening every step of the way. Contact our senior partner John Bloggs now to find out how we can get you safely to the other side.

Another—powerful—technique for emphasising benefits is to pose questions and then answer them:

Are you restructuring your business? Will you have to cut your workforce? We can guide you through the whole process, helping you follow the correct redundancy procedures and making sure all your staff understand what's happening every step of the way. Contact our senior partner John Bloggs now to find out how we can get you safely to the other side.

Either way, the message is clearly about what's in it for the client, with the firm's features—the lawyers' ability to do the job well, the name of the person to contact—used only to reinforce the benefits. And the sub-text here is that this firm will not only get the law right but they'll hold the client's hand and equip them to keep communications civil with their staff, thus reducing the risk of unfair dismissal claims.

The tone is welcoming and informal but also has authority. To give this some context, imagine for a minute that you are the proprietor of a modest SME, forced, for the first time, to fire people you personally hired not that long ago. You are under pressure, you're feeling vulnerable, you have a superficial understanding of the 1996 Act, but you're in uncharted waters and terrified you'll get something wrong and end up before a tribunal. At the same time, you don't want to be made to look or feel ignorant, stupid, or out of your depth. Which of these two approaches do you think would be most reassuring, most likely to encourage you to keep reading and find out more? And which one is more likely to get the firm past the obstacles of indifference?

We cannot emphasise enough how important it is for you to park your neutral, formal lawyer's style and get into the habit of using natural, conversational language to promote the benefits of your business whenever you are writing promotional copy. It doesn't matter whether your target client—as in our example—is a modest SME or whether they are a global player, a charity, a club, or just a member of the public. The principle remains the same because we are all hard-wired the same. As John Carlton says: "Use the word 'you' in almost every sentence. You're talking to a human being."

5.2 Clear out the clichés

Clichés, jargon and gobbledegook: they're everywhere! And lawyers are right up there among the worst offenders when it comes to harnessing meaningless phrases to sell themselves.

Some common (way too common!) examples are…

- client-centred; client-focused; client-based *(where else would you be looking?!)*

- committed to…; dedicated to…; commitment to clients *(as above!)*

- a full range of services *(as opposed to what—a pretty feeble range of two or three threadbare ones?)*

- proactive service *(looks good, but what does it **mean**?)*

- cost-effective service; competitive service *(as opposed to a grossly over-priced ineffective rip-off?)*

- wide / extensive / broad experience *(against a maximum couple of years' PQE or a complete lack?)*

- support at all levels *(levels of what?)*

- tailored solutions *(as opposed to something you toss indiscriminately in the general direction of all your clients?)*

- innovative solutions *(in preference to stale, obsolete, can't-be-bothered solutions? There are way too many "solutions" out there anyway—the word has lost its value).*

There are plenty more, and we have all—us included—been guilty of using them in both our writing and our speech when we just can't be bothered to find the right words to articulate what we want to say, or because we're succumbing to emperor's new clothes syndrome: we do it because everyone else does it and it must therefore be OK.

But it isn't. The problem with using vacuous terms and phrases is that almost everyone now knows full well that they're vacuous. They can easily trigger your prospective client's blah detector and stop your copy getting past the obstacles of indifference. Suffice it to say—and we'll look at this again in Chapter 14—that you've only got about eight seconds to grab and hold the attention of a visitor to your website.

So **copywriting rule number 3** is to keep the road through your copy clear of rubbish.

Do not, however, confuse stilted clichés and jargon, which have largely lost whatever meaning they once had, with colloquial turns of phrase and expressions that we all use. Including the language of ordinary conversation can—when employed sparingly and in the right context—help your copy flow and make it more accessible.

You'll find examples of the sort of everyday phrases we mean throughout this book. Here are just a few from this chapter:

- Get your message across.

- Tell the same story.

- This is good news because...

- ... engage your audience's attention.

- On the receiving end...

- ...how this translates into...

- ...in uncharted waters...

If you're at all sceptical, it's worth noting that top copywriters routinely—and very deliberately—employ this technique and urge the rest of us to do it too. Do you think they'd bother if it didn't work?

There are a couple of final points about using straightforward language. Always avoid two or more words when one will do, and don't use long words when short ones work just as well. See the Resources section for examples.

For more about the use—and abuse—of our language, visit the Plain English Campaign's website (**www.plainenglish.co.uk**). Another site we recommend is **http://gobbledygook.grader.com**, which analyses your website for excessive use of jargon (and helps you realise quite how bad copywriting can be).

5.3   Breaking up your text

Which of these is easier to read? This?

> When you're writing copy to market your business, you need to break up the text to help hold your reader's attention. There are various ways of doing this. These include using boxes or sidebars to focus on a particular point you want to make, using sub-headings, using bullet points and numbers to separate ideas into lists, and using bold or italic text for emphasis.

Or this?

> When you're writing copy to market your business, you need to break up the text to help hold your reader's attention. There are various ways of doing this. These include using...
> - boxes or sidebars to focus on a particular point you want to make
> - sub-headings
> - bullet points and numbers to separate ideas into lists

- bold or italic text for emphasis.

We have used sub-headings, bold and italic text, bullet points and numbered lists in this book to make it easier for you to read.

Bullet points and numbered lists are also easy to write and they force you to communicate concisely—all leading copywriters employ them. But you should only use them where your text separates out naturally. Don't force words into bullet points or numbered lists for the sake of it. This, for example, doesn't work:

- Are you restructuring your business?

- Will you have to cut your workforce?

- We can guide you through the whole process.

- We can help you follow the correct redundancy procedures.

- We will make sure all your staff understand what's happening every step of the way.

- Contact our senior partner, John Bloggs, now to find out how we can support you.

The flow, intimacy and natural progression of the original paragraph is lost and the tone has become hectoring instead of engaging, as though the reader is being shouted at and ordered about rather than invited into a conversation.

5.4   ... It's still not about you!

Lawyers are often badly let down by poor, feature-heavy writing in their practice descriptions—the copy usually found somewhere prominent on a website home page, near the front of a brochure, on a directory listing, or in an advertisement. Even though this *is* about you, it should still be focused on your *benefits* and not on your *features*.

Let's consider five examples from real solicitors' websites, chosen entirely at random. The copy is verbatim but the names have been removed as this is not an exercise in naming and shaming. All punctuation, emphasis and spelling are exactly as they appear on the webpages.

Example 1

[FIRM'S NAME] can trace its roots back to 1910, when [FOUNDER'S NAME] was admitted as a solicitor and started practice in [NAME OF TOWN]. From those early days our reputation has become firmly established. And our ethos is still the same.

> *"To help clients resolve their problems and achieve their objectives in an approachable efficient and cost effective way".*

Please browse our website which will tell you about [NAME], its people and business. We hope it will answer your questions. But nothing will convince you fully, until you instruct us to represent you. Only then, will you be able to experience for yourself, how [NAME] has become such a well respected, specialist, firm.

Example 2

[FIRM'S NAME] was established in [CITY] over twenty five years ago and have gained a reputation for high professional standards and a partner-led service to our business and entrepreneurial clients.

What we can offer:

- Expert advice in all our practice areas
- A high level of service and communication
- An understanding of commercial realities as well as the legal aspects of transactions
- An ability to act quickly
- A proactive approach in all aspects of the transaction always trying to increase the benefit to our client.

Example 3

[NAME] and [NAME] started in partnership in 1992. Although the partnership is relatively new in [NAME], its origins go back further. Both Partners were formerly with established practices within the area, [PARTNER'S NAME] being the resident Partner in the [TOWN] office of [SECOND FIRM'S NAME] since it's opening in 1970. In 1992 the firm also acquired the former [TOWN] practice of [THIRD FIRM'S NAME] which had been established since the early 1950s.

Both Partners are well experienced in most of the usual legal problems Clients are likely to encounter and can offer advice on a wide variety of subjects. They are supported by an able and helpful staff most of whom followed the Partners from their previous practices.

Example 4

WE are a quality legal practice based in the centre of [CITY]. WE provide practical, straightforward legal advice which is cost efficient and client orientated. We're not too big to provide a friendly, approachable and really personal service to all our clients but not too small to provide a professional, experienced team of lawyers offering a first class service. Whilst [FIRM'S NAME] has a strong tradition, it lives in the present and plans for the future.

WE hold a franchise from the **LSC** assuring you of quality care.

Example 5

[FIRM'S NAME] combine experience with innovative approaches. We are proud of our past, but embrace modern technology and look forward to a dynamic future.

You may contact us by e-mail should you require more information or wish to arrange an appointment.

As you browse through the [FIRM'S NAME] website, you will find that we provide a comprehensive range of legal services. With three offices in the [AREA] we have the capacity to provide a service that is "local" in feel across a large geographical area. We value our close links, established over many years, with the communities we serve.

Action

This time you're going to do the work! Look again at these pieces of copy and see how they "perform".

First apply the three copywriting rules:

1.   You and yours.

2.   Benefits not features.

3.   Clear the clichés.

Then see if they get past the obstacles of indifference:

1.   Who cares?

2.   So what?

3. What's in it for me?

Look as well for unnecessary verbosity and, while you're at it, poor grammar and punctuation! Once you've done this, compare your critiques against ours, which you'll find in the Resources section for this chapter.

Action

Next, put your own practice description to the test, going through exactly the same processes.

Action

Now review *all* your existing and recent marketing materials against these criteria. This may include copy on your website, in emailings, in newsletters (printed or electronic), advertising, and in your PR material, such as news releases.

Yes, this may take some time, but it *is* worth it because you'll be in a better position to tackle the final task in this section.

Action

Return to the summary that you wrote at the end of Chapter 4 (the **Action** where you refined your USP, your other top two benefits, the key features of your firm, and the key features of your employment law team).

Use your summary to write a new practice description. Then:

1. Test it against the copywriting rules.

2. Test it against the three obstacles of indifference.

3.   Check it for poor grammar, spelling and punctuation.

(See Resources for ours, but please finish yours first!)

Unless you were already a copywriting whizz—or you have been employing one—your new practice description should serve you significantly better than whatever went before. Use this exercise as a springboard for everything you write from now on, including daily communications with your clients and colleagues. You will all reap the rewards!

As we said at the start of this chapter, good copywriting is a skill, not an art. You now have a sound (though basic) overview, and like all skills it's something you'll refine through practice, picking up tips and ideas as you go. And there is no shortage of those, particularly from American copywriters, who have an ability to use the most disarmingly simple language to quite awesome effect.

We recommend some good sources in the Resources section for this chapter.

6

The best publicity is free publicity

6.1   An introduction to the old rules (and the new)

We all know what good PR is. It's when you get publicity for free, when journalists say nice things about you and deliver a healthy helping of that third-party testimony you need to help build credibility with your clients, both current and prospective.

And the only way you can achieve this is by sending out lots of news releases, chasing journalists, and keeping your fingers crossed, right?

Not any more. As with so much in our lives, the internet is changing the rules. Specifically, it's changing how journalists look for ideas, how they build on them, how you fit into their new way of operating, and—crucially—it's creating channels of communication that can take your news direct to your audience, bypassing the media altogether. Note that we say "changing". While the realignment is well under way, it's by no means complete, and for many on both sides of the media fence the "old rules" are still producing excellent results.

So what are these "old rules"? David Meerman Scott, bestselling author of *The New Rules of Marketing & PR*, has been one of the first to quantify this seismic shift in the mechanics of PR.

He lists the following among the "old rules":

*   The only way to get publicity is through the media.

- Businesses communicate with journalists through news releases.

- The only way the public finds about the news release is if the media uses it for a story.

- The only way to measure the success of a release is by monitoring what's been published or broadcast.

And these are among the "new rules":

- PR is for more than just a media audience.

- PR means using news releases, blogs, podcasts and other online content as PR tools to communicate directly with clients.

- PR is about your firm being recognised across the Web, not just one night on local TV.

Does this mean immediately abandoning tried and tested ways of dealing with journalists? Not at all: nothing beats great media coverage for raising your profile and enhancing your reputation—with your clients and with your peers. But it's no longer the only way of achieving this, and it's essential to see the bigger picture before deciding on the best strategy for you.

This chapter focuses on the traditional route to a journalist's heart, and gives you the chance to hone your copywriting skills while they're still fresh in your mind (we'll look at the new rules of PR in Chapter 12). However, before going any further, let's step back and look at what PR actually means.

6.2   The great 20th century invention: the origins of PR

The public relations industry—and an industry it is, with the Chartered Institute of Public Relations representing 9,500-plus UK practitioners and at least as many more outside—traces its origins back to the charismatic Edward Bernays. He was born in Vienna in 1891 and with his family moved to New York a year later. He styled himself as a "public relations counsel" and between 1919 and his retirement in 1963 was responsible not only for numerous high-profile campaigns of his own, but for putting in place many of the techniques now embedded in PR, and particularly in media relations.

Among these is the lynch pin: using third-party authority to get your message across. He pioneered harnessing "expert" opinion—in a classic example he promoted bacon eating by publishing his own survey of physicians who recommended eating large breakfasts and then circulating this to 5,000 other doctors, together with publicity material for his client's pork products.

Bernays also understood well the power of the picture. In 1928, he organised a "photo opportunity" to showcase the dour President Calvin Coolidge as a warm and sympathetic character. In what is also believed to be the first instance of a US president engaging a PR professional, Bernays rounded up a star-studded cast, including Al Jolson, for breakfast at the White House followed by photos on the lawn.

Bernays died in 1995, aged 103, but his ideas are alive and well and appearing daily in a media outlet near you.

6.3 Why should you use PR?

As Bernays recognised, all of us tend to accept the word of a neutral third party over that of someone with an obvious, partial agenda. Advertising is, by definition, partial. That's its function—to promote your product or service. Intelligent media relations, on the other hand, puts a disinterested messenger— the media itself—between you, what you're promoting and the public.

Does this mean we shouldn't advertise at all? No, but you may want to rethink how you do that as well. (We look at traditional advertising in more detail in Chapter 18.)

Before you begin any type of publicity campaign—involving the media or otherwise—you need to be sure you have clearly identified your goal, which brings us back to the fundamentals of marketing discussed in Chapter 2:

1.   Who are my clients?

2.   What do they want?

3.   How do they want me to provide it?

American legal marketer Tom Kane puts it like this: "If a firm doesn't know where it wants to end up, who its target audience should be, and what clients it really wants to serve, then any advertising or public relations campaign is premature." Assuming you do now have those objectives identified and in place, Kane identifies the three main differences between the two traditional approaches:

Advertising	Traditional public relations
Paid for (and can be expensive)	Free (unless you're using a PR agency)
You specify your message	Message is controlled by the media outlet
Comes across as a sales pitch—which it is	More credible as the pitch is made by a third party

He favours PR over advertising for the reasons Bernays identified, as does UK marketer Chris Cardell, whose claimed successes include generating coverage off the back of one press release that would have cost £1.5 million in advertising fees. "I love PR because it's free and it lets you reach thousands or millions of people", he says.

Few law practices are likely to achieve an audience in the millions using the media alone (unless it's on *News at Ten* for entirely the wrong reasons!), but into the high thousands is well within everyone's reach with the right approach.

6.4   Catching the media's eye using the old rules

You can attract the media's attention via two main routes:

1.   Give them a good story.

2.   Give them yourself.

We'll look at each of these in more practical detail shortly, but to clarify the difference between them let's first use examples featuring our fictional West Midlands discrimination practice:

1.   Story-led PR—the practice appoints a new partner and employs two new solicitors, and issues a news release.

2.   Expert-led PR—the Court of Appeal issues its judgment in a high-profile sex discrimination case. One of the team comments on the outcome during a local radio news programme.

We'll explore how to use these strategies following both the old PR rules (in this chapter) and the new (in Chapter 12). First, an example of PR that combined both of these, close to our hearts, is a campaign launched by one of the authors of this book in 1999 when he wrote a book entitled *Avoiding Unfair Dismissal Claims*, a 200-page guide on the art of dismissing employees lawfully. A single press release triggered enormous publicity, including a double-page spread (with a very unflattering photo) in the *Independent* newspaper, as well as radio and TV interviews. Indeed, for one hour (and one hour only!) the book reached the number 1 sales slot on **www.amazon.co.uk**, knocking a certain celebrity chef to a well-deserved second place! The press release took less than an hour to write, and it took a further hour to phone about 20 national newspapers and journals and ask for the email addresses of the "industrial correspondent". A very successful investment of two hours' time!

6.4.1 Steering clear of the spike

When you hit "send" and despatch your news release to a media outlet in the traditional manner, you stand only a one per cent chance of it seeing the light of day. Here's why.

You may in your travels have heard one journalist discussing with another journalist the fate of a story: "That went straight on the spike." To "spike" a story means it's not going to see the light of day and has, with the click of a mouse, joined all the others in a graveyard folder adjacent to every newsdesk inbox (for the term's origins, see the Resources). A depressing 99 per cent of items—incoming news releases among them—get spiked.

So how can you raise your odds of being among the tiny minority who not only get read, but get used? By putting yourself in the shoes of the journalist. It doesn't matter whether they're the news editor of a national newspaper, a duty editor at ITN, an online editor for the BBC website, the district reporter for a group of weekly papers, the editor of a specialist trade weekly, or in sole charge of a small local radio station. They all face two unrelenting challenges:

1. They're under constant pressure to fill their empty spaces or airtime.

2. They're constantly seeking ways of achieving it.

And this means they're all looking for the same thing: a story. But not just any old story—a story that will interest *their* audience (which is *your* audience too, of course) and give them the edge over their rivals. They're not remotely interested in you or your firm *per se*, but offer them something that will entertain or inform their readers, viewers or listeners, and you're in with a fighting chance.

But before you think this is a breeze, there is one extremely important factor you have to remember, and it's one that neither you *nor the journalist* has any control over. The late Tory prime minister Harold Macmillan was (possibly inaccurately) reported to have replied when asked by a journalist what blew governments off course: "Events, dear boy, events." And it's events—the drama and emergencies of life, global or otherwise—that can end up dictating what happens to your story, particularly in the mainstream media. The converse of this, of course, is that if it's what's known as "a quiet news day"—or week, or even month—you can find yourself getting much more attention than you could normally expect, and your story given a much larger headline. (There's more about the influence of events in Resources.)

6.4.2 Getting your foot in the door

Because they're always under pressure (and we do mean always), journalists don't suffer fools gladly, or indeed at all. Unless you're already a few stages down the relationship-building road, all they want to know is whether you're offering them something they want. They respond exactly as a prospective client might to, say, your website message, and you need to get them past those three obstacles of indifference we discussed in Chapter 5:

1. Who cares?

2. So what?

3. What's in it for me?

Again, you have to focus first on *benefits* rather than *features*, though in a slightly different way than you do when addressing your audience direct—a journalist is looking for the benefits to *them* in your story, not at the benefits you bring your clients. You therefore need to find what's known as a "hook" or an "angle" to make what you're offering at the very least intriguing and ideally compelling.

So let's build a story. You need to tick these five boxes (we'll call them W5) on the journalist's basic checklist:

1.   Who?

2.   What?

3.   When?

4.   Where?

5.   Why?

Let's return to our West Midlands practice appointing a new partner and employing two new solicitors. We'll call them Adams, Brown and Curtis. Their senior partner is John Adams, the new partner is Anne Jones, and the two new solicitors are Bill Smith, who will be based in the main office, and Carol Davis, who will work from the branch office. Bill has made age discrimination his speciality and Carol has made sex discrimination hers. The appointments were all made in February 2009, and Adams, Brown and Curtis was established in 1999. We've put all this information into Table 3.

The next step is to identify the elements in this information that constitute news:

1.   The practice is 10 years old in 2009.

2.   The practice is expanding because the workload is expanding.

3.   The workload is expanding because the scope of discrimination law has widened.

Table 3   Using W5

Who?	What?	When?	Where?	Why?
Adams, Brown and Curtis	Employment law practice specialising in sex discrimination; clients are local SMEs	Established 1999	West Midlands	To meet growing need
John Adams	Senior partner	1999	Birmingham	
Anne Jones	Partner	Joined practice in 2003; appointed partner in February 2009		Practice expanding because scope of employment law widening
Bill Smith	Solicitor; age discrimination specialist	February 2009	Head office in Birmingham	Practice expanding (as above)
Carol Davis	Solicitor; sex discrimination specialist	February 2009	Branch office in Wolverhampton	Practice expanding (as above)

4. More fee earners are needed to match the growing workload, so two new solicitors have been appointed.

5. Anne Jones is appointed partner to reward her contribution to the firm's growth.

To this we can add *features* that may add substance but are not intrinsically anything new:

1. John Adams is the senior partner.

2.   The head office is in Birmingham; there's a second office in Wolverhampton.

3.   Adams, Brown and Curtis is a niche employment law practice.

4.   It specialises in defending sex discrimination claims.

5.   Its clients are primarily West Midlands SMEs.

6.4.3 Getting your news release right

These are the main reasons why 99 per cent of the copy submitted to any media outlet ends up spiked:

1.   The story's inappropriate—a mother and toddlers' group fundraiser in Nuneaton isn't going to make it onto *Newsnight*!

2.   The story's incomplete—it doesn't tick all the W5 boxes; for example, the location of the firm is missing, or there's no clue why the senior partner has won the award.

3.   It's confusing—the ingredients are there but in an illogical order that makes it hard work to unravel and tease out a story.

4.   There are no contact details—it's astonishing how often this happens! Journalists aren't clairvoyant and they are busy. If you don't tell them how to get in touch, don't expect them to track you down.

5.   The story is just plain boring—it's like all those other dreary, fact-laden offerings that also fail to see the light of day, a significant proportion of which are written by people employed by PR agencies. There's no hook or angle, nothing to inspire a journalist to even read beyond the headline, never mind find out more. It instantly triggers the obstacles of indifference and fails entirely to pass the AIDA test outlined in Chapter 5 (attention, interest, desire and action).

Returning to our West Midlands practice, here's a news release written primarily with the local media in mind. It stands a high chance of hitting the spike!

Law firm announces appointment of partner and two new solicitors

Adams, Brown and Curtis solicitors announce the appointment of Anne Jones to the position of partner.

Mrs Jones has been with Adams, Brown and Curtis since 2003 and will continue to be situated at the office in Birmingham.

Joining the firm are Bill Smith, who will be based in Birmingham, and Carol Davis, who will work in the Wolverhampton office.

John Adams, the senior partner, said Mrs Jones was being made a partner in recognition of her contribution to the firm and that extra work had made it necessary to employ Mr Smith and Miss Davis. They are solicitors who specialise in age discrimination and sex discrimination law respectively. All the changes in the firm are taking effect in April 2009.

Adams, Brown and Curtis was established in 1999 and is an employment law practice that specialises in defending sex discrimination cases. Mr Adams said the caseload had grown due to the changes in discrimination legislation.

ENDS

What's wrong with this? At first glance, it appears to tick most—if not all—the boxes. We know *who*, we know *what*, we know *where*, *when* (more or less), and we know *why* (just).

But the information is scattered about and begs a lot of questions. Let's dissect it as though we're an over-stretched journalist working for a local weekly newspaper somewhere in the West Midlands:

1. Paragraph 1—Where is this practice? Who is Anne Jones? Should I care?

2. Paragraph 2—Good for Mrs Jones, but so what? Oh right, they're based in Birmingham.

3. Paragraph 3—Who are these people? Where have they come from? Wait a minute, is the main office in Birmingham or Wolverhampton?

4. Paragraph 4—Good for Mrs Jones (again), but so what? What's caused this extra work? It's mid-April 2009 now. Have they been appointed yet or not?

5. Paragraph 5—Oh look, it's the firm's tenth anniversary. Wonder why they didn't mention it. Can I be bothered to find out? Nah—what's in it for me? Oh right, the extra work's due to more legislation. Wonder what that actually means? Sounds quite interesting given the downturn in the economy, and there might be a story there, but I've got another 90 releases to plough through before lunch and anyway there's no contact details. Spike.

And that's assuming they got past the headline!

You could get lucky, of course—it might be a quiet news week and you'll get some coverage. But it will be dull coverage, because what you're offering is dull, and you'll fail to engage with your target audience because the readers—you'd be unlikely to get listeners or viewers for this—will in turn put the three obstacles of indifference in your way.

So let's turn this around and give our grumpy journalist something a bit more newsworthy. To do this, we'll engage all the principles of effective copywriting we discussed in Chapter 5, in particular using AIDA and plain accessible English.

PHOTO OPPORTUNITY:
9 April 2009
Thursday 16 April @ 10am
Centre House, King Street
Birmingham

Lawyers celebrate milestone by taking hard way down for charity

A group of lawyers will next Thursday (16 April) abseil down a Birmingham office block in a £10,000 fundraising celebration of their firm's tenth birthday.

The ten solicitors from employment law specialists Adams, Brown and Curtis will be joined by lawyers and clients from across the city in the charity challenge at the firm's head office in King Street at 10am.

Senior partner John Adams said: "This is a fun way to mark the firm's milestone and our continued expansion. We're raising money for the local children's hospice, and we're hoping to hit a target of £10,000—£1,000 for each of the past ten years."

Mr Adams said Anne Jones was stepping up to partner level after six years with the practice. "Anne has made an enormous contribution to our business—particularly in her specialist area, which is defending sex discrimination claims for local employers.

"We've seen a steady rise in our workload due to the broader scope of discrimination law, and Anne will now get extra support from Carol Davis who also specialises in sex discrimination work and will be based at our Wolverhampton office. She joins us from Coventry law firm Duggan, Edwards and French.

"We're also welcoming Bill Smith who will handle our rapidly growing portfolio of age discrimination work from the Birmingham office. Bill comes to us from Gee & Harris in Stafford."

Mr Adams added: "Both Bill and Carol have volunteered to join us in the abseil even though it'll be their first week with us—something of a baptism of fire!" The practice has set up a donations page at www.justgiving.co.uk and there is more information about the fundraiser on their website, www.abcemploymentlaw.co.uk.

ENDS

More information from John Adams on 0121 111 3333;
john.adams@abcemploymentlaw.co.uk

NOTE TO EDITORS: Adams, Brown and Curtis is a niche employment law practice specialising in defending discrimination claims for West Midlands SME employers.

www.abcemploymentlaw.co.uk

Let's dissect it as we did before, from the journalist's perspective:

1.   A photo op—good start. Headline's quite intriguing... what's the first part saying? Birmingham lawyers celebrating their firm's tenth birthday with a charity abseil. Makings of a good picture story... *(Attention)*

2.   Paragraph 2—okey dokey, tick the boxes: we know *who* (the law firm), we know *what* (charity abseil), we know *when* (10am next Thursday), we know *where* (firm's office in King Street), and we know *why* (to celebrate firm's anniversary). And they've got some clients coming—I wonder who? *(Interest)*

3.   Paragraph 3—that's clever: £1k for each of the ten years, plus we've got the senior partner saying it all in quotes, which saves me a lot of time. A bit of a cut and paste and away we go. *(Interest)*

4.   Paragraphs 4, 5, and 6—ah, right, they're throwing in some extra back-patting stuff here. But that's OK because we've got a nice story and it'll add a bit of weight. This growth in employment law looks interesting—might be worth following up for a feature. Who's the contact? The senior partner. Good. That'll save being passed around. And there's a note to editors saying exactly what they do. Handy. *(Interest / desire)*

5.   Paragraph 7—I was just wondering when these newbies were starting, and I see it's next week. Fine. Sorted. Oh, and they've got a justgiving.co.uk page as well. I'll go have a look at that when I check their website. Could get two stories out of this, actually—a pre-piece and then a follow-up with the picture next week... Let's see how we're looking for space... *(Desire / action)*

You see the difference. This copy clears the obstacles of indifference, ticks all the journalist's W5 boxes by the end of the second paragraph, and passes the AIDA test. There is a proper story, a good angle, a hook. Now there's a high probability that the firm will get two bites of this cherry—depending of course on those events beyond everyone's control—with the essence of this release appearing in the first week, and a photo of the abseil and another story in the second. The reporter was also sufficiently intrigued by the firm's growing portfolio to start thinking about writing a longer article, and if that did happen then this one release could end up producing three separate chunks of positive free publicity.

Not only that—because there's something visual on offer, this is the type of story that could also interest local TV, and local radio might send along a reporter or do a telephone interview. And there's more! The specialist trade press is also always looking for human interest stories, so this release could bear fruit there with a minor tweak—instead of sending the story ahead of the event, the firm would need to get their own quality photos taken on the day and then send those along with a version of the release written in the past tense.

Yes, the partners have had to do some lateral thinking, and invest some time, energy and resources to attract this media attention. But the abseil is an excellent profile-raiser and morale-booster in itself, showing the firm understands the importance of community involvement and corporate social responsibility. The event is good PR all round and also cements relationships by involving existing clients.

You obviously can't use this exact formula for everything you want to publicise, but the basic structure works whatever you're saying. When you're primarily aiming at the media, follow these golden rules of release writing:

1. Always look for a way to offer a photo opportunity. Study the illustrated stories that get published or broadcast by your target media for inspiration.

2. Write an intriguing headline. Your headline alone can mean the

difference between publication and the spike, so look carefully at those featured in your target media and mirror them as closely as you can. Look also at the headlines of the American copywriting greats (see the Resources section for Chapter 5 for where to find examples).

3. Match your language to the outlets you're targeting. Study them and copy their style.

4. Use simple sentences following the copywriting principles in Chapter 5, and no more than 25 words for the first paragraph. Avoid jargon and clichés!

5. Clear the obstacles of indifference, ideally by the end of the first paragraph.

6. Get all the W5 boxes ticked, ideally by the end of the second paragraph.

7. Trigger AIDA with the headline and interest in the first paragraph. The journalist must be committed to taking positive action before the end of the release.

8. Aim to include a quote from a named individual with authority—a senior partner or similar. But avoid empty words and phrases like "I am delighted that…" "We are pleased to announce…" (See Resources for other examples.)

9. Always include full contact details for a named individual, ideally the one you have quoted.

10. Keep the release to the equivalent of one A4 page unless there's some truly compelling reason not to, and don't drop your text size lower than 10pt.

Action

Using Table 4 (the W5 grid in the Resources), the copywriting principles from Chapter 5, the approach discussed here, and the Adams, Brown and Curtis news release as your basic template, have a go at writing your own news release. You're doing this for real, so keep looking at it from the journalist's perspective while you write, and when you're finished, get a colleague to apply the W5, obstacles of indifference and AIDA tests.

6.4.4 Knowing who to contact

We'll come on to nurturing relationships with individual journalists shortly, but first you need to know who you're looking for and where to find them. It's important to get this right. Using a scatter-gun approach is not only a waste of your time and resources, it can actually engender ill-will if you keep sending employment law related material to a specialist in an unrelated field—a motoring correspondent or economics editor for example. (And yes, obviously there are occasional overlaps—we're talking about a general rule!)

Who you target is going to be dictated by several basic factors including...

1. the size of your practice

2. your type of practice

3. where you're located.

This will of course vary enormously. If yours is a multidiscipline high street practice in a small town, a worthwhile proportion of your target audience will read, watch or listen to the local media. If, on the other hand, you're a substantial corporate city centre practice, your general target clients may read *The Times* or the *FT*, listen to the Radio 4 *Today* programme, and watch *Working Lunch* or *Newsnight*. And they may read, watch or listen to their local media as well, which if they're commuters could widen the scope beyond the city limits. You can also expect them to consult specialist media—trade publications for their industry or profession, along with associated websites—just as you do. Where would our West Midlands practice Adams, Brown and Curtis fit into this sliding scale? Here's a recap:

1.   It's a small to medium-sized firm (10 solicitors).

2.   It's a niche employment law practice specialising in…
       a)   representing employers
       b)   handling discrimination cases.

3.   Its target audience is SMEs in the West Midlands.

With our example release we've already identified local print and broadcast media as good targets. This story was also worth sending to the legal media because of its human interest angle, but would there be any mileage in this firm ever seeking publicity in, say, the *Daily Mirror*? Or *News at Ten*? Only in the most unusual of circumstances, such as involvement in an attention-grabbing case of national significance—and if it's that interesting, the media will already be on to it. Were Adams, Brown and Curtis to launch a new service specifically targeted at, for example, independent financial service SMEs then it would be worthwhile targeting that sector's trade press, and remember that consumer magazines are also always looking for new angles.

For the larger city centre practice with major corporate clients, if the story is broad-based and interesting enough there are not only many more potential media targets, but they're also more diverse—add to the list national daily newspapers, regional and even national broadcast media. We explore the wider online role of releases when we turn to the new PR rules, but for now—and whatever the size and type of your practice—don't overlook the many news and specialist websites out there which are also engaged in a constant quest for new, interesting stories. Even where they are satellites, do approach them, as they may give you space when their mainstream media parents can't or won't.

How do you find all these targets and how do you find out who to contact? There are three main ways of doing this:

1. **Do it yourself!** Work out your target types of outlet—local, regional, national, trade, print, broadcast, online, etc—and then narrow your list down to what is a manageable size for you. Try **www.mediauk.com** as an excellent starting point. You should find most of what you're looking for here, and even the tiniest outlets now have websites. You may not get the names of individual journalists for all the media you select; many may only list generic newsdesk email addresses and phone numbers.

2. **Invest in a media guide**, such as the annual Benn's Media, which goes into forensic detail and does so at an eye-watering price— £412 on Amazon (http://tinyurl.com/n2jo28)! You could spend a day at the local library, of course.

3. **Subscribe to a media contacts service** such as Vocus (**www.vocus.com/content/index.asp**) or Cision (**http:// uk.cision.com/**). They do all the hard work and not only identify and maintain bespoke contacts lists for you, but also—among other options—distribute your releases. Unless you're putting out a news release practically every day, this is unlikely to be cost-effective. (There's more about these services in Chapter 12.)

Once you have your list of contacts, you need to introduce yourself. Before making the initial call or despatching your news release, phone each of your target media's newsdesks and find out who is the right journalist to approach. You may not be offered a name because the outlet doesn't have anyone specialising in law-related stories, instead being told to "just go through the newsdesk".

So you have your list of contacts, you have your release written and ready to go.

Imagine for a moment that you are in the shoes of the person tasked with distributing the Adams, Brown and Curtis's abseil news release. For a story like this, which is flagging up a future photo opportunity, aim to get the release out at least a week in advance. This increases the chances of it being put on the newsdesk and picture desk schedules.

Here's an outline of the full process, including the initial phone call:

1. Phone the newsdesk and say that you're sending a release shortly "about a charity abseil taking place next week to raise money for the local kids' hospice". That's of much more initial interest than anything to do with you. If asked for more information, focus on the photo opportunity and the fundraising first and then explain why you're doing it—to celebrate the firm's anniversary. At this point, ask for the name of the person you're talking to and ask if you should send it direct to them or to the newsdesk. Ask for a direct dial number—you may get one, you may not.

2. Send the release. If you do have a name, personalise the email and run the news release text within it. Don't attach anything at this point.

3. Leave it a few hours, or overnight, then call the person you spoke to and ask if they've got it OK. If it's been read and the journalist is sounding interested, ask if they need any more information or would like to talk to the senior partner. If it hasn't been read, you're flagging up its presence in the inbox. If it's been read and they're not interested, politely ask why. You may not get much of an answer. That will depend on why it's been spiked—lack of space, already got a charity or a law firm story lined up, just plain not interested.

4. Even if it appears to have bitten the dust, send out a modified version of the release the day before the photo call—something

may fall through and your original release is long gone. In the email subject line write: "Photo opportunity reminder—charity abseil tomorrow." Also include this at the top of the text: "Photo opportunity reminder—tomorrow (16 April)" and change all the "next weeks" to "tomorrows", but keep the date in the text!

5. On the day itself, if you've not already been told it won't be used, call first thing to check if anyone is coming. Specifically ask whether, in the case of print media, they're sending a photographer and reporter, or just a photographer. A photographer on their own will not generate anything new in the way of copy, so you may want to call your named reporter after the event to let them know how it went. For broadcast media, ask if they're sending a TV crew or radio reporter—if they are, give yourself a big pat on the back and make sure everyone is smiling!

Should you follow up after you've got coverage? If you've been dealing with an individual rather than the amorphous newsdesk then dropping them a quick email to say thank you helps oil the wheels. Don't phone, though. Unless you've got something new to say, you're just eating into their day and you risk losing goodwill. And this brings us on to the next stage of relationship-building.

Action

Compile a list of five media targets, including at least one print, one broadcast and one trade. Follow the procedure we've just outlined for establishing contact, sending your release, and following up.

6.5 Making friends with the media

Nothing beats being able to pick up the phone and say, "Hi, I've got a great story for you", and the journalist on the other end not only hearing you out but knowing you well enough to trust your judgment. As with all mutually beneficial relationships, this takes work—particularly to get to the point where it's an equal partnership and you're as useful to the journalist as they are to you.

You start at a significant disadvantage. A journalist is trained to take nothing at face value, leans towards the cynical, is under pressure, is bombarded with unsolicited information, and you could be anyone. When you're giving them something they want, they'll be your very best friend. But as soon as they've got it, you become just one of the scores of people who pass through their working lives and you're quickly forgotten—unless you make it your business to be remembered!

6.5.1 Getting inside their world

Let's assume that you're with Adams, Brown and Curtis and your abseil news release has generated some good publicity. In the process you were in touch several times with a local newspaper journalist and you now want to start building on that connection.

We'll begin with the practicalities. The exact routine obviously varies, but essentially everyone working in the media is driven by a deadline of some sort: monthly, weekly, daily, hourly—right down to half-hourly for radio newsrooms. There's no let-up—the space or airtime has to be filled and it's always against the clock. To call a reporter on, say, an evening paper about something that's happening next week when they're ten minutes from that day's deadline triggers more expletives than practically anything else in the newsroom! So before you say anything, you need to find out the best times and the no-go times—all you have to do is ask and most journalists will be pleasantly surprised you're bothering.

You may already know a bit about the journalist you want to cultivate, but we urge you to find out more. If they're a print reporter, read at least ten of their most recent stories before you next make contact. If they're a broadcast journalist make sure you watch or listen to them whenever you can. Google them. Do they have a LinkedIn or Facebook page? Do they use Twitter? Have they got a blog? Depending on their seniority, you may be able to track their career. Look too for interests you share, work-related or otherwise. Your aim here is not to quote their life story back to them, but to give you insight into how they think and operate and to identify areas of common ground. If they're interested in what you can bring them, they'll be doing exactly the same (more about this when we get to the new rules in Chapter 12).

6.5.2 Touching base again

Now you need to find a reason to get back in touch, a fresh angle.

Wearing your Adams, Brown and Curtis hat, you could call to let the journalist know how much the abseil actually raised (only if it's on or above the target, of course!). Say that the publicity made a big difference, thank them again, and follow that up with a confirmation email which includes a short quote, something like:

> Senior partner John Adams said: "Everyone is very pleased we've raised so much for such a worthy cause and would like to thank all those involved—our own Adams, Brown and Curtis team, other lawyers from across the city, and our many clients who either took part on the day or have been so generous with their support."

You're now back in the reporter's inbox, they have some copy they can use, and contact has been re-established. Your next objective is to find more ways to keep the channels open and to gradually morph into an "expert".

You'll recall that our reporter showed interest in the firm's growing workload, but of course wearing your current hat you don't know that! The reporter's memory has now been jogged by your call and because you've been so civil and helpful, there's more than a 50–50 chance they'll want to follow up. If they do, invite them to lunch. Yes, really! Invite them to lunch (or maybe breakfast—find out which suits *them*). They may decline—some offices have a hospitality ban—but let's assume our reporter accepts. This gives you an unrivalled opportunity—not to do anything that smacks of a pitch, but to illustrate on neutral territory the *benefits* to the journalist of having you as a contact.

Let the journalist do the bidding—they are chiefly interested in picking your brains. But to do that, they will have to ask about the firm and your background (remember you'll have already been Googled, as will your colleagues!), and this is your chance to do a little showcasing. The journalist will come away with the bones of a story and you'll come away knowing you've been put in their contacts book. And there, unless you do something very foolish, you'll stay. What's more, you'll go with the journalist if they move on, which could prove even more beneficial in the future.

6.6 Becoming an expert

It's now a few months down the line. The story about the growth in employment law work has been published—lots more free publicity for you—and now you're in fairly regular touch with the journalist. You're still doing the legwork—perhaps sending in an email reminder about the latest rise in the national minimum wage, or a short statement commenting on new statistics showing a sharp rise in local redundancies. And then you get your real chance—remember our example of an "expert-led" story (in Section 6.4)?

Well, let's put you in the shoes of the senior partner at Adams, Brown and Curtis. The Court of Appeal decision is out, there's a local connection and when you call the paper and offer to comment, the reporter bites your arm off. Next time they'll call you and all your groundwork is repaid because now you've become an expert and the traffic is two-way.

Tom Kane says: "By getting to know media contacts, they may call you when they need a lawyer's perspective. They are always looking for good sources of information, particularly when they are covering a case or on deadline with the latest, hottest breaking news. They won't think of calling you unless they know who you are."

And the media needs a constant supply of experts, particularly experts who are good talkers and happy in front of a camera or microphone! Your contribution will be dictated by who is calling. The depth and technical detail needed by your local newspaper or radio reporter is going to be very different from the insight expected by a journalist from *The Times* on one hand or *The Lawyer* on the other. Once again, getting to know your media contacts and their audiences will make it much easier for you to judge the response they need.

With this shift in emphasis comes new protocols, and you do need to be on your guard, no matter how cordial your relationship with the journalist. When they come to you, the main thrust of their story may well be already mapped out. Your role is to help "stand it up"—justify their stance. You therefore need to be wary about being ambushed into saying something you don't actually mean, or saying anything that could be taken out of context. Lawyers are fortunately better trained and experienced than most to recognise the pitfalls.

These tips should also help:

1.   Return the journalist's call as soon as you can—you don't want them going to anyone else.

2.   Immediately ask when their deadline is—that way you can gauge the urgency of the inquiry.

3.   Politely ask whether they're recording the call or taking a shorthand note. Be specific about this—not just a note, but a shorthand note. If they're not taping and they can't do shorthand, your words are more likely to be paraphrased, you're more likely to be misquoted, and it's harder to prove

either way. If the inquiry touches on something controversial—with the scope to damage your personal or corporate reputation—consider recording it yourself or say that you'd rather answer their questions by email instead. Yes, they may go elsewhere and you may lose a bit of short-term goodwill, but they will be back and you're meanwhile spared some potentially unwelcome attention.

4. Never, ever say "no comment". You may mean that you've no view on the matter, but what the journalist hears is a lawyer with something to hide. If you just don't have the answer at hand, say you'll find out and call back. For something outside your remit, instead say: "That's not a topic I know anything about—I can give you the name of someone who does." Should the journalist be asking about a matter directly concerning you or your firm, it's even more vital to give a proper answer: a "no comment" never prevents a negative story. In this situation only begin the conversation if you're well prepared.

5. Don't assume anything you say is "off the record". Journalists are under colossal pressure to deliver and it can be hard to resist the temptation to "stand up" a story with something said in confidence when there's nothing else at hand. By all means agree in advance what is, and is not, for publication, but always assume that everything you're saying could reach a wider audience.

6. Never assume you'll get copy approval—you very rarely will unless the journalist is seriously out of their depth and needs you to check they've got hold of the right end of the stick.

7. Once the story has been published or aired, and you're happy with it, drop the journalist a friendly thank you email. If you've been misquoted, you need to weigh up your response. If no damage has been done, let it go. Journalists quickly lose

patience with contacts who nit pick, and the mistake may anyway have not been theirs but introduced somewhere further down the editing line. If it's more serious, then you must let them know. When debating how far to push it, bear in mind though that printed apologies largely serve only to draw fresh attention to the original misrepresentation, which can exacerbate rather than remedy the error.

Action

Select one of your new contacts and start building a relationship with them (including lunch!) as we've described.

Your goal is to become their expert, and when you've achieved this once, repeat the process until you're on the expert contacts list of at least one print, broadcast and legal trade journalist.

We asked our profiled firms to tell us about how they use PR.

"I used an outside agency for PR, but it didn't generate much—a few articles in the *Financial Times* and the *Evening Standard*, a few mentions here and there, but it didn't actually do a sausage in terms of business. Part of the problem with our business is that PR people are interested in the cases. But it's not in our clients' best interests to go blowing to the press, so you can't say anything. Ninety per cent of cases are settled on confidentiality agreements anyway."
Alain Cohen, director, Ashby Cohen

Tom Walker, head of employment law at Manches, worked closely with Colemans-ctts' marketing team when he was in the same role there: "For example, when the law on constructive dismissal changed quite heavily in favour of the employer, I gave it to our marketers to give to a local business journal and it was used to raise our profile. My whole approach is to write positive articles."

"We're ambitious and we do want to spread the good news, but I think you need to do PR properly if you're going to do it at all and at the moment it's all hands on deck. We would need to use an external agency."
Mark Ellis, CEO, Ellis Whittam

Raising your personal profile through publicity unconnected with your practice can be highly effective. *Ronnie Fox, principal at niche City employment firm Fox*, is particularly accomplished at this—see Fox's profile at the start of the book for more details. But he also gets coverage on employment and partnership law matters in both the mainstream and the legal press, some of which he generates himself and some of which now comes through his PR consultants. Fox initially built his contacts with the media "simply by being prepared to speak to journalists and befriending them", and uses hospitality to oil the wheels.

"If you've come for an interview, I might say: 'Shall we go for lunch afterwards? I'll take you to a place you've never been before'." He has made it his business to find out how they work, and what they need: "I help them meet deadlines, and I'll introduce them to others when I'm not the right person." Now the balance with his contacts is 70:30—they come to him 70 per cent of the time, and he goes to them 30 per cent.

Members of the *Lewis Silkin* employment law team are widely

quoted by both the mainstream and specialist media: "The media come to us and we get a lot of word of mouth referrals. Our lawyers are often approached as 'experts', for example James Davies on age discrimination."
Mirella Sikorski, senior marketing executive

"We don't use the media at all—it's not part of the business model at the moment."
Dean Morris, principal, Morris Legal

"PR is something I'd associate with those who have either a larger or broader range of stakeholders where relationship to brand values is important *en masse*—Nike, or Microsoft, or Ferrari. I'm not saying it can't transfer to B2B but the instruments need to be sharper and more focused and while we occupy a niche in an employer sense, all our client organisations are disparate and it would be a real challenge to find those sharp, focused instruments that would promote our brand."
Darren Maw, managing director, Vista

7

Time to get out more

We stressed the importance of visiting and entertaining your clients in Chapter 3, as a means of maintaining fruitful relationships and generating fresh business.

Now we're going to explore other ways of boosting your income simply by getting out more and going online—marketing tactics particularly worth honing when times are tough because they can bring significant dividends for very little outlay other than your time.

Until very recently networking meant meeting prospective clients face-to-face the old-fashioned way, but the phenomenal growth in social networking websites is changing all that. In the space of just a few years there's been a paradigm shift in how we all communicate, and we are all on the same learning curve as the highly sophisticated and flexible Web 2.0 technology opens up more and more possibilities.

However, before you jump in, do be careful. It would be very short-sighted indeed to switch all—or even most—of your networking attention away from the real world, just as it would be foolish to pretend online networking has no role to play in a 21st century law firm.

At the heart of using any kind of networking as a marketing tool is the concept we've already explored—that ultimately people buy people and we all make myriad decisions every day on that basis. For this reason networking should never be equated to hard selling. Your aim is to showcase your expertise and knowledge, to give freely, and never to directly pitch for business. In time you want to become recognised as the dependable expert to whom people turn, not a pushy sales person fixated on talking about yourself.

If you're already an accomplished networker—virtual or otherwise—congratulations! But don't skip this chapter as you may well discover new ways to build on what you're already doing and the inspiration you need to expand your networking horizons.

If, however, you're among the many lawyers who find the whole concept anathema, take heart. Networking is—like copywriting—primarily a learned skill. And—again, like copywriting—while it comes more easily to some people than it does to others, it really is something all of us not only can do but need to be doing right now.

We'll look first at traditional networking before exploring the virtual version in Chapter 9.

7.1   I hate networking!

How often have you said it or heard someone else say it? It's almost a badge of honour to declare that you hate structured networking, or you're no good at it, or you'd rather pull your eyelashes out one by one than be dragged to a networking event. Or you may come at it from the time angle—you're just too busy trying to bring in the fees to fit in networking. Yet networking is an essential part of any professional's life, whether your principal aim is to build your personal reputation or it's to source the new work your firm needs to grow or just stay afloat. Either way, it's time to embrace networking as part of your remit, take a deep breath and get yourself out there.

The good news is that it need not be an ordeal. Gwenllian Williams and Michael Farrell, of UK legal training consultancy deWinton Williams, say:

"Many lawyers are introverted, reflective and dislike self-promotion. Pushing themselves forward in a networking event, standing in front of an audience and socialising with people they do not know can be deeply uncomfortable. Such events raise the spectre of social discomfort and rejection. The reality is that this rarely happens, but the fear of being unsuccessful is sufficient to keep them away from profile-raising events."

Will Kintish, a former chartered accountant who now provides networking skills training for lawyers and other professionals across the UK, goes a step further. The word "fear", he says, breaks down (in a particularly apt acronym for lawyers) into:

* false
* evidence
* appearing
* real.

He offers examples of the sort of conversations we have with ourselves when confronted with people we don't know:

"Nobody's going to talk to me."
"What if I'm asked something and I don't know the answer?"
"I'm not going to remember anybody's name."
"I'm bound to tip my drink over somebody."

We all have these irrational anxieties, which boil down to fear of rejection, fear of embarrassment and fear of failure, not anything remotely life-threatening. And think about it—if you're going through this process, so too will everyone you're about to meet. Have you *ever* been subjected to ridicule or abuse at a business-related networking event? Do you know anyone who has? You may come across the odd person who's discourteous and dumps you for someone they consider more interesting, or someone the worse for wear, but we're generally all on our very best behaviour because we are all there for the same reason.

Kintish says: "To be a good networker, one has to be approachable, friendly, affable, agreeable, likeable and personable. The list goes on but at the end of the day 'nice' says it all." OK, but how do we overcome our fears and achieve this "niceness"? Let's return for a moment to Chapter 4 when you were homing in on what first drove you to become an employment lawyer, and then on identifying your ideal client. We said there that doing the type of work you enjoy best for people you like and respect is ultimately not only the most fulfilling, but also the most lucrative in the long term.

So before you attend any networking event you need to focus again on...

1.   your target client

2.   what they want

3.   how you're going to provide it.

You are rarely—if ever—going to find yourself in a room full of your ideal clients, but that's not the point. It's being able to identify very clearly the type of work you're already doing that brings you the most satisfaction, and what you're ultimately seeking that matters. Once you have that clear in your mind, it's going to make it much, much easier for you to talk with ease, confidence and authority. Note the use of the word ultimately. Remember, you're not there to pitch for anything. As Williams and Farrell say: "Lawyers need to understand that they are not selling in the true sense—they are demonstrating experience and expertise which lead clients to feel safe with them, they demonstrate a commercial sense which makes clients trust them, and they create a rapport which makes clients want to work with them."

In other words—and where have you heard this before?!—it's not about you. American marketer Barbara Walters Price, who confesses that she detests networking, says: "Never enter any situation asking 'what's in it for me?' Go ready to serve and serve humbly. That's the golden secret to effective 'networking', if you want to call it that. I prefer the term effective 'servanthood'." Will Kintish says: "Give first and receive second should be the attitude. If you only think 'what's in it for me?' you are likely to become unpopular. Think more, 'what's in it for you?'" And he quotes author and poet Elizabeth Asquith Bibesco: "Give without remembering, receive without forgetting." In other words—and where have you heard *this* before?!—it's all about benefits.

Not only is it about benefits, it's not about features. And your job title is a feature, not a benefit. So when—as can be guaranteed to happen—you are asked: "And what do you do?", the last answer you want to give is a bald, "I'm a solicitor". Why? Not least because it's a conversation stopper—as you say it you're likely to start feeling defensive because lawyers are not, as we know, universally adored, and this will be reflected in your body language. But primarily because it's a feature and the person you're talking to is busy erecting the three obstacles of indifference. They're also not going to be interested in the fact that your practice was established in 1946 by the senior partner's grandfather or that your offices have recently been refurbished. Remember:

1.   Who cares?

2.   So what?

3.   What's in it for me?

So what should you say? Enter the elevator pitch, quintessentially American in origin but universal in relevance.

What we're talking about is the succinct but compelling response we give when asked what it is we "do". One simple way of structuring it is: "I help (your clients) to (the problems you solve for them)." For example, if you were one of the West Midlands solicitors from Chapter 4 you might say: "I help local small businesses stay up to date with all the changes in discrimination law." Another twist is to focus just on the challenges you address: "I work with (your clients) who (the problems they face)." So: "I work with local small businesses who find it hard to keep up with all the changes in discrimination law." The other person will then say something like: "How do you do that?" To which you reply: "I check in with them at least once a week to keep an eye on how it's going and I also let them know immediately if anything's happened that could affect their business." The other person will hopefully then say: "That sounds useful—tell me more." You could then respond: "Well, for instance only yesterday…" and give them a genuine example of a problem you've solved that has wider application. And if you still feel absolutely compelled to say "I'm a solicitor" when asked what you do, at least qualify it by saying: "I'm a solicitor, but what I actually do is…", and use the rest of the formula.

Whichever route you take, the conversation should now open up, and you'll be holding the other person's attention because they can see there may well be something in it for them—benefits—or if not for them, for someone they know. Instead of an uncomfortable impasse eventually filled by you asking what *they* do, you've taken the initiative.

Now, though, you need to start listening. As Will Kintish says: "Spend more time in a conversation being interested rather than interesting. People love talking about themselves; nice people let them." And American lawyer Lisa Landy—voted Interlaw's Interlawyer of the year in 2006 and an acknowledged networking expert—says: "The best way to meet people and make a good impression is to let the other person talk. The idea is '80 per cent they talk, 20 per cent you talk'." Take the opportunity to offer advice freely—remember, you're not there to sell—and start building the relationship. (For help in producing your elevator pitch, see the Resources for this chapter.)

Ronnie Fox, principal at niche City employment and partnership firm Fox and one of our profiled employment specialists, is an accomplished networker. He makes no secret of the fact that he enjoys it, accepts a lot of invitations, and does a great deal of socialising in contexts where business and fun overlap. "It's no good being the best lawyer in the world if nobody knows who you are. You're not going to get any business that way."

Action

Compose your own elevator pitch by referring to the dialogue outlined above and following the guidance in the Resources. You must finesse it until you're comfortable delivering it and you're getting the responses you're looking for. Then keep on refining it. As with all elements of successful marketing, testing is critical.

7.1.1 How do I choose who to talk to?

Which of us hasn't had this experience? You arrive at a networking event, recognise not a soul and hover near the entrance wondering what to do. Depending on the time of day, you might grab a coffee or a glass of wine, and then you'll hover with that, perhaps tucked away in a corner, sipping from it at regular intervals as displacement activity. You know you should be circulating but you're rooted to the spot, partly by the conversation in your head that we described above, and partly because you genuinely don't know how to begin.

Will Kintish offers valuable advice on "working the room" in his booklet, *How to Become a Confident and Effective Networker*. A good starting point is to identify which groups of people are "open" and which are "closed" through their body language. Pairs which are open will be standing side by side, while those that are closed will be facing each other. Obviously you don't want to barge into what's become a private conversation, so focus on the open twosomes and ask their permission to join them. The same applies with groups—approach where there's a gap and wait until you've caught the eye of whoever's speaking and smile. They'll almost certainly smile back, the others will turn to face you and welcome you by introducing themselves. Ask their permission to join the group and stay quiet. Don't change the subject, just wait until an opportunity arises and then contribute to the current topic. If there's no gap, and the body language shows you the group's happy as it is, move on to the next one.

When you first go up to someone else on their own, start off by asking if they mind you joining them and introduce yourself. Then stand side by side so that you can signal to others that they'd be welcome to come over. Only close up and face one another if you want an exclusive conversation. However, you're there to network, not find a soul mate, and you need to keep moving. Kintish suggests using exit strategies such as: "It's been great meeting you. I just need to go and see Joe over there—would you like me to introduce you?" "I'm going to get another drink—do you want to join me?"

7.1.2 How do I remember their names?

This will no doubt also chime. You're introduced to somebody at a business event and instantly forget their name. In fact, you probably haven't even heard it as you're busy focusing on shaking hands and reading their body language. Never be embarrassed to ask them to repeat it. Our own names are very precious to all of us and they will be pleased that you're sufficiently interested in them to take the trouble to get it right. Once you've got it, use it several times in the early stages of the conversation to make sure it's committed to memory. If you're with someone else and they don't introduce you when a third party joins your group, it's almost certainly because they've forgotten your name—just do it yourself and spare everyone's blushes.

A useful tip is to wear your badge on the right so that when you shake hands your name is clearly visible without the other person having to move their line of sight far from your face. Those of us who are right-handed generally stick a badge on the left in an instinctive move, so you may need to consciously remind yourself the next time you're doing it.

Before you part company, make sure you ask for a business card. Will Kintish says: "Read it carefully and comment. This shows you're interested in your new contact. Ask permission to contact them in a few days to find out more about them and their business." He then suggests that you write the date and time you've agreed you'll be calling on the back of the card—within their sight. "This shows commitment and links to the next stage." Later, back at the office or at home, make a note on the card of where you met and anything particularly interesting about them. You also need to offer your own card, even if you're not asked for it, not least because they're more likely to remember you when you call.

Ronnie Fox has designed a folded business card specifically for networking events—especially bigger ones. It acts as a mini-brochure for his firm and also carries Fox's photo. A more recent addition to his networking arsenal is an LED lapel badge which he tested at the 2008 International Bar Association annual meeting in Buenos Aires. It read: "I'm Ronnie Fox ... talk to me." And they did. "Having fun and prompting amusement is a part of my life and I believe that good humour helps to resolve situations. There are four thousand lawyers who go to the IBA. Most of them will return with a hundred cards and will forget who gave them three-quarters of them. I've got a special card—it doesn't look like anybody else's except those of a couple of people who've imitated it. That's the card I use at conferences. People will remember—'oh, he's the guy with the flashing badge... His card's got a picture of him, so I can remember who he is'."

7.1.3 You must make that call!

It's now a few days later. You're back in the office with a colossal to-do list and the thought of phoning someone you barely know with what feels like a thinly disguised sales pitch is filling you with a mix of irritation and dread. But to capitalise on what you've already invested, you must do it, and it's much easier if you approach it as a challenge rather than a chore, an extension of your conversation rather than anything to do with selling. So phone at exactly the time you agreed, re-introduce yourself, focus first on what you talked about at the event and then see where that takes you.

Your prime objective is to set up a meeting to explore further what you can do for this prospective client, but always take your cues from them. If they're not ready to do that, don't push it. Maybe drop them an email with a copy of your latest newsletter, or flag up a seminar your firm is organising that they might find useful. Follow up at intervals—from what you've found out about them (at the networking event and subsequently) you can identify issues that will be particularly relevant to them. If there's a significant EAT judgment, for example, let them know in a personal email how it might affect their business. Only when they specifically tell you that they're not interested should you let them go.

7.2   Where should I go?

The networking opportunities for meeting other people are legion. The opportunities for meeting the *right* people for a defined purpose are narrower, and it's crucial that you don't waste your time in the wrong places. Focus in once again on your ideal target client:

- What are they looking for?

- What am I offering them?

- Where will I find them?

There are two main directions you can take. Either network through a business-based organisation that attracts your ideal clients, or find one that's focused on something you're personally enthusiastic about which will lead you to them by more circuitous means. In the first group, we're principally talking about...

- national business networking organisations

- local business bodies

- trade/professional organisations.

And in the second...

- lawyers' organisations

- charitable or not-for-profit organisations

- leisure, sport and/or special interest groups.

We recommend that you concentrate on events such as business breakfasts or lunches, along with seminars and workshops, rather than anything where you're the audience. Lectures—unless accompanied by provision for socialising—involve too much one-way traffic and visits are too specific. There are benefits and drawbacks to every networking combination, but for optimum results it ultimately makes sense to spend most time where you'll feel most comfortable. Lisa Landy says: "Select one or two organisations you are passionate about because it won't feel like work."

Let's look at the categories we've listed so that you can weigh up how they might work (or not work) for you and your firm.

7.2.1 The national networkers

There are several UK-wide organisations for which networking is the raison d'être rather than one of a portfolio of functions. We're focusing on two.

Business Network International (BNI) was launched in the US in 1985 and can now genuinely call its reach global. There are more than 550 "chapters" across the UK, with each meeting once a week over breakfast and all operating to exactly the same agenda. (In fact, the 20-point agenda is identical wherever you are in the world.) The organisation's UK website **www.bni.eu/uk/** claims that referrals generated in 2008 through BNI "led to business worth £190 million". Only one representative of any trade or profession is allowed to join each chapter and all members act as ambassadors for their colleagues, handing out each other's business cards and making personal recommendations.

Here are the good points:

- You can build relationships quickly within a fixed and defined group of largely local business people, and work as a team to promote everyone's interests.

- There are tough compliance rules, which ensure a disciplined and motivated membership.

- It's a results-driven organisation.

- You'd be the only employment lawyer in the chapter.

- You have access to BNI's wider network and trainings.

- The authors can point to good evidence that BNI membership does work for some businesses!

And here are the downsides:

- The organisation is very structured and meetings follow a rigid format.

- You're expected to attend all meetings—and speak at them—and may face expulsion if you miss too many.

- There's no control over who's already on board. It's up to the chapter membership committee who gets in, so you'd need to be elected to that to have a future say.

- By definition, it's pretty parochial at the practical level so may not match your ideal target client.

- For such a large organisation, BNI's websites are astonishingly amateurish and difficult to navigate, making it harder than it should be to find out whether there's a chapter near you.

The second dedicated organisation we're looking at is **4Networking (or 4N)** at **www.4networking.biz**, which has at its heart an excellent multifunctional website that puts BNI's online presence to shame. Very much the new kid on the block (it was launched in early 2006), 4N at the time of writing only has a small presence in Scotland and none in Northern Ireland so can't claim to be truly UK-wide. The 4N philosophy is to mix breakfast meetings with online networking—including a forum, blogs, the opportunity to post articles, and be featured—and the structure is much less rigid and formal than BNI's. 4N had just under 200 breakfast groups in mid 2009.

Here are its good points:

- There is breakfast networking with more than one set of business people (the premier membership package allows you to attend up to four different meetings a week, anywhere that has a group and there's also a one-group option).

- There are no sanctions for not showing up.

- It harnesses numerous online options (further details in Chapter 9), so it's not geographically defined.

- It's less serious and formulaic than BNI—the stated balance is 50/50 work/socialising.

And here are the downsides:

- There are few groups north of Newcastle upon Tyne (as yet).

- Breakfast meetings are less structured, focused and results-driven than BNI's.

- The breathless, informal, in-your-face, we're-all-best-mates "work is fun" approach isn't to everyone's taste.

7.2.2 Keeping it local

Say "local business organisation" to most people in business and the chances are they'll reply, "chamber of commerce". All chambers act as local information interchanges and are in business to promote business. They usually have good links with the local authority and government agencies, and manage networking diaries to a greater or lesser degree. How much you'll get out of attending their events is going to depend on the quality of your local chamber, and if you were also to explore the BNI or 4N route you would undoubtedly see a lot of the same faces. However, whatever the size of your practice and wherever you are based, if even some of your prime target clients are likely to be in the local chamber, then you need to be a member yourself. Perhaps you already are, in which case now is the time to put your fee to good use!

All UK chambers are listed on the British Chambers of Commerce website (details are in the Resources).

Here are their good points:

- You get to meet a range of local business people (the exact make-up will vary from place to place, but SMEs always feature heavily).

- You get to meet local councillors and dignitaries.

- There are different venues and event themes.

- You can build your presence as a reliable employment law expert.

- There's access to training and other CPD options.

And here are their downsides:

- Depending on location, they can be a little parochial.

- Some of them may have a too overtly-political agenda.

- The quality of events is variable.

Look beyond your chamber for other local or regional business-orientated bodies. Our West Midlands discrimination law specialist might, for example, find value in joining the Warwickshire Business Club, one of many such groups across the UK which act as a local or regional networking hub. (Just Google "business club" to find out what's close to you. There are, incidentally, four firms of solicitors in the Warwickshire club.) Other options for our specialist employment lawyer could include attending events organised by the West Midlands Business Council, the Staffordshire and West Midlands region of the Federation of Small Businesses, or the Professional Institute Network for the West Midlands.

7.2.3 Trade and professional events
How useful this type of event is to you will again depend on the type of client you're targeting, but what you're looking for is the opportunity to join business people engaged in a specific trade or profession—engineering, say, or accountancy or medicine. Most of their events will be members-only, but if there's a topic of particular relevance—a workshop on workplace safety, say, or the tax implications of redundancy—why not just get in touch with the organisers and ask if you can attend? You could even offer to formally contribute to the discussion (see below for more about public speaking).

If you're coming from the other side of the employment relationship, our emphasis thus far is less relevant, but the principles are the same. To use the redundancy example again, is your Citizens Advice Bureau organising a workshop or seminar, either for volunteers or open to the public? If so, what could you add? Or perhaps a local trade union branch is arranging a series of events for members focusing on fallout from the shrinking economy. Again, ask if you can attend or, better still, be involved.

A bit of lateral thinking can also yield a wealth of possibilities. American lawyer Lisa Landy became the Florida affiliate for the Organisation of Women in International Trade some five years after she went into practice. Five years later, she was global president and has continued to hold key board roles since. "It generated lots of clients for me, because I was in the newspaper a lot, I was interviewed on radio, I was interviewed on TV, and it got me a lot of credibility among my peers."

On the positive side, trade and professional events mean that you can...

- home in on target clients very specifically

- raise your profile as the "expert", especially if you're actively involved in the event

- forge sector links.

And here are the downsides:

- It could be time-consuming for you as homework is involved.

- The events can be very specialised, so although a pool of potential clients is defined, it's also smaller.

- You may have to stand up and speak!

When Ronnie Fox founded the Association of Partnership Practitioners in 1989, it was to raise the profile of this area of work. And he designed the association's meetings to encourage networking: "I built social interaction into the structure of the meetings. A typical workshop starts at 5.45pm, and when you arrive you get a cup of tea, you meet a few people and then at 6pm we go into the meeting itself. The meeting's over at 7.15pm and then there's drinks and canapés so that you get to talk to people. It's a multidisciplinary organisation, it's not just lawyers, and it's deliberately structured to allow people to network."

7.2.4 Talking to yourself—lawyers' organisations

Ah, that's better—back in the comfort zone. You know where you are with other lawyers, give or take. Nobody's going to look down their nose at you or ask you those duh questions. And it's great to talk shop, share experiences, find out how others are riding out the economic storm, and swap ideas.

The only problem with all this is that while you may go home with lots of new business cards, you're highly unlikely to directly meet many—or indeed any—prospective clients. So while there are of course myriad benefits associated with membership of, say, the Employment Lawyers' Association (ELA), the Discrimination Law Association or the Industrial Law Society, they are mainly for your professional benefit, via CPD and by raising your profile through getting involved, election to office, speaking at events, and so on.

Over the longer term, you may well get referrals—from those you meet and through enhancing your reputation—and we're not for one minute suggesting that you abandon the ELA or any other professional body you belong to (indeed, one of us has been heavily involved with ELA for many years). Just be mindful, when you're measuring out your valuable time, of your marketing priorities, and be careful not to indulge in any self-deception.

In summary, then, lawyers' organisations are good for...

- raising your profile

- CPD

- networking with other lawyers

- getting an overview of what's happening in your specialist corner

- improving your networking and speaking skills

- letting your hair down.

And here are the downsides:

- Prospective clients are exceedingly thin on the ground.

- There's a risk of kidding yourself that you're busy marketing your business when in fact what you're largely doing is (no doubt very usefully) investing in yourself.

Ronnie Fox's client base includes a significant number of other legal practitioners, and so for him going where the lawyers go does makes a lot of straight business sense. He offers as an example the role networking played in facilitating a successful high-profile merger. "American firm Kirkpatrick & Lockhart Preston Gates Ellis—then called Kirkpatrick and Lockhart— came to see me and said: 'Ronnie, we want to set up in London.

Not by opening an office, but by taking over a London firm. We'll be back to you when we've got the negotiations seriously under way.' They came back in a month. 'Well, actually, it's all fallen through but we're talking to others.' Came back in another month. 'Nothing's worked, but we're on the look-out.' I went to one of those legal awards dinners and I sat next to Michael Johns, who's the chairman of Nicholson Graham & Jones. At that time, negotiations with Pinsent Masons had just fallen through and he was saying, 'Well, it didn't work out...' And I said, 'Well, maybe you've had a lucky escape—who knows?' 'Well, we've decided to merge. That's the right thing for our present position.' 'Would you ever consider talking to an American firm?' 'No.' 'As a favour to me, would you talk to Kirkpatrick and Lockhart because Peter Kalis, the chair, is an Anglophile, he has an English law degree and he's not like the rest of the Americans I've met.' Met him once and the result was Nicholson Graham & Jones merged with Kirkpatrick and Lockhart. It was very successful, and I got the legal work doing the merger."

7.2.5 Give and ye shall receive: charitable and non-profit organisations

So far we've focused on largely commercial, transaction-focused contexts, but there is a whole other side to networking that's a lot less intimidating for those of us who feel uncomfortable doing any kind of business over breakfast. And that's because you're not actually doing business at all.

What you are doing is offering your time, energy and skills as a volunteer, working alongside other like-minded people towards a goal, usually to do with fundraising. Instead of feeling that you're chasing down work, you're building genuine relationships with people from a variety of backgrounds. You're happy to share your expertise, offer advice and guidance, and in time referrals flow from your generosity.

This works. It is the ethos underpinning the best-known business people's voluntary organisation, Rotary International, which has the motto "Service Above Self" and lists among its objects "high standards in business and professions". You must meet exacting criteria before you can be invited to join. The emphasis is slightly different with the Round Table, where personal growth is allowed to explicitly share the spotlight alongside serving the community. (There are, however, age and gender-related constraints: you have to be aged between 18 and 45 and a man—the women's equivalent is the Ladies Circle. Perhaps not the ideal audiences for a talk about extending the scope of the age regulations—or then again!)

These are among the best known arenas for slow-burn business building through volunteering, but there are myriad other avenues to explore. When you're not being a lawyer, what's the one thing you do that you're really enthusiastic about? Do you have a pastime, or a hobby, or take part in a sport, or is there an area of interest that can keep you completely absorbed and about which you know a great deal?

For example, if you're already a member of your golf club and you've never considered standing for office, why not put yourself forward at the next annual meeting? Or perhaps your next project is rebuilding a classic car—consider finding out if there's a local branch of the marque's owners' club and then get involved. Maybe you relax by reading post-modern fiction—is there a book club nearby you could take part in? We know none of these examples may resonate for you. That's not the point. The idea is to get you thinking imaginatively about bridging the professional/personal divide in a painless and potentially rewarding way.

The good points about networking in this way are that…

- it's pressure-free networking

- it's about building relationships naturally and slowly

- you're making a real contribution to your community

- you're having fun.

The downsides are that...

- there are no quick returns

- it may involve a heavy time commitment.

Among Ronnie Fox's voluntary titles is Past Master of the City of London Solicitors' Company. He held the post of Master in 1998–1999 and continues to sit on the Court. He also wears the Company's award for distinguished service. "I joined many years ago because I wanted to align myself with what they were doing to promote City solicitors. I started going to working meetings, became a member of committees, and got interested in the social side—the livery side—because they do a lot of worthwhile charitable work. And, of course, there are the other lawyers—the vast majority are interesting people who are enjoyable to meet."

And don't forget your own social network. Keith Ferrazzi says in his book *Never Eat Alone* that "personal contacts are the key to opening doors". That may not be a particularly revolutionary observation. What is surprising is that the beneficiaries barely ever met as many as 28 per cent of these catalyst contacts. So, says, Ferrazzi, "it's not necessarily strong contacts, like family and close friends, that prove the most powerful; to the contrary, often the most important people in our network are those who are acquaintances".

Why should this be? Because the people you mix with most by definition move in roughly the same circles as you. Those at the edges, by contrast, are "hanging out with different people, often in different worlds, with access to a whole inventory of knowledge and information unavailable to you and your close friends". The secret to tapping this wealth is what Ferrazzi calls identifying the "super-connectors"—the people in your network who know hundreds, if not thousands, of people. Key among them are restaurateurs, head-hunters, lobbyists, fundraisers, PR people, journalists, and—unsurprisingly—politicians. So who do you know who's a potential super-connector?

Action

Make a list of all the contexts in which it's feasible for you to network, based on where you live and work and how much time you are prepared to commit.

Then, following the example grid in the Resources section, assess each option for advantages and disadvantages—using our guidelines and your own knowledge—and refine the list until you have three to five front-runners. At least one should be primarily business-focused and one voluntary in nature. Then whittle it down to one of each. Then go make your presence felt!

7.3   Going the extra mile

Legal marketer Tom Kane says he's heard many a tale of woe from lawyers who say they belong to several organisations, professional and otherwise, but claim it's a waste of time. "However, when examined further, one finds that although they are 'joiners', they are not 'doers'. Being active in an organisation requires just that—activity."

His checklist for reaping real rewards includes you...

- being more than a joiner—make a meaningful contribution

- seeking leadership positions—volunteer often

- believing in the organisation's mission, so you will remain interested and active.

Public speaking is one area where it's easy to make a meaningful contribution. All organisations, whatever their complexion, are always looking for interesting people with stories to tell—an easy starting point is your own existing clients, and in turn their clients.

Why then do most of us recoil in total horror at the prospect of standing up before an audience? We're back to the fear factor. Will Kintish says: "The main cause of the problem appears to be that we are simply unaccustomed to speaking to more than one person, or to a very small group of people, at a time." And the solution? As with the other techniques for successful networking, it boils down to practice. Joining a speakers' group such as Toastmasters International, where you can hone your skills and overcome your nerves, may well be a good investment.

Action

Take the elements of your elevator pitch and expand them into a five-minute presentation. Focus again on benefits, but broaden it to embrace how employment lawyers in general support their clients. You could for example differentiate between corporate and individual work, and then look in more detail at your own areas of expertise. As before, this isn't a sales pitch. Assume your audience knows nothing of what you do! Use props—PowerPoint, flip charts, etc—or not, as you wish.

The main object here is to get you to focus on opening a window on your world in an engaging and accessible way, so pay close heed to the copywriting golden rules from Chapter 5 when you're at the writing stage. Rehearse and practise as often as you can, run it past colleagues or friends, and then seek out a platform from which to test it for real.

PART TWO
Making connections:
New ways of communicating

8

It's not called the Web for nothing

British computer scientist Sir Tim Berners-Lee said in 1995 of his invention, the World Wide Web: "I had (and still have) a dream that the web could be less of a television channel and more of an interactive sea of shared knowledge. I imagine it immersing us as a warm, friendly environment made of the things we and our friends have seen, heard, believe or have figured out. I would like it to bring our friends and colleagues closer, in that by working on this knowledge together we can come to better understandings."

With Web 2.0, his vision has come to pass, no doubt in myriad ways that he couldn't have predicted. Never before have those of us fortunate enough to have routine access to his web been able to communicate so quickly, effortlessly and in so many ways, jumping continents in an instant to find people, products, services and information we could never otherwise have known existed. (If you're a little hazy about what distinguishes the internet from the web—and the two have become conflated in daily use—and you're not sure what Web 2.0 is, there's a brief guide in the Resources for this chapter.)

For all of us on the right side of the digital divide, a world without this frontier-free online dimension seems unimaginable and truly archaic. And if you're a Generation (Gen) Y (or Millennial)—born after 1980—then the internet, web and mobile technology have run like a thread right through your life, woven into your education and every facet of your socialising. That's how you do much of your business, stay in touch, and make your consumer choices. You know no other way, and the rest of us ignore your reality at our peril—not only because of the actual logistics, but because of the paradigm shift in thinking that now underpins them. Here's a beautifully clear insight into the Gen Y perspective.

The view from Gen Y...

Social media marketing consultant Shama Kabani is highly respected as one of this burgeoning business area's trailblazers. Her business—Click To Client (http://clicktoclient.com)—**attracts customers from around the world, including the UK.**

She says on her Facebook profile:

> When I first launched my company, I was unsure of how people would respond to the owner (me!) being part of Gen Y. For the longest time, this remained a fear. I figured none of our clients had figured out my age, or they just plain didn't care. Either way—I was happy, they were happy, and the business flourished.
>
> Imagine my surprise when our biggest client announced to me 'we chose you out of all the companies because you get the online world like NO OTHER. You practically grew up with it'. I was pretty stunned as I hung up the phone. Literally a week later, another client exclaimed how choosing us was a natural choice because I was at the helm. I noticed this to be a growing trend…and then it hit me. Being Gen Y was an advantage!

Shama then lists some "secret weapons that Gen Y can leverage for success":

1. **Adoptability**: One of my favorite professors in college, Dr Daly, once shared with us the biggest advantage of being young. He said it's easy to get adopted. It's much easier to find mentors and people to take you under their wing when you are Gen Y. Every generation wants to see us succeed.

2. **Their second nature = technology.** The internet didn't come about when Gen Y was in the middle of a career. We didn't have to learn the keyboard. Most of us grew up with it! Technology is second nature to most Gen Y'ers. And as the world continues to become more virtual, this continues to be an immense strength.

3. **Less baggage, more support**. Most Gen Y'ers are the result of supportive families and encouraging teachers. While some might deem us the 'coddled' generation,

---

we are also an extremely positive generation. And have less baggage compared to other generations. Strong support systems are the hallmark of our generation.

4. **Your own definition of success is accepted**. Every generation before ours has had success defined for them. A traditional family, a 9–5 job, one career, etc. Not any more. We are the first generation to have the freedom of defining what success means to us. And, it's fully accepted! Just like the favourite answers on our exams, the answer here is: there are no right and wrong answers.

8.1   Now everyone has a say

We saw in Chapter 3 that disgruntled clients already have a platform from which to vent their spleen (**http://solicitors.info** and the more downmarket **www.solicitorsfromhell.co.uk**). These, as with the countless other customer review sites out there, are built on real people with real views—you, your clients, us and ours. And it doesn't stop there. Through what is labelled social media we can have our say in a huge array of contexts, including commercial sites (Amazon and eBay showed the way here), through social networking, via blogs and forums. We can do it in writing; we can do it with video: according to Wikipedia, in 2008 an estimated 13 hours of new videos were uploaded to YouTube every *minute*, and in 2007 the site consumed as much bandwidth as the entire internet in 2000. What's important here is not the quality of what's uploaded—yes, we agree, most of it is dire—but the quantity. It's now routine for many millions of people around the world to share their lives and their opinions in ways that were unimaginable even ten years ago.

Web 2.0, coupled with the spread of broadband (which means most of us are connected 24/7), has triggered a whole shift in the balance of attention and power. In the old marketing model it was one-way traffic—you as the business owner could largely control the message, through advertising, direct mail, telesales, networking, and so on. And if you didn't always manage to deliver exactly what you had promised, the damage done was likely to be small-scale and the grumbles easily contained.

Not any more. Now your clients are able, if they wish, to heap praise on your practice or pour scorn on your services pretty much at will, and they don't need a dedicated site like Avvo to do it. Pete Blackshaw, executive vice-president of strategic services at internet market research analysts Nielsen Online, and founder of PlanetFeedback, says in his book, *Satisfied Customers Tell Three Friends, Angry Customers Tell 3,000*: "This is the era of what I call consumer-generated media, or CGM. What exactly is CGM? It is the currency of a new commercial relationship between business and consumers. It is the endless stream of comments, opinions, emotions, and personal stories about any and every company, product, service or brand, which consumers can now post online and broadcast to millions of other consumers with the click of the mouse."

In the world of CGM, positive postings give you the very best type of free publicity, but an angry rant can just as easily arrive in the public domain in an instant, and your marketing message and reputation then take a hit. Blackshaw cites as just one example what happened to Dell. The computer giant stood by and watched after journalism professor (and *Media Guardian* columnist) Jeff Jarvis made his views public from his blog in 2005. Within days, the web was awash with negative contributions about Dell, soon followed by the mainstream media, which by covering the furore in turn prompted fresh online vitriol. The same thing happened to internet service provider AOL, and Blackshaw says that it wasn't just down to both companies' disgruntled clients having established blogs and being able to let off steam in style. "In reality, it was the companies' lack of credibility that was responsible for the backlash. What did in AOL and Dell was the fact that they hadn't fostered open, trusting relationships with their customers; they simply weren't credible—and they were summarily punished for it." And the memory lingers on, because online everything leaves behind a trail: Google "Dell sucks" today and Jarvis's original posting comes up on the first page, only upstaged by the follow-ups it spawned.

Credibility—as Pete Blackshaw stresses—is crucial to how you build customer relationships in any context, but lies right at the very heart of what happens online. He identifies the six "critical credibility drivers" as...

1.   trust

2.   authenticity

3.   transparency

4.   listening

5.   responsiveness

6.   affirmation.

He puts trust first because he sees it as the most important. "Trust implies confidence, dependability, and faith in a company or product. It is achieved through honest, ethical, straightforward, consistent, and predictable business practices", he says. "To be truly credible in today's digital world, the claims a company makes about itself or its products must be affirmed by the things consumers are saying to one another through message board comments, online reviews, blog posts, shared photos and videos, and so on...Credibility rules the day, and if a company's 'story' doesn't foster trust, if it doesn't convey transparency and authenticity, if it isn't informed by listening and responding to customers, and it isn't positively affirmed by what consumers are saying to one another, then it's just another phoney story. And consumers will see right through it."

Clearly, there are significant differences between the type of big-brand, high-maintenance, high-profile business that Dell and AOL run, and yours, but the principle is universal. You can't control the catalyst posting, and you can't control how many other people read it or how many add their two-pennyworth, but you can have a say in what happens next. By making a conscious decision to get involved in the online conversation as part of your wider customer care strategy, you can better capitalise on the good news, greatly reduce the likelihood of bad news, and be there to mitigate if the worst happens.

8.2   The building blocks of an online presence

Whatever your present understanding of online marketing is, we are assuming that because you're reading this, you agree that all law firms now need slightly more than a one-page website and an email address to effectively showcase their business. Building a successful online presence is not only important for the reasons outlined above, but it can also be highly cost-effective. However, because it's a constant work in progress, there's an inevitable time commitment—how big this is depends on the complexity of your strategy, and that's something you should be better able to gauge once you've assessed the options.

In this part of the book we'll look at the key elements of the current online mix and then pull these together to show you how to use them to achieve a single marketing and PR goal.

With all that in mind, where exactly *are* we taking you? *Towards an effective online profile centred on a website which is nourished by your involvement in social (or customer-generated) media.*

We've explained why above, so the next question is how? You obviously know what a website is and we'll be looking in detail at how to maximise the potential of yours. Social media is, as we've said, the label attached to those parts of the web where we can all join in the conversation, principally...

- social networks (for example, Facebook, LinkedIn)

- blogs (for example, BabyBarista, The Barrister Blog, CharonQC, Employment Law Blog)

- microblogs (principally Twitter)

- photo sharing (for example, Flickr, Photobucket)

- video sharing (principally YouTube, Seesmic, Metacafe)

- wikis (of which Wikipedia is the best known).

Linking to and underpinning them are...

- email

- podcasting.

We'll be discussing each of these, some in more detail than others, but we'll first expand on that overall aim:

- Your website is your hub, where all your initiatives—online and offline—meet, and your foremost goal is to make it a valuable source of *information* for...
  - existing clients
  - prospective clients
  - the media
  - social media participants, principally bloggers.

There is of course overlap, there are grey areas, but those are your four principal audiences. And there's an additional benefit—getting you higher up Google's rankings. We look in depth at building information resources in Chapter 11, and then at your website itself in Chapters 13, 14, and 15. We look at the role of email within your website and more generally in Chapter 16.

- Through involvement in social networking you enhance all your marketing initiatives by...
  - building on face-to-face networking connections
  - raising your personal and professional profile

- establishing a platform for exchanging ideas
- linking back to your website and blogs.

Social networking is developing at breakneck pace—in Chapter 9 we identify the more effective sites for business-building, consider tactics you can use, and point you in the right direction if you're seeking a more forensic understanding of this phenomenon.

- Everyone may seem to be doing it, but surprisingly few are doing it really effectively. A well-written, thoughtful, topical blog can be an immensely powerful business-building tool. Add to the benefits of social networking...
  - enhancing your reputation as an "expert"
  - floating new ideas
  - connecting with other law bloggers in the UK and further afield.

We'll explore blogging, and its first cousin microblogging, in Chapter 10, and we look at how to pull together all these social elements to deliver powerful "new rules" marketing and PR in Chapter 12.

There's logic to how we're leading you through this online maze. To get your website fully up to speed, you need to understand how your role in the wider web feeds into it. That's why we discuss the mechanics of enhancing your own site *after* we've explored your social media choices. But before we begin unpacking all this we do just need to clarify three points:

1. Nothing we're exploring in this part of the book is intended as a substitute for what we've already discussed or the ideas to come in Part 3—your aim remains to select a balanced range of tools that will work best for *you*. As Dave Evans says in *Social Media Marketing: An Hour a Day*: "The social web, used correctly, is all about what your community of supporters can do to help you build your business ... social media is a

complementary extension of all of your other marketing efforts."

2. The ways in which we communicate online are changing all the time—sometimes quickly and dramatically, sometimes more slowly and subtly. What you're reading about today and what works for you tomorrow may be quite swiftly overtaken by events. To continue to reap the rewards, you need to remain alert and make a clear commitment to keeping your online presence relevant and fresh.

3. Following on from that, we must stress that we are not techies, geeks or website designers, nor do we have a crystal ball. Our aim in this part of the book is to give you a clear *overview* of the options currently available which when drawn together could significantly lift your visibility and give you access to a great many more potential clients.

8.3   Social media etiquette—good manners are a must

One of the most intriguing aspects of how social media is growing and developing—particularly for anyone interested in human behaviour, and lawyers generally are—is the surprisingly unanimous consensus that has emerged over etiquette. Before you join the conversation, you have to learn the rules, and be aware of the two major online no-nos:

1. Trying to sell. For now you must in effect park "here's what I've got, here's what it will do for you…" and focus solely on "here's who I am". You will be ignored or cast out into the cold if you use any of the main social media pillars to blatantly push your marketing message.

2. Failing to disclose an interest. If you're taking part in any kind of online discussion and you have a direct involvement in what

you're contributing or recommending (a new service you're launching, or a link to a briefing paper on your website, for example), *you must say so*. If you don't, be certain that you will be found out. Your credibility will plummet and your input will no longer be taken at face value.

Only on websites specifically focused on business building (we look at some of these in the next chapter) is it acceptable to take a more direct approach, but even there the "give to receive" premise underpinning face-to-face networking still prevails.

Dave Evans says: "*How* you conduct your campaign in a social context is critical to success. The key is not so much to 'let the guests make the rules' but rather to work with those already in the community and to become part of it, to establish your value and develop a shared sense of respect. If you're a newcomer, watch and listen and then join in. Become part of the community. You have plenty of places where you can shout, persuade, and exert claims *outside the social web*. Within the social networks, you've got the responsibility of conduct that comes with being a guest—and in particular a guest who would like to be invited back some day. In return, you have the opportunity to engage your audience at a level that you simply cannot match elsewhere."

9

Networking the 21st century way

We looked in Chapter 7 at traditional networking—meeting people in the real world to build new business relationships—and now we're going to explore the online version.

Online networking is growing at an exponential rate. A survey in autumn 2008 by website WeCanDo.biz found that although face-to-face networking was still ranked as the most effective for generating new business, of those already networking online 67 per cent believed it had brought them closer to their target audience and 52 per cent planned on doing more in the next 12 months. Focused business sites scored highest—82 per cent said they networked there—while 52 per cent said they used mainstream social sites. Over half—59 per cent—had already won business through networking websites, and 92 per cent would recommend it as a marketing tool to their professional contacts.

In this chapter we'll give you an overview of what social network services offer and suggest ways of harnessing them. Even if you're one of the millions who already have a Facebook or LinkedIn presence, you may get a fresh perspective.

9.1 Social networking—beyond Friends Reunited

The origins of the personal social networking going on today can be traced back more than a decade, with Classmates.com among the first to appear from the US in 1995 and the UK equivalent Friends Reunited five years later.

Since then, there's been an explosion, with the three that will probably be most familiar—Facebook, MySpace and Bebo—all launching between 2002 and 2004. As of July 2009, Facebook was the most popular in the UK, and had overtaken both MySpace in the US and Bebo in Ireland. Many millions of people use these sites every day, and not just to share aspects of their personal life when they should perhaps be working. The popularity of individual sites waxes and wanes, but predictions that social networking's days are numbered appear unfounded, as borne out by the WeCanDo.biz survey. Indeed, we may well see the scope instead widen significantly as Web 2.0 matures and mobile phones become more sophisticated and interactive.

Action

If you have never looked in detail at any social networking sites, or perhaps only bothered with the one you decided to join, spend an hour or so exploring what's out there.

This Wikipedia listing offers a good selection: **http://en.wikipedia.org/wiki/List_of_social_networking_websites**.
Focus on actual social networks (we'll come on to blogs and microblogs in the next chapter). Note the two sites that interest you most and then find out more about them here: **www.socialnetworkingwatch.com**. There's also more information about the sites we mention here in the Resources.

9.2   Is it natural for lawyers to do this stuff?

So how does social networking on sites like Facebook and Twitter fit into marketing an employment law practice, which is, after all, why you're here? Are we suggesting you now channel all your energy into building up an enormous circle of online friends? No. What we're suggesting is that you consider the implications.

Paul Lippe is founder and chief executive officer of Legal OnRamp, an online community primarily targeted at corporate lawyers. He says: "Some lawyers tend to dismiss new developments like Facebook as shallow and trivial—that is a mistake. The growth of online collaboration promises to be an important development for law because, in many ways, online communities reflect its traditional community model."

He lists ten reasons why, chief among these being that:

- *Law is a social profession.* "From barristers' chambers to one of a thousand professional societies and groups, law is honeycombed by social networks."

- *Legal content and expertise are shared and developed socially.* "Before Wikipedia, lawyers developed the Common Law—a linked, multi-authored, 'emergent' codification of best practice."

- *Using a social platform is the easiest way to go global.*

- *Social platforms will change law's competitive dynamics.* "If Partner Smith from Abu Dhabi has hundreds of connections and recommendations online, then it does not matter if Partner Jones in Abu Dhabi considers himself a better lawyer. Partner Smith will gain the reputation and therefore the business."

- *Social platforms are about people.* "Clients want to connect to trusted experts, not documents. Technology is not a silver bullet, but judicious use of it can better align firms and clients, reducing costs, improving value and enhancing everyone's satisfaction."

In part modelled on Facebook, Legal OnRamp is a deliberately exclusive community to maintain high security, with membership by invitation only, and was launched in 2007 by a consortium of nine bluechip companies led by techie giant Cisco. Lawyers from more than 40 countries have access to a database of all members as well as forums for sharing information and documentation. Big players on both sides of the Atlantic, such as Allen & Overy, have been quick to start using it to stay in touch with their clients' legal teams and showcase their expertise to other potential clients. Indeed, Allen & Overy has gone further, making a financial investment in Legal OnRamp in early 2008, not many months after doing a U-turn and allowing staff to access Facebook at work. Among the justifications given for lifting the Facebook ban was that it offered business opportunities.

Legal OnRamp had something of a monopoly on global legal social networking until autumn 2008, when the American Bar Association (ABA) unveiled LegallyMinded, a free-to-join, open-to-all, site (Charon QC was an early recruit) offering a full set of resources. The ABA's manager of interactive services, Fred Faulkner, says his aim was to fill a niche. "We looked at a lot of the professional and social networks, and the gap we found was that there truly wasn't a good site that was a cross between professional and personal networking. We want to do something for the profession as a whole and highlight a bunch of content that the ABA and other sites publish. We took some ideas off Facebook and LinkedIn but added wikis, opportunity for members to have blogs, and content within the legal profession."

Unlike Legal OnRamp, LegallyMinded is not exclusively for lawyers, which broadens (or conversely dilutes) its appeal. Faulkner says: "It's for lawyers, paralegals, law librarians, law students and others. If you're in the legal market, it's a place to access content and network with other professionals with whom you have similar interests."

A particularly useful feature is the people map. Based on the details in your profile, you get a diagram showing other members with shared areas of expertise or interests (see Figure 1).

Individual firms are also using the Facebook model for restricted-access internal social networking projects. In DLA Piper's case its "Inside the Tent" is a portal for future trainees.

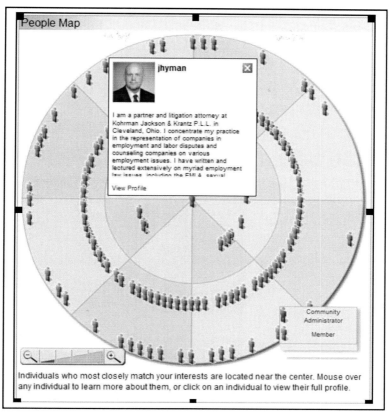

Figure 1 LegallyMinded's people map puts you in the centre

Meanwhile, the variety of general business and professional online networking options continues to grow, and that's what we'll explore next. We'll start with the most interesting of those websites actually labelling themselves as tools for "business marketing".

9.3   The virtual business breakfast

In Chapter 7, we looked briefly at **4Networking** (or **4N**), which unites online social networking and the real-life variety through business breakfasts—and does so effectively, judging by its growth. As discussed,

4N is driven by its very sophisticated and easily navigated website, offering a range of tools such as searchable member directories (around 100 solicitor practices and half a dozen employment law advisors were listed at the time of writing), and several forums and communities. Basic online membership is free and allows you to create a listing and Google-friendly profile, submit articles, and contact other members directly. Other levels are pitched at different pricing points depending on the benefits provided, including a two-month trial which allows you to attend up to three business breakfast meetings before signing up. Given the findings of the WeCanDo.biz survey discussed at the start of the chapter, and the shift towards just this type of mix, 4N looks likely to emerge as a very significant player, particularly once it achieves full UK coverage.

Here are its good points:

- There are a range of online networking options, which are all easy to access and use through a well-designed website.

- There's an upgrade option for breakfast networking (you can attend up to four different meetings a week, anywhere that has a group, or confine yourself to one).

- There's a glossy magazine!

These are the downsides:

- Its informality may jar.

- There are no doorkeepers, so you may attract interest of variable value from some people you don't know (though this has not been flagged up as a problem anywhere, and anyway, isn't that why you're in business?).

- Membership mainly comprises SMEs at the moment, which may not match your target client profile.

Eight years before 4Networking's launch came **Ecademy.com**. It's also British in origin, one of the first social networking sites, and possibly the first anywhere to focus on business networking. The aim is the same (the slogan is "connecting people"), and Ecademy now has members in more than 220 countries (exactly how many isn't posted, but it's estimated at around 170,000 and millions of visits are logged every year). The website is nowhere near as user-friendly as 4Networking's but the spread is far wider, and there are also options for face-to-face meetings through events organised by Ecademy or one of its members' clubs, based on locality or topic. With free membership you get a profile, but you can only respond to online messages from other members; you need to upgrade before you can actually start a conversation or join many of the online clubs (there are several for—or run by—lawyers; others cover aspects of doing business and yet more are purely social). Upgrading a level also allows you to take advantage of Ecademy's blog, create a Google-friendly profile, and to attend (and create) monthly networking meetings, and advertise. The top level brings additional benefits, including access to an autoresponder service for a range of incoming messages, upgraded advertising and listings, membership of exclusive clubs, and one-to-ones with Ecademy directors.

Here are Ecademy's good points:

- It has a global reach and breadth of member interests.

- It's great for forging new personal as well as business relationships.

- It has a wide range of bells and whistles such as blogging, setting up clubs, posting testimonials for other members.

These are the downsides:

- Free membership benefits are fairly restricted and fees are quite substantial.

- The website is frustrating to navigate and it's not always easy to work out what you can access or what you're allowed to do when you get there.

9.4   No sausages involved

The site behind the **WeCanDo.biz** survey is entirely web-based and is focused more on the contacts-book model—you primarily find services through recommendations made by people in your own network. Basic membership is, again, free (though rather confusingly there are two varieties: "consumer" and the more useful "business"), and once you've created your profile, you upload your own contacts book (web-based or from your files), see who's already signed up, endorse trusted business colleagues, and start collecting your own endorsements. You can also seek help and advice from other members, a significant proportion of whom are based outside the UK, especially in the US and Europe. Other useful free features include contacting other members, receiving leads, and looking at the other businesses that are listed when someone does a search for your services. Upgrading brings further features, such as being able to publicise WeCanDo.biz endorsements on your own website, listing networking events, and accessing forums.

WeCanDo.biz was launched in June 2008, and a year later had fewer than 3,000 members listed, very few of them offering legal services of any kind. It's therefore hard to judge how useful it might be. However, given that you can access a lot for no financial outlay and the endorsements for the site itself are all positive, we'd recommend having a look.

Here are its good points:

- It's a good website—easy to use with logical navigation and layout.

- Lots of features are available for basic membership, so there's no upfront commitment, and a clearly defined business focus.

These are downsides:

- It was only launched in summer 2008, so the network is still limited.

- Having two types of free membership is more confusing than helpful, though this may be a work in progress.

The best-known global professional networking site remains American-owned **LinkedIn**, which by summer 2009 was boasting a membership of more than 43 million members in over 200 countries, at least 2 million of them in the UK. The company claims that a new professional joins every two seconds; the average age is 41 and more than half are decision-makers. LinkedIn was a pioneer of the contacts-book networking model, and this is more rigid and tightly policed than the WeCanDo.biz version.

According to Patrick Crane, LinkedIn's vice-president of marketing, the system is based on the six degrees of separation, the same concept harnessing the "super-connectors" in your life (which we mentioned in Chapter 7). "The idea is that LinkedIn does not take away the face-to-face; it speeds up the way to find the right person to do the face-to-face with", says Crane, who predicts that more than half the world's professionals will be LinkedIn members within the next five years. "Every LinkedIn profile will become the manifestation of you." The LinkedIn model—and that used by the smaller German-based Xing, which has six million-plus members worldwide—has been shown to be particularly effective for those wanting to take a step up the career ladder. Christine Pilch, writing in *BusinessWest*, also points to LinkedIn's potential for rapid network building: "Remember that your network grows exponentially when you add a connection because you then have access to their connections (second tier) and people they are connected to as well (third tier), and vice-versa. It is entirely possible to build up a network of about four million people within three months by making smart connections with well-connected professionals."

However, how useful those four million people are to you is another matter. LinkedIn's emphasis on the individual, their CV, and their existing contacts rather than on their business, its services and benefits, and establishing links outside established circles, may not make LinkedIn as effective for sourcing new custom. Basic membership is free. There are three other levels based on the number of, respectively, introduction requests made, internal emails sent, and number of results displayed per search.

Here are its good points:

- Its colossal worldwide membership increases the likelihood of building a network of contacts quickly.

- Useful features include professional groups (there were at the time of writing eight—mostly north American—for employment law).

- It raises profiles by answering questions posted by other members. This is a recent example: "Would walking out of an after work office meeting be considered grounds for dismissal?"

- It's an excellent resource for building lists of names for use in other marketing contexts.

The main downside of LinkedIn is that you're initially dependent on your existing contacts. If you don't have many contacts that are already on LinkedIn or prepared to join, you're not going to get very far very fast. LinkedIn often takes a firm hand if you make several approaches to tenuous contacts and they're all rejected—you may find yourself labelled a spammer and severely restricted in what you can do. To avoid pitfalls and get more from membership, try these independent tips compiled by a member: **http://blog.linkedin.com/blog/2007/07/ten-ways-to-use.html**.

9.5   Where the wealthy go

To match their gated homes, the uber-wealthy have their own gated online communities. These are invitation-only sites, prime among them being **ASmallWorld.net**. It was founded in 2004 by Erik Wachtmeister, a banker and the son of a Swedish diplomat, who told *Forbes* magazine in 2008: "I realised there was an existing community of people who are connected by three degrees of separation: They stay at the same resorts when they travel, frequent the same restaurants and have similar lifestyles. They needed a platform to share and receive information—it was a huge untapped opportunity."

ASmallWorld has around 320,000 members, 65 per cent of them in the UK, Italy, Germany and France, 20 per cent in the US, and the rest in the Middle East and Asia. Is it worth becoming a member (assuming you might know anybody on the inside who could invite you in)? If wealthy A-list business people are your target clients, then obviously yes. The forums are used extensively for business networking, featuring questions such as: "Anyone with good lawyers in Phuket, Thailand? I'm building a sustainable-apartment development and need some UK–Thai contracts written up for an investor." Once you're on the inside, membership is free as the site is underwritten by advertisers such as Cartier, Moet & Chandon and Patek Philippe. Enough said!

Its main good point is that you're networking with the world's business elite in a highly-defined, closed marketplace—if that's your target market. The main downside is getting in!

There's information about other online business networking sites in the Resources.

Action

Investigate the business networking sites we've featured here (plus the others that are in Resources) and pick out the one that looks as though it will offer you the most benefits for your business.

If there's a free sign-up, opt for this while you test the water. Be prepared to invest initial time in getting your profile looking as thorough and professional as possible, and then in building your network.

Then see what happens—and please let us know!

9.6 Facing up to Facebook—making the most of a mainstream social site

And then there are the rest, the ones that you most likely already know about, particularly if you're a Millennial lawyer who came of age with the internet.

We're going to focus on Facebook because it's...

* the fastest-growing social networking site in the world (700,000-plus new users a day in summer 2009)

* ranked fourth in the world for traffic by internet intelligent and navigation company Alexa

* the most popular social networking site in the UK.

The statistics speak for themselves: see www.facebook.com/press/info.php?statistics#/press/info.php?statistics

Facebook was launched in February 2004 solely for Harvard students. Within a month, more than half the university's undergraduates had signed up, and within a year the platform was extended to other Boston colleges. Then Facebook's scope was widened to take in all US universities, then US high schools, and then—by the end of 2005—UK universities.

The doors were finally opened to everyone in September 2006, and that's when it really began to take off worldwide.

Getting started is free and simple. To use Facebook at its most basic all you need to do is…

- create a profile—you can only have one account, and it must be in your own name.

- add some content—you're offered a list of standard settings which you can include, exclude and modify, and you can write something about yourself (see below to find out about adding photos).

- start building a network of online contacts through "friend requests"—approaching people you know who are already members, or asking friends and colleagues who aren't to join in. You will also receive "friend requests" (which you can accept or decline). Only "friends" can see your full profile, find out what you're doing, and leave comments.

Should I use my photo?

Generally speaking, the answer is "yes" because, of course, people buy people, and if you're featured on your practice website then it would be inconsistent not to. But for some there may be sound reasons not to—on religious grounds, for example, or perhaps because of problems arising from past relationships.

If you do decide against using a portrait, don't just use the default image provided by the social networking site. In Social Media Marketing: An Hour a Day, Dave Evans suggests using an icon instead. "You can express your personality graphically even if you don't choose to use your face. Mikons (www.mikons.com) is a social site where you can create your own personal icon in a few minutes." Or you could create a cartoon of yourself at **http://makeacartoonyou.com**.

Your profile is your showcase, with brief "status updates" as the centrepiece. These can be purely personal—what you're doing, where you're going, who you're meeting—or point your friends in the direction of something interesting. Your friends can comment on your updates, you can comment on theirs, and you can leave messages on each other's "walls", or communicate directly via personal messages. You can post photos, video and audio files, and imbed these on your profile page, and you can list upcoming events. Everything you and your friends input within your network is "fed" to you, and herein lies the real value. In time your network entwines with other networks, the size of your Facebook contacts list grows, and you are linked—albeit loosely in most cases—to a potentially enormous number of people.

So where does any of this fit in with marketing your practice? As we said in Chapter 8, the emphasis when using social media like Facebook is precisely *not* on marketing, it's on building relationships and raising your personal profile. It's on making suggestions, flagging up links to interesting web pages, becoming the employment law "expert" in your particular network. However, for all that Facebook is primarily used as—and marketed as—a means for keeping in touch and having fun, it is nonetheless very cleverly structured to also be harnessed as a more commercial business tool. Most obviously, you can advertise (more about online advertising in Chapter 15). Less obviously there's a catalogue of built-in resources and applications which when woven through your profile can become a significant means of reinforcing your credibility.

According to social media marketing consultant Mari Smith, the following are of most potential interest:

1. *Notes*, which can be used to expand on your profile, add personal or professional content, host a blog, or as a platform for an imported blog. Friends can add comments, and everything posted there goes into your own feed and those of your friends.

2. *Events*—you can list your own upcoming events, to which friends are invited, and monitor your friends' events.

3. *Groups*—as the owner of a "group", you can send messages to up to 5,000 other Facebook members who've chosen to join. Groups can cover an enormous range of topics (and do!). There are, for example, more than 40 which include "employment law UK" somewhere within their general remit. Among them are groups set up by both traditional practices and by advisors. Smith says groups are particularly useful if you're launching something new, as you can use your members as an early test board and offer them information to download. There are three types of groups: open, where anyone can join; closed, where the owner or administrator has to approve membership; and secret, where only the members and people they invite to join even know the group exists. To get better insight on how groups work, start by joining a few and getting involved in their dynamics before you consider creating one.

4. *Pages*—this is a more specific Facebook business marketing tool. To create and maintain a page, you must be "an official representative" of the business or individual that is its focus. Rather than having members, pages have "fans". President Barack Obama's main page (there are many others), for example, has nudging 3.5 million fans. In a rather different league, but still impressive, a Miami criminal attorney has 150 fans, some of whom have posted glowing testimonials on his page, and a Tampa law firm has more than 280. (Lawyers in Florida seem to lead the way, but there are many others with listings, including a few from the UK.) Unlike groups, pages are indexed, which means they show up on Google, and you can also have an unlimited number of fans. Are pages therefore better than groups in pure marketing terms? Smith suggests you go for both as they serve different purposes.

These are just the principal building blocks. The best way to explore what else you can do is by signing up and doing it! As with any type of marketing, including when you're being more overt within an area you've created, like a page, you must always focus on benefits. Social media marketing consultant Shama Kabani sums up a successful strategy thus: "If you would possibly tell a friend about it, it can be marketed on Facebook." David Meerman Scott says: "Facebook is emerging as a primary way that many people keep in touch with the people and the organisations that are important to them. In the 2008 US presidential election, Facebook profiles of the candidates and supporter groups [were] an important way for people to be involved, and for many companies Facebook is a marketing tool."

Take a look at the Resources section for further details about Facebook and how to use it effectively, and information on other social networking sites.

Action

If you haven't already done so, join Facebook and start building your profile, your network and other features. As with the business networking site you join, you need to keep track of what does and doesn't produce a response, and whether they're the type of responses you want. Test different approaches and refine your tactics as a pattern begins to emerge. It's highly unlikely you'll get nothing back. If you do, please look again at what you're doing before you write off online networking as a marketing tool, because it's not going to go away any time soon! Both the authors have been using Facebook for years, so don't forget to look us up!

9.7   Wikis—knowledge bases for the 21st century

You'll no doubt already be familiar with Wikipedia (we've directed you towards several entries already in this book), and this is the most widely used "wiki". Wikipedia defines a wiki as "a page or collection of web pages designed to enable anyone who accesses it to contribute or modify content...". The definition adds: "Wikis are often used to create collaborative websites and to power community websites. The collaborative encyclopaedia Wikipedia is one of the best-known wikis. Wikis are used in business to provide intranet and knowledge management systems."

Search "employment law" in Wikipedia and you'll arrive at a page giving an overview of the basics across a range of nations: **http://en.wikipedia.org/wiki/Employment_law**. If you spot a glaring mistake, or want to add to the entry, you are free to do so. Among the links on the page is one to "British labour law" (**http://en.wikipedia.org/wiki/British_labour_law**), and again, you can change the text simply by clicking on the "edit" link. You can do the same with LexisNexis's wikis, among them human resources law, though you need subscriber access, and if you want to dip a toe into more academic waters, you could be the first to start a UK employment law thread at **http://en.jurispedia.org**, a global collaboration of universities "devoted to worldwide law, legal and political sciences".

By doing so you will, not surprisingly, leave a trail, but unless you arrive with malevolent intent this should not be an issue.

Many US—and an increasing number of major UK—law firms are now creating their own Wikipedia pages, for example Eversheds, Clifford Chance, Allen and Overy, and Charles Russell. Individual US lawyers also increasingly feature, for instance see **http://en.wikipedia.org/wiki/Ben_Brafman**, **http://en.wikipedia.org/wiki/Marcia_Clark**, **http://en.wikipedia.org/wiki/David_Boies**. However, this trend is only slowly being picked up on this side of the Atlantic. What are the benefits? Wikipedia entries routinely feature right at the top of search engine results, so if somebody were to Google your firm's name—or, indeed, you—and saw you had a Wiki listing, they would be highly likely to have a look. Wikipedia—although only in existence since 2001—has acquired a remarkable online presence which has brought with it a high degree of (occasionally misplaced) authority and credibility.

Wikipedia apart, how can hosting or contributing to wikis help you? As part of your intranet (if you have one)—and not therefore as a direct marketing strategy—you could use the concept to pool experiences, information and strategies. Looking outwards towards your clients, you could for example use a wiki to track a piece of legislation on its journey from first announcement to the Statute Book, and beyond. You could link to your own observations on the topic, link to external contributions, and invite visitors to your website to add to your wiki. UK law firms have yet to grasp the potential of this pillar of social networking, so here's an excellent opportunity to do something different. There's more about wikis in the Resources for this chapter.

Action

Explore the world of wikis, starting with Wikipedia and then looking further afield. You won't find much to do with the law, and next to nothing focusing on employment or labour law. But don't be deterred! It's the *concept* we're urging you to explore and then consider as another way of lifting your firm's profile.

10

The era of the ego—how to harness the power of blogging

One of the most marked developments heralded in by Web 2.0 technology has been the rapid blossoming in popularity of the blog (the abbreviation of weblog, a web-based journal) as a means of communication. You'll no doubt be familiar with the concept, and you may well have a few among your bookmarks, but unless you're one of a tiny minority (of the estimated 180 million-plus blogs logged by monitoring website Technorati in 2008, fewer than 3,000 were written by lawyers), it's less likely that you've ever considered writing your own.

Why, after all, would you want to? What would be the point? You're a lawyer, not a diarist. And who would be interested in anything you have to say anyway? The answer to the last question is a potentially significant number of people—and precisely because you *are* an employment lawyer. The point of the exercise is to give those people the opportunity to hear what it is you've got to say in a context where they can become part of the discussion. It is this that underpins the phenomenal success of the blogging formula and takes it outside the confines of conventional written communications—the two-way conversational traffic, a reflection of the inclusivity that threads through all the social media we're exploring.

10.1 The blog basics

How should we define a blog? American writer and journalist David Meerman Scott has been a blogger since 2004 and is now an acknowledged expert in harnessing the power of this medium as part of a "new rules" approach to marketing and PR (we look in further detail at this in Chapter 12). He describes a blog like this: "It's just a web site. But it's a special kind of site that is created and maintained by a person who is passionate about a subject and wants to tell the world about his or her area of expertise." Fellow American Tom Peters, a veteran management consultant and author, began his blog in 2004 and is unequivocal in his enthusiasm. Blogging, he says, has changed his life, his perspective, his intellectual and emotional outlook, and no other single thing has been of more professional importance to him in the past 15 years. "It's the best damn marketing tool by an order of magnitude that I've ever had", he says.

All very inspiring, but what are the specific benefits for you as an employment lawyer and for your practice? Former US trial lawyer Kevin O'Keefe now runs LexBlog, a Seattle-based company dedicated to building legal blogs—or blawgs—and hosts Real Lawyers Have Blogs, his own blog which also acts as an excellent information hub. He says: "While there are many personal blogs online that are like journals of all aspects of the author's life, legal blogs are a completely different story. The publisher of a legal blog is generally an individual lawyer or a practice group in a law firm. Well-run legal blogs usually focus tightly on one niche area of the law and/or jurisdiction. The aim is to provide the legal blog's readers with a constantly renewing source of news and insight about that topic. "You and your legal blog provide something very valuable to current clients, prospects, the public and the media: a constant watch on a particular topic. A legal blog establishes its author as a reliable, helpful authority on the subject matter, and builds and enhances the reputation of its publisher. Your legal blog does the work, compiling and passing along updates as they occur—and for visitors with some vested interest in your topic, this brings them back again and again. Visitors often come to rely on information from the legal blog for quality information and commentary. For professional businesses, like lawyers, achieving this level of loyalty among visitors, the monetary rewards can be great."

Rewards in the form of fresh instructions, either from existing clients made more aware of the depth of your expertise, or from new ones.

As O'Keefe says, blogging is a simple and highly cost-effective way of raising your personal profile and enhancing your reputation as an expert—or to use the jargon, a "thought leader"—in your field:

- It's a flexible and fast platform for exploring new ideas and shaping opinion—and for responding quickly to important judgments and policy announcements.

- It's an easy way to monitor what people—including current and potential clients—think about you.

- It's an unrivalled means of channelling online traffic back to your firm's website—and search engines like Google love blogs!

To reap the rewards, however, you need to be committed to some key blogging ground rules:

- Keep updating. If you leave your blog unattended for much more than a week, you will lose your readers' interest and confidence.

- Be prepared for negative comments. Go ahead and blitz spam or profanity, but as your aim is to get a conversation going, let your detractors have their say.

- Be authentic, honest, ethical and transparent. Use your own voice and never let your blog become a faceless corporate mouthpiece.

The three key things a blog should never be are...

- a replacement for balanced journalism

- a platform for a traditional sales, marketing or advertising pitch

- solely a means of improving your search engine listing.

As Scott says: "The blogger's usual focus of promoting a single point of view is dramatically different from the journalist's goal of providing a balanced perspective." But there is ample room for both, and rather than view—as some media professionals still do—the web as a sprawling newspaper, Scott favours thinking of it as "a huge city teeming with individuals, and blogs as the sounds of independent voices, just like those of the street-corner soapbox preacher or that friend of yours who always recommends the best books". And journalists are increasingly using blogs—particularly those written by respected professionals— as information sources (more about the role of blogs in PR in Chapter 12).

By far the most popular blogs are those written by an identifiable individual who is not making any kind of blatant bid for anything other than their readers' interest and attention. Journalists are not alone in viewing with some distrust those blogs which are little more than ads for a business or a service. Learn to distinguish between what Lithuanian internet marketing consultant Linus Simonis labels "corporate" and "business" blogs. "The biggest difference between the two is that the business blog is a personal blog about the company, business or practice which the blogger manages. The corporate blog dilutes a person and puts the corporation in first place. Yes, posts are signed by real people, but they reflect corporate rules. Bloggers are often hired in order to write and manage corporate blogs."

Underlying this is the same basic premise—people buy people, and anything carrying an exclusively corporate hallmark will have to work significantly harder to win readers' loyalty. Indeed, a survey by Forrester Research, a US market research specialist, found that only 16 per cent of consumers trust company blogs; regular readers of blogs are slightly more forgiving at 24 per cent. In his report on the survey, Josh Bernoff says:

"When consumers say they mostly don't trust corporate blogs, you can interpret their response similarly to when they say they don't trust TV commercials or corporate spokespeople. Even as consumers ramp up their blog reading, they seem to believe company blogs created to further corporate goals are not balanced and are basically an extension of a company website."

So does this mean that you shouldn't have a blog on your firm's website? Not at all, though you can choose to have it hosted elsewhere and linked back to your website. We would urge even large practices to adopt the Simonis business model over the corporate, and to make your blog original, thought-provoking, ethical, entertaining—and personal. O'Keefe says: "A legal blog tends to become closely identified with the lawyer or practice group who creates it. Readers get an honest feel for the people behind the legal blog, and form a stronger bond with the blog publisher than with a law firm that just publishes a website."

Not everyone has got this message. He cites as an example of how not to do it one Texas PI attorney's blog, which comprises little more than cut-and-pasted news reports about accidents and injuries onto which is tagged a stock paragraph saying: "If you or a family member has been injured because of the fault of someone else; by negligence, personal injury, slip and fall, car accident, medical malpractice, trucking accident, drunk driving, bad product, toxic injury etc then please contact xxxxx. For a no obligation, free case analysis, please call xxxx ..." As well as making a desperately unsubtle bid for business, this lawyer is using his blog to try to push his website up Google's listings by littering the text with popular keywords. (We'll look in detail at more intelligent search engine optimisation tactics in Chapter 15.) O'Keefe says: "To the majority of bloggers, the media, and sane people, the lawyer looks like an idiot at best. To me, he's an embarrassment to our profession."

10.1.1 The building blocks of a blog

We're not going to get technical, but it's worth familiarising yourself with the key elements of every blog post, as identified by Wikipedia:

- The **title** is the main title, or headline, of the post.

- The **body** is the main content of the post.

- The **permalink** is the URL (uniform resource locator, or address) of the full, individual article.

- The **post date** is the date and time the post was published.

Most blogs also include…

- comments—where readers can correct errors or give their opinion on the post itself or the subject matter

- categories (or tags)—the subjects discussed in the post

- trackback and/or pingback—links to other sites that refer to the individual post.

We'll look next at how to get started, but first we urge you to immerse yourself in the legal blogosphere—or blawgosphere—and in the world of blogging more generally.

Action

Search first for—and bookmark—legal blogs that…

- you feel a personal affinity for

- attract reader comments (supportive and adverse)

- are regularly updated

- include links to other interesting blogs or websites.

Check out how different blogs handle the essential elements that we identified above.

Then identify blogs that...

- you're not personally drawn to

- aren't updated regularly

- attract little in the way of feedback

- are making a direct marketing pitch.

Compare the two sets to give yourself a clear overview of what does and doesn't work in general, and what works for *you* personally. From this analysis you're aiming to emerge with the formula you need to build your own blog. The globally accepted blog format puts the most recent post at the top of the page with earlier pieces running chronologically beneath it; be cautious of any sites that use a different layout.

Be prepared to spend some time on this exercise, and to follow links from one blog to the next. That way you'll find more sources of inspiration, and there's every chance you'll discover lots of other useful things along the way!

In the Resources for this chapter you'll find some suggestions, including blogs with which you may already be familiar.

Action

Following on from the first exercise, pick out a handful of the legal blogs you rate most highly—between five and ten—and commit to visiting these frequently. Most good blogs will offer you the option of signing up to an RSS feed (more about RSS in Chapter 15), or automated email updates telling you when something new has been posted. Once you've been checking in regularly for a week or so, start contributing to the conversations. This helps you overcome any inhibitions you may have about writing in this context and sows the seeds for you launching your own blog. Getting seen and being read not only helps establish you as an expert, but also increases the likelihood of other blog owners linking to yours in the future. And there is another useful benefit—by keeping in close touch with what others are writing about, you can more easily monitor what they're saying about you and your firm. Scott says: "Most of the time when I mention a company or product on my blog, I do not get any sort of response from that organisation. However, about 20 per cent of the time, I'll get a comment on my blog from someone at that company or a personal email. These are the 20 per cent of companies that monitor the blogosphere and react to what's being said. You should be doing this too, if you're not already."

Remember what happened to Dell and AOL...

10.2   What should I say and how should I say it?

We'll assume that you now have at least a passing acquaintance with what's working well for other lawyers and law firms (and for professionals more generally), and a good idea of how not to blog.

Now it's your turn to have a go. But don't start downloading software and looking at designs just yet—spend some time getting organised and rehearsing. Before you go live with your blog, you need to be 100 per cent confident that you will...

- have enough *material* to create new posts at least once a month, preferably much more often

- have enough *time* to write and publish your posts at least once a month—and respond quickly to feedback.

We can't tell you exactly what to write, but employment law offers a constant source of news which by definition is rich in human interest and appealing to a broad audience. If you specialise—like our hypothetical West Midlands discrimination practice—then put your focus there to more easily build your status as an expert in your field. And always feel free to borrow and comment on other people's ideas. Part of the blogging ethos is to stay constantly tuned in to what's being said and flag up anything interesting you find to your own readers. Just make sure you always acknowledge—and link to—your source. However, avoid posts that do nothing but link to another blog or website—your readers are looking for your views, not a directory. Simonis says: "Post only when you have something worth saying in your specialist area. Post only when your post will be helpful to your target audience and will prove your difference in your target audience's mind. And link only when the link helps your reader to better understand your point of view."

As other general pointers, we would suggest...

- that if you do specialise, you focus your blog posts there as much as you can—the narrower the niche, the more quickly you can grow your reputation

- that you go for a mix of information-rich posts and more opinion-led pieces—always remember that your readers are interested in your interpretation, not just the bare facts.

To blog well, you need to find your blogging "voice". That's why we urge you to do a great deal of research and as many dummy runs as it takes for you to feel comfortable before going live. The best example we know of is Tim Kevan who, three years ago, launched an anonymous blog called "BabyBarista" (**http://timesonline. typepad.com/baby_barista/**), a young, machiavellian Horace Rumpole character manoeuvring for tenancy in his chambers. *Times Online* picked it up within months (and Bloomsbury have published it as a novel; see **http://tinyurl.com/buqy5j**).

Clearly you have to park your business writing style, and you also need a different approach for this genre than for writing conventional marketing copy or media releases. You are of course still a representative of your firm, and you want your readers to know that, but that's not your principal aim here. This is just you talking—not you as lawyer to existing client, lawyer to prospective client, or lawyer to journalist. That said, your blogging needs to have discipline and structure, and not be studiedly casual or colloquial. We suggest you stick to these copywriting and news release basics:

- Wherever possible write in the first person and address your readers as "you" (you and yours).

- Remember the obstacles of indifference—they apply here as well:
  1. Who cares?
  2. So what?
  3. What's in it for me?

- Keep posts as tightly-written as possible, but if there is a lot to say, go ahead and say it, and try breaking up the text with bullet points.

- Pay particular attention to your titles to grab and hold attention and to help your Google ranking.

- Avoid clichés and jargon.

- Use your news release checklist—you want to number journalists among your readers:
  1. Who?
  2. What?
  3. When?
  4. Where?
  5. Why?

You may also find it helpful to have your ideal reader/client in mind. First, picture them sat at their screen Googling for your employment law speciality, and then follow them as they click on the link to your blog for the first time, remembering always that you've only a matter of seconds to grab and hold their attention. Then picture them bookmarking your blog, returning to you, leaving comments, and becoming one of your regular followers.

(An essential part of getting a high Google ranking in the first place is using keywords in the blog post title and text. We'll look at this in Chapter 15 when we discuss making your website work.)

Action

Practise your blog writing until you feel you've found your "voice". We're not going to give you a target number of posts—you may find this easy, you may find this a challenge. Either way, do spend time identifying and bookmarking good sources of employment law news and discussion, and experiment with different approaches to transforming your raw material into blog posts.

10.3 Where should I do it?

You can add your blog to your website or you can run it separately, either on another site you control or under the umbrella of a host such as major players Wordpress and TypePad, or a specialist such as Kevin O'Keefe's LexBlog. (There's a link to Wikipedia's list of hosts in the Resources.) There are advantages and disadvantages to both approaches.

*   Keeping your blog on your own website is…
    *   good for enhancing your corporate identity
    *   good for providing content and depth to your website
    *   less good for establishing you as an independent voice.

- Hosting your blog on a specialist website is...

  - good for promoting yourself as an independent thought leader, away from your corporate branding

  - good for picking up extra readers—visitors to other blogs on the hosted site may well find their way to yours

  - less good for projecting yourself as speaking for your firm, but then you want to avoid doing that too overtly anyway!

Either way, the software is now so sophisticated and user-friendly that you don't need to be any kind of a techie to design and maintain a successful blog using the content management systems they all feature. If you go for the in-house option, all you need to do is download your blogging software of choice (again, Wordpress and TypePad are the leaders here) and either set it up yourself or get your technical team to do it for you. It's worth devoting a chunk of time to thoroughly exploring and adapting theme options to echo your website design—there are literally thousands to choose from. If you go for the external hosting option, again take your time to pick a design you're happy with. A word of caution—moving from one host to another can mean leaving behind your archive or engaging in some costly redirecting, so make sure you're entirely happy with your choice before signing up.

Your blog should also ideally include all these elements from the start:

- An "about" section—your readers want to know who you are and what you do.

- At least one photo—your readers want to know what you (and your colleagues if it's a practice group blog) look like.

- Clear, fixed links to your firm's website and other relevant sites—you will add to these as the blog develops.

How a blog put one employment lawyer in the media spotlight

Mark Ellis, CEO of employment law consultancy Ellis Whittam (and one of our profiled firms), has first-hand experience of what can happen when a blog post grabs the limelight and is picked up by the media. In January 2007, he floated the idea of largely dismantling the UK's web of employment law, saying: "Sure, as a responsible society we need a set of basic laws/rights that guarantee the safety, dignity and minimum wage for all workers. But I suspect that I speak for a silent majority of employers when I say that silly amounts of compensation awarded to a sacked employee, particularly against a small employer, are bad for business, can put an entire business at risk, and are bad for UK plc."

Within hours, he had comments from several employers supporting his view, and one against from a trade unionist, which in turn sparked a stream of further comments. Some backed Ellis's stand, others the shop steward's, and one from Conservative Central Office managed to do neither! The thread ran on for nearly a year (into January 2008), attracting media attention for Ellis's "cult following" on the way and forcing the then Department of Trade and Industry to put out a defence of the unfair dismissal legislation.

What spurred Ellis into going out on a limb in the first place? He initially set up the blog—which he hosts himself—as a means of driving traffic to his main website. "It was simply to get some optimisation, and the blog was a good way of doing it. My style anyway is very matter of fact and frank with no legalese and I suppose I like to be a little bit controversial sometimes, challenging conventional thought processes." So the post was solely to attract attention. "I did it deliberately, knowing what I was doing, looking for a reaction because I knew the reaction would assist in my aim. To be honest, I have no idea how it was then picked up by some of the media, but it was. So I really just tried to fan the flames of controversy by drawing it to the attention of the Conservative Party myself, looking for a reaction. Then there was a reaction from the Labour Party, stimulated I think by Personnel Today's pieces on it, which included an editorial. It was just one of those things that ran itself, really, and that was fine—it suited my purpose."

A significant number of the links created at the time, such as that from Personnel Today, still exist, driving traffic to Ellis's website.

Nothing he has posted since has had the same impact, and he admits that he has not been as diligent as he could, something he is already addressing. "The blog adds quality to the website, and it adds something we haven't got anywhere else, which is the personal touch."

Ellis's original post and the subsequent thread can be found here:

www.elliswhittam.com/blog/?p=5

His follow-up posting is here: **www.elliswhittam.com/blog/?p=6**

The *Personnel Today* coverage is here:

www.personneltoday.com/articles/2007/02/14/39248/dti-rejects-calls-to-scrap-unfair-dismissal-law.html

Action

Take a tour of the blog hosting and software sites listed on Wikipedia (the link is in the Resources). From there investigate the huge range of design themes available. Even if your blog will be an integral part of your website, visit the hosting sites for design ideas and advice. Decide which software best suits your needs and then get to work on building your blog.

10.4 The new kid on the block—Twitter

Before we leave blogging, it's worth remarking on the truly phenomenal rise of microblogging site Twitter, which recorded 343 per cent year-on-year growth between September 2007 and September 2008, from 533,000 users to 2,359,000. And it's still growing fast. Although there are other microblogging sites (see the Resources for the Wikipedia link), Twitter is head and shoulders above all the rest, in terms of both functionality and popularity.

The California-based privately-owned site calls itself "a service for friends, family, and co–workers to communicate and stay connected through the exchange of quick, frequent answers to one simple question:

What are you doing?" Sign up, and you can "follow" people, and they can "follow" your 140-word updates—Tweets—via the web or mobile phone. Twitter was launched in 2006 as a fun adjunct to mainstream social sites. Now its role is changing and it's increasingly being used as another way of flagging up something new, and for the rapid dissemination of information. During the terror attacks in Mumbai in November 2008, for example, a significant number of eye witnesses used Twitter to alert the world to what was happening—and were often markedly quicker in their information-gathering and disseminating than either the authorities or the media.

Our favourite employment Tweet is UK Employment Law (http://twitter.com/ukemploymentlaw), the author of which describes herself as "a London-based employment lawyer defending companies in employment tribunals". She seems to spend most of her time throwing Harvey at her hapless trainee, moaning about LexisNexis, and battling her partners to manipulate redundancy selection criteria for her firm's secretaries. She acquired hundreds of followers in just a few weeks (and if anyone knows who she is, we'll "out" her in the next edition of this book!). Since she launched in 2009, several dozen 'lookalike' employment lawyers have begun their own twitter pages.

How does it work? Joel Comm, a high-profile US internet entrepreneur and marketer, calls Twitter "the water cooler of the 21st century". He says: "Initially, no one will see your Tweets. That is, until you begin 'following' other people's. This is accomplished quite simply by clicking a user name and then clicking the 'follow' button under the name. If you follow another member because you find their content interesting, they are more likely to follow you. If you reply to a member's Tweet personally, the reciprocal 'follow' becomes even more likely. The more active you are and the more willing to interact with others, the more followers you will acquire."

As of summer 2009, Comm had more than 70,000 followers. Because of Twitter's uniquely informal structure, you can seamlessly jump from purely social to purely professional Tweets without jarring. Comm says: "One day my Tweets might consist of 'Upgrading to iPhone 2.0! Hope it goes well...' But the next day I might Tweet 'Heading to LA to speak at an event. Come see me for free on Sunday!'"

When you sign up, you get your own Twitter page where—in line with the site's dedication to brevity—you're given just 160 characters for your profile. O'Keefe, who hosts the LexTweet Twitter legal community, has as his: "Legal media publisher. CEO of LexBlog." UK blogger Charon QC has "Blawger and Rioja drinker" as his.

You can Tweet from the web and from your phone, and you can use a staggeringly varied range of applications that have been developed to make Tweeting even easier. You can inbed your Tweets on your blog as a news feed, and within other social media such as Facebook, all facilities which together help give this microblogging facility its high profile. O'Keefe says: "Interesting thing about Twitter, and I don't think most lawyers or firms are ready to use it, is that the people who may follow you are heavy influencers of others. They are people who blog and otherwise virally spread what they hear. If you are providing insight on a niche through Twitter, word can be spread very rapidly. You can benefit from Twitter in three ways that I see today. First, a way to socially network with people, some of which networking may lead to work, speaking engagements, and the like. Two, a means to amplify your message, i.e., spreading what you may be blogging, writing, or speaking on. Three, if you blog, you are going to get news from other bloggers whose content you may want to reference in your blog or work."

The (anonymous) US lawyer who hosts LawyerKM adds: "Twitter shouldn't be seen as a billboard on which lawyers declare their ability to trounce insurance companies and win large settlements for injured clients. It should be a way for lawyers to engage in conversations and form relationships, which may lead to trust, confidence, and maybe— just maybe—a new client or more work from an existing one."

The authors do, however, confess to a small disagreement over the usefulness of Twitter. Eugenie Verney agrees with all of the above, believing that Twitter offers a highly effective social media platform for building your online presence. You could, for example, Tweet to alert followers that a landmark European Court decision has just been posted on the ECJ website, and ask for reactions. Or you could remind them the national minimum wage goes up shortly, point them in the direction of a new post on your blog (or better still somebody else's), or flag up an event you're taking part in—and then Tweet from the event! People buy people, and Twitter is all about people.

Daniel Barnett, by contrast, believes that Twitter is a temporary fad which is already saturated (there are dozens of employment law and employment consultants tweeting updates, most of which are just website links and none of which says anything new). It's only Stephen Fry aficionados and stalky teenagers who follow Tweets with any real interest. Most people get bored within a few weeks by an inability to sort the wheat from the chaff amongst the huge volume of turgid material thrust upon Twitter users.

Time will tell which one of us needs to tweet our words…

Action

If you're not familiar with Twitter, go and have a look: http://twitter.com. Use the search facility (at the foot of the home page) to look for people who may already be members. Try searching using the # facility to, say, look for a specific event or topic (for example, one that got well used early in 2009 was #uksnow). Use the section to help navigate around the site and find out more, and also Google for other ideas about how to use Twitter. These are constantly changing, so we're not offering any links.

Signing up for a Twitter account is free and doesn't commit you to anything. We suggest you do, just to explore whether this is another marketing tool you could put to good use, if not right away then at some time in the future. Meanwhile, you can keep a close watch on how Twitter grows and matures, and who else is signing up.

11

Making your website a rich information source

This chapter focuses on the information and material you use on your website to give it depth and interest. We're not looking at any other aspects of website design or function (we'll return to those in Chapter 13), just at the elements that comprise what is known as *content*. Here is why these are vitally important:

- A large library of relevant, regularly updated and free content turns your website into a valued resource. It helps you build your personal and corporate reputation with your existing clients, prospective clients, other lawyers and the media.

- A rich seam of content is essential for driving visitors to your website. The more material you have that meets the search engines' ranking criteria, the higher you'll climb in their listings.

What do we mean by *content*? In addition to the copy that appears across your website, you should be aiming to include at least some of the following:

- news releases

- regular updates, for example client newsletters and briefing notes

- guides

- white papers

- e-books

- video and podcasts.

We'll look at each of these in turn and how you can use them to enhance your online presence, and we'll also consider how you can add more depth to your site by buying in material.

First, a note of caution that applies to anything you post. The overwhelming bulk of your content should ideally be original. If you're using anything that's already been published online, be aware that even if you acknowledge the source the search engines may nonetheless still rank it as somebody else's. When they find any kind of direct duplication, search engines—including the all-important Google—will automatically label the earliest online publication date as the original, and downgrade or leave unranked any further appearances. This does not, of course, mean that second-hand material has no value, just that its value is diminished as a means of enhancing your search engine visibility. It goes without saying that if you use graphics or images, you also need to check their copyright status before publishing.

11.1 An extra role for news releases and newsletters

News releases used to have a very limited lifespan. They'd be written, sent out, read, responded to (or not), a story appeared (or not), and that was the end of that.

Now, not only can they live indefinitely (we'll look in the next chapter at their role in "new rules" PR, and how to format them for maximum online impact), they can also play a very useful part in giving your own website some extra value. They give visitors a good overview of your firm's achievements and aspirations, as well as providing a pool of practical information. And the search engines love them!

We suggest you create a specific area of your website for news releases and make sure you post a web-optimised version of each one you generate at the same time it's distributed to the media. You need to build a searchable archive and make old releases accessible by subject and by publication date. They're usually presented as individual web pages rather than as PDF downloads, but either—or indeed both—will meet your visitors' expectations. Put a link to this section on your home page, but only post extracts there if you're going to be updating frequently. Old news releases are a very significant turn-off, as indeed is any other time-sensitive material afforded a prominent position, especially on your home page.

11.2   Adding value to regular updates

You may already be generating regular updates that you email to your clients. If you're not, we explore this in more detail in Chapter 16. Either way, this is another easy way to build up website content, as you are largely only finding a new role for something you're already producing.

As with news releases, create a separate area for them, and archive them in the same way to ensure consistency. Updates are most likely to take the form of client newsletters—produced at regular intervals, usually monthly or quarterly—and briefing notes, which follow an event such as a key judgment or the announcement or implementation of new legislation. Because newsletters often follow traditional hard-copy design rules, they lend themselves particularly well to downloading as printable PDFs, but make sure you carry web page summaries that the search engines can find easily as well.

With briefing notes you again have choices. However, you would normally only be writing them as a swift response to something, and restricting them to web page format highlights the sense of immediacy better than a PDF. They definitely need flagging up on the home page, but once again be meticulous about removing anything past its sell-by date. One further—but important—rule about briefing notes (and any other written online material) is to never use the words "today", "yesterday", "this week", "next week", and so on. There is nothing worse than reading something that, for example, starts: "The Government today announced plans to..." and be given no idea of when "today" was. Just use the date: "The Government announced plans on 1 May 2009 to ..."

11.3   Guides that focus on facts

What's a guide in this context? Well, just that—something straightforward that throws light on a topic, most usually a piece of legislation or a process, and how it works. Guides are not discursive. Their role is to give your readers the facts rather than provide detailed analysis or advice, and there's no prescribed size. Ideally make them downloadable for use as a reference tool.

Here are a couple of examples of how our profiled firms use guides on their websites.

Colemans-Ctts's website features a series of employment guides. "We have web guides which are very short best practice for the key situations you find— ill-health, poor performance, redundancy, and so on. And although we've the disclaimers not to rely on them, they just tell people what they need to know."
Tom Walker, former head of employment law at Colemans-ctts, now in the same role at Manches

Dean Morris includes a range of detailed online guides on his got-the-boot.com website: "Most people do actually go in and have a look—experience tells us they do actually read it. I had an email from somebody I couldn't help, but he commented that it was a fantastic site, incredibly informative."
Dean Morris, principal, Morris Legal

11.4 White papers—out of Whitehall and onto your website

The online "white paper" has its origins in the Whitehall version, typically a government paper arguing a specific position or offering a solution to a particular problem. Over the past decade or so, the web has seen new definitions emerge, with the technology sector taking the lead.

Law firms in the UK have—like other professional sectors—been quite slow to explore the full marketing potential of the white paper, which Michael Stelzner, executive editor of *WhitePaperSource Newsletter*, describes as "... a persuasive document that usually describes problems and how to solve them... It is a crossbreed of a magazine article and a brochure. It takes the objective and education approach of an article and weaves in persuasive corporate messages typically found in brochures".

Most white papers...

- are between 5 and 12 A4 pages in length, though they can exceed 50

- largely comprise text with few graphics, but may include diagrams, charts and illustrations

- are free, but often only made available in return for registering an email address.

Stelzner says in his book, *Writing White Papers: How to Capture Readers and Keep Them Engaged*: "White papers usually provide valuable information to their intended audience, yet readers of white papers generally understand that the sponsoring company is marketing to them. The marketing aspect of a white paper is typically a very soft sell." In other words, when you write a white paper for your website, your principal aim is to give your readers something of factual, practical use—information which you hope they will act on by engaging your firm. It is not to lay out a stark list of what you do. "The goal of a white paper is to lead the reader toward the conclusion that your service will best meet his or her needs", says Stelzner.

The use of online white papers is growing fast (a Google search in early 2009 produced more than 26 million results). Stelzner says that this is because they "are able to fly under the radar and penetrate most organisations' anti-marketing defences because they are sought after and brought into the organisation by decision-makers. If they are well-written, white papers will not only reach their target, they will influence them".

So how should you go about writing them? Stelzner surveyed hundreds of white paper writers, and found a general consensus that an effective white paper should…

- first address problems, challenges or needs, rather than presenting the solution

- educate as a top priority

- contain practical, useful information

- focus on benefits more than features

- avoid direct selling

- avoid using humour.

This in large measure returns us to many of the essentials of effective copywriting identified in Chapter 5. As with blog writing, what's primarily involved is a shift in style rather than a fundamental shift away from the basics. With white papers, you need to take a fairly formal tone, write in the third person, and—as Stelzner's survey respondents agreed— steer clear of using humour (or irony) to make your point. You must have a compelling headline, and you need to finish your white paper by giving your reader clear direction on what they need to do next. "The title encourages readers to stop what they are doing and read your masterpiece. Similarly, the call to action entices those same readers to take a very specific action", says Stelzner.

Should you label your white papers as white papers? Not necessarily, though a significant number of visitors to your website will now understand what they're getting if you do. Alternative titles could include "briefing paper" (as opposed to the shorter, more event-initiated briefing note), "discussion paper", or "special report". White papers are definitely takeaways, but you should always include summaries—for your visitors and the search engines—and make a feature of them on your home page. There's more about how to produce white papers in the Resources.

11.5 E-books—exploring ideas in depth

The term e-book is now used to cover several types of material, including electronic versions of hard-cover classics and full-length books published in this format only, for example, co-author Daniel Barnett's book written with Kate Palka: *Age Discrimination: An Analysis of the Nature and Impact of the Employment Equality (Age) Regulations.*

We're obviously not looking at those here. The type of e-book we're interested in is written exclusively for free distribution via a website but is more than just an expanded white paper. One key way to differentiate between the e-book and more formal white paper is in its design: an e-book can be in landscape, rather than the more traditional portrait format. Other suggestions include...

• using engaging graphics and images

• writing in a lighter, more conversational style than you would in a white paper

• opening with a story, and using examples throughout

• paying particular attention to the title to ensure it grabs the reader's attention.

We also recommend using a professional editor and a proofreader, to which we add the optional extra of a designer. Producing an e-book involves a higher investment in time and resources than any of the other content we've discussed, but can also bring greater, quicker rewards. A well-written, attractive and topical e-book can draw more visitors to your website than just about anything else, because you're offering something of obvious value for free, and word will soon get around. We'd suggest you only publish one e-book at a time for maximum impact and be sure to give it plenty of attention. Put links featuring the front cover across your website and on your emails, refer to it in your blog and whenever the topic comes up in conversation, at networking events for example.

Action

First explore what others are already doing, and then start thinking laterally and looking for a topic that lends itself to one of the following:

1. A *briefing note*—that is, a quick response to a judgment or legislative change.

2. A *guide*—a process (such as redundancy procedures) or the

elements that comprise a claim (unfair dismissal, for example).

3. A *white paper*—here you need topics around which you can construct an informative discussion that leads the reader naturally towards wanting to find how you can help.

4. An *e-book*—for this you're looking for subjects that lend themselves to a longer but lighter and less constrained analysis than a white paper.

(We've not included news releases or newsletters as these are covered elsewhere.)

Your next task is to have a go at writing a briefing note, drawing on the guidance in this chapter and the copywriting rules from Chapter 5. If you're already producing these, or want more of a challenge, try your hand at one of the other categories—a guide, white paper or e-book.

11.6   The power of broadcasting

So far we've looked at how written content can enhance your website. Now it's the turn of audio and video—the fastest-growing media across the internet, as the YouTube statistics we quoted in Chapter 8 clearly demonstrate. We're focusing both on material your visitors can access on your website and subscribe to, download and keep.

We particularly like the use of audio testimonials. Co-author Daniel Barnett's two companies make use of this at **www.emplawservices.co.uk** and **www.cpdwebinars.com/testimonials.php**.

Using this type of media does involve more commitment than producing the written material we've discussed so far, but need not be either expensive or excessively challenging. (We are not qualified to go into any very technical details about producing and posting audio or video content, but we've included some excellent sources of techie information in the Resources.)

But why should we bother? Well, because we are all becoming more and more accustomed to absorbing information through what we hear and—particularly—what we watch rather than what's put in front of us to read. As a lawyer, you are one of the exceptions. This is a profession still biased towards working with the printed word, but a significant proportion of your current and future clients may well no longer be. When they reach your website, you need to be sure you grab and hold their attention in as many ways as you can, and you need to pay particular attention to harnessing video.

11.6.1 A picture is worth...

In *Social Media Marketing*, Dave Evans says: "As the saying goes, 'a picture is worth a thousand words' ... a video can convey very precise meaning and can engage an audience in ways that words alone sometimes fail to do. This is particularly important when you consider the multitasking 'scan'-oriented consumption of digital content."

The growing importance of video emerged strongly in a survey at the end of 2008 of 400 advertising, marketing and media decision-makers by online video host PermissionTV. Among the key findings was that...

• 71 per cent believed using video would help build brand awareness

• 67 per cent identified online video as a primary focus for their 2009 marketing campaigns

• 64 per cent said a primary goal of their online video initiatives would be strengthening relationships with existing clients.

Matt Kaplan, vice-president of Solutions, and Chief Strategy Officer with PermissionTV, said: "These survey results demonstrate the strategic importance of online video in the overall marketing mix, as well as a growing requirement for more sophisticated video experiences."

Specialist journalist Chris Crum, from online magazine webpronews.com, put it in plainer English: "Online video is consuming the web whether you like it or not. Some prefer text content over video in most cases, and that's OK too. I don't think text is going anywhere, but demand for video is on the rise from both consumers and businesses looking to stay on top of their marketing." The secret then, is to give your visitors something in a video that they can't find anywhere else, says Crum. "The best videos provide a user experience that simply can't be duplicated in text."

How can you apply this to your own business? As with the rest of your marketing materials, the precise content will obviously depend on the type of client you represent. A video appropriate for a leading corporate practice is clearly not going to work if your primary targets are no-win, no-fee claimants. However, the principle should be the same—you're aiming to bring the law to life, and one of the most effective ways of doing this is through scenarios.

Taking our West Midlands discrimination law practice as an example, they could complement the written material on their website by featuring one or more videos focusing on commonly-encountered problems. For instance, one video could centre on a woman returning to work after maternity leave whose employer wants to assign her to different duties. The narrative could highlight the potential minefield the employer was entering, following the drama until the point where real conflict threatened. A significant proportion of viewers—current or prospective clients—should be sufficiently unsettled to want to find out more.

Would this work better than just offering a written guide? Almost certainly. We recommend you visit profiled firm Vista's website at www.vista-online.co.uk/ and look at the scenarios featured there. The significant downside of using video this way is the investment—this has to be professionally produced. Unless you have access to some talented amateurs happy to perform for free, you can't put together a convincing drama as part of a DIY project! Nonetheless, this does remain probably the most effective use of website video for employment lawyers.

Beyond the reach of all but the bigger hitters is something like Pinsents's highly impressive HR Network TV, a subscription podcast service targeted at HR decision-makers which helped win the firm the 2008 Law Society Award for Excellence in Pioneering Legal Services. However, you could use video more modestly to highlight important judgments or legislative changes, provided that whoever makes the presentation is comfortable and effective doing so. There's nothing worse than watching stilted, wooden performances from lawyers (or indeed anyone else unaccustomed to speaking before a camera), and there's a risk of the message getting lost in the delivery. You also could experiment with Question and Answer sessions, and involve several members of your team. Another obvious way of harnessing video is to record any seminars or training you host, but be careful—without intelligent (and probably professional) editing and producing, these can be very tedious! Scott also sees growing potential for incorporating both audio and video into blogs: "While your competition is still trying to figure out 'that blogging thing', you can leverage your existing blog into the new worlds of audio and video and leave the competition way behind."

Wherever you use video, aim to keep it succinct. Chris Crum says: "Length is often a factor. As a rule, people generally do not want to watch lengthy videos unless they are either entertaining or truly useful to them. From a business standpoint, I believe you are going to have greater success from making the content as useful as possible in as little time as possible." We would also advise you to do the following:

* Focus on one topic at a time.

* Write a script, but don't read from it. Rehearse it and polish it before going in front of the camera.

- Think carefully about your backdrop. What image are you aiming to project?

- As with written material, don't use "today", "yesterday", and so on. Stick to dates, or if the video is generic don't use dates at all (this applies equally to audio clips).

11.6.2 The YouTube phenomenon

There's no escaping YouTube, and you shouldn't want to. Remember, around 13 hours of new video were added to the site every minute in 2008. Try a search for "employment law UK" on YouTube and you're likely to get fewer than 20 results, a significant number of them uploaded by Legal Training TV (**www.legaltraining.tv**). Take the "UK" off your search, and it shoots up to well over 500. Although in the wider YouTube context this is still a drop in the ocean, it nonetheless indicates that North American law firms and legal marketers have already begun to recognise the power of YouTube to widen their reach. We strongly urge you to explore this platform as a way of broadening yours as well.

If you're unfamiliar with the concept, it couldn't be simpler. The official description reads: "YouTube is a free online video streaming service that allows anyone to view and share videos that have been uploaded by our members." All you do is...

- create an account

- upload a video

- decide who can see it—everyone, or those you choose to supply with a link.

As a Web 2.0 social media platform, YouTube allows you to invite people to leave comments about your video, and this can (as with a blog) be a valuable source of feedback—good and not so good. You can also "embed" a YouTube video within your own website, a blog, or a Facebook or MySpace page, widening still further the site's usefulness as a marketing tool, and providing useful linking for the search engines. YouTube, only founded in 2005, has, since late 2007, been a Google subsidiary. YouTube says of the arrangement: "The exciting and powerful platform YouTube has built complements Google's mission to organise the world's information and make it universally accessible and useful." In other words, if it's on YouTube, it will be viewed favourably by Google. At the time of writing, most of the employment law videos from both sides of the Atlantic were pretty dull, largely featuring a collection of talking heads. The first UK law firm to upload a well-researched, well-produced scenario video that mixes elements of humour and pathos with clear guidance could, we predict, really clean up. We have found one in the US, produced by employment consultancy Manpower. It's called the "Employment Law Sing-A-Long Song" and is very, very funny. It's at http://tinyurl.com/bvrm3u

Action

If you're not familiar with YouTube, visit **http://uk.youtube.com** and spend some time looking around. See what other lawyers—within your specialist area and in other fields—are doing, and identify those videos that you think work well and those that don't.

Open an account (all completely free) and set up search parameters so that you can stay in touch with what's being uploaded with an "employment law" tag attached. If you're going to embrace video as part of your marketing mix, consider seriously including YouTube as an important way of reaching your audience.

11.6.3 Putting photos to use
Where YouTube dominates the video upload market, Flickr does the same for still photos.

At first glance photos may not appear to offer the marketing opportunities of video, and that is largely true. However, look upon Flickr as an adjunct to your website, somewhere you can make available a large number of images featuring present and prospective clients—at events you have organised, for example, training sessions you have hosted, or networking sessions—and the perspective changes. You wouldn't want to clutter up your own website with photo galleries like this (they eat up a lot of server space for a start), but they can be an easy way of growing and maintaining relationships and building goodwill. All you need to do is point visitors in Flickr's direction. And as Flickr is very Google-friendly, if you learn how to label your images effectively they will rank highly in the search results.

Action

Again, as with YouTube, if you're unfamiliar with Flickr, visit **www.flickr.com** and explore how the site works.

If you have a set of photos from a recent event, open an account, upload them, and either link to them from your website or restrict access and send the link to the people featured. If you go for the second option, and this applies equally to YouTube, you will miss out on the pictures being found by search engines.

If you don't have corporate photos, these are an absolute **must**. Remember, people do business with people. See Chapter 14 (14.2.2) for some guidelines on photos.

11.6.4 Podcasting

How does a podcast differ from an audio clip or a video? It doesn't—it's all about delivery, and we've deliberately deferred looking at audio in any detail so far as we believe that it's most effectively used in podcasting rather than as a static website feature.

What do we mean? You'll no doubt be familiar with the podcast concept. The BBC, for example, has for several years been offering free downloads of selected radio programmes in MP3 format. This allows, say, Archers fans to catch up with events in Ambridge whenever they wish by subscribing to automatic updates fed direct to their PC, laptop or hand-held device. The BBC also offers a more limited, mainly news-based feed of video podcasts— or vodcasts. The term podcast derives from a conjunction of iPod and broadcast, reflecting the fact that it was Apple's pioneering MP3 player for which the first podcasts were formatted. A significant number of UK law firms are already using audio clips on their websites, with varying degrees of success, but very few are using podcasts consistently. Again it's Pinsents (with "radio station" Outlaw.com as well as HR Network TV) that is among those showing the way. Scottish firm Maclay Murray Spens has also fully embraced the concept, and Charon QC uses it for audio interviews with people within the legal and marketing professions.

There are two main benefits of providing a podcast service:

- Because subscribers sign up for your podcasting service, and receive updates automatically, it's significantly easier for you to build a relationship. The principle is the same when you gain their consent to email them information (which we return to in Chapter 16).

- You're offering online visitors another valuable resource that adds depth and authority to your website.

Audio podcasts are easier, quicker and less expensive to produce than videos, so you may want to consider focusing more of your energy here to start with. Their subject matter can also be more contemporaneous. You could record a briefing note as an audio clip and add it to your podcast pool at the same time as you put together the written version. As with videos, keep them tight and as short as possible, although people are generally more forgiving with audio as it lends itself so well to multitasking!

We'll discuss in detail how your website visitors can subscribe to your podcasts and other online material in Chapter 14, but the most usual way is by offering sign-up through an RSS (really simple syndication) feed. You may already be using RSS to access other people's services.

Action

We're not going to ask you to go away and make a video or record a podcast—at least not yet!

As with the written content, you first need to look at what others are doing, particularly law firms who specialise in the same areas as you. See how they use video and audio, and always approach their websites as a potential client would, not as a rival lawyer. Consider the following questions:

• Is the content timely and relevant?

• Does it grab your attention immediately?

• Are the videos or audio clips too long? If so, how would you edit them?

• Are the videos or audio clips well presented and professional in feel? If not, how would you improve them?

Drawing on your research, put together a programme of…

• three videos, including at least one scenario

• six podcasts, including at least one based on a briefing note.

It would be over-ambitious to attempt to introduce both onto your website at the same time, so next weigh up the pros and cons for you, taking into account both your resources and your target audience. Would video reach more potential clients, or setting up a podcasting service? What are your rivals doing? More likely than not, they're doing nothing, which gives you a very useful advantage.

11.6.5 Paying for added extras

The final area of website content we're looking at in this chapter is using third party material from an outside supplier, which you pay for.

The best known and most widely used service for employment lawyers is DiscLaw Publishing's Emplaw (**www.emplaw.co.uk**). Among others, Conscious Law also provides quality content, in their case through regularly updated news feeds.

There are advantages and disadvantages to doing this. On the plus side...

• you're offering visitors a wealth of information and guidance you would never have time to produce yourself

• you're adding significant depth to your website, which both enhances visitors' perception of its value and increases your search engine visibility (with the caveat mentioned above about re-published material)

• updating is done automatically and often daily, eliminating the embarrassing risk for a busy practice of having out-of-date information on their website (for example, old compensation limits).

And these are the disadvantages:

• The material isn't unique. It can obviously be found on rival websites and this may be an issue for some visitors, though probably a minority.

• Your control over what's made available is limited. It's likely to be largely off-the-shelf and may not always reflect your practice's style and approach.

Jonathan Golden is managing partner and head of the employment group at west London firm Solnick LLP. He and his colleagues have been using emplaw.co.uk as a reference source since 1999 and made it a website feature in 2002 when DiscLaw first marketed it to reflect host websites' branding. "Many firms will be concerned about placing content over which they have no control on their website", he writes in *Internet Newsletter for Lawyers and Law 2.0*: "This has not been an issue for us because we were already using and trusted this product, and we have a clear copyright and disclaimer message which shows this to be a DiscLaw Publishing product. So are we worried that people will spot that we don't write this service ourselves? In truth, I don't think anyone has ever noticed, and I doubt they would care. What people care about is that the information is available, free and part of the service we can provide."

Golden says the Emplaw material is there to provide employment information clients don't want to pay for, and the firm "uses that introduction to develop a relationship of trusted advisor". You can see it at **www.solnick.com/employment.html**

Action

Have a look at websites featuring Emplaw (another example is **www.employment-relations.co.uk**), and material from Conscious Law, and see how it's being used—and by whom.

Would it add the type of value that would work well for you? Do any of your competitors use it? If so, how? What would be the advantages and disadvantages for you?

12

Playing the PR game
to the new rules

In Chapter 6 we showed you how to use the "old rules" of PR, so you now have a blueprint for working with the media in the traditional way. This will continue to serve you very well, but we now want you also to embrace the sea change best defined by David Meerman Scott's "new rules", and start looking at ways to take your PR message to a much wider audience—one that includes the media but is no longer restricted to the media alone. Scott says: "The media have been disintermediated. The web has changed the rules. Buyers read your news releases directly, and you need to be speaking their language... This is not to suggest that media relations are no longer important; mainstream media and the trade press must be part of an overall communications strategy. But your primary audience is no longer just a handful of journalists. Your audience is millions of people with internet connections and access to search engines and RSS readers." Just to recap, these are the key new PR rules:

- PR is for more than just a media audience.

- PR means using news releases, blogs, podcasts and other online content as PR tools to communicate directly with clients.

- PR is about your firm being recognised across the web, not just one night on local TV.

We'll look at how you make this happen, pulling together in an example some of the different social media strands we've explored so far, along with a "new rules" news release. And we'll start by looking at how journalists are already modifying the way *they* operate in response to Web 2.0 and other changes.

12.1 The view from the journalist's screen

Just as Web 2.0 is offering you new ways of spreading your message, it's also changing how journalists go looking for stories, particularly the specialists. The two are becoming closely intertwined, which is why it's so important that you also understand how to establish yourself and your firm as a reliable source of information with quality website content.

Not that many years ago, a journalist looking for information about, say, the statutory definition of redundancy and how it worked would have had to go to a library—their employer's or the local public one—fish out a legal handbook, get hold of a copy of the legislation, possibly do some time-consuming photocopying, look through a pile of cuttings, phone a legal contact or two, and make a very large number of notes.

And now? Well, you know what happens now. They do what we all do—they Google. There is something of a chicken and egg issue here, but the fact is media organisations of all sizes worldwide are closing in-house libraries and disposing of their archives, so accelerating the shift, and of course cutting costs as they go. Whether destroying the planet's hard-copy media heritage serves any of us well in the long term is a separate issue. There are clearly inherent dangers just as there would be if the Law Society or Inns of Court decided to empty their libraries and channel all research online. However, for now and for you, there are some unrivalled PR opportunities to be grabbed by becoming a rich and reliable source of employment law information.

"But lots of people are already doing it", you protest. Yes, quite a lot of people are—some a great deal better than others. And we're not suggesting that you even try to challenge Emplaw (**www.emplaw.co.uk**), for example, or Delia Venables (**www.venables.co.uk**) in terms of depth, breadth, scope and detail, or indeed approach. We are instead looking at what *you* do *best*—that niche you identified in Chapter 2, revisited in Chapter 6 as part of your traditional media approach, and what you need to do under the "new rules".

12.1.1 Winning trust as an online resource

Google *employment law* and you'll get in excess of a million UK results. Search for *employment law discrimination* and it falls to 350,000. Then change it to *employment law sex discrimination* and youre down to 200,000. Then change the search to *dismissal during pregnancy* and it drops to 10,800; put it within quotes—"dismissal during pregnancy" or "dismissed during pregnancy"—and you've got around 1,500. Be a bit more specific still—"dismissed during pregnancy" + legal rights—and you'll get 75 or fewer.

Now put yourself back in a journalist's shoes. This time she works for a national broadsheet and she's researching the background to a case concerning a high-profile woman sacked while pregnant. The Court of Appeal hearing attracted a lot of media attention and the judgment is due any day. The journalist is already quite knowledgeable but wants to add some flavour to her story and is looking online for new angles on the topic, for something she hasn't found in the most obvious places. Like most journalists, she's an experienced Googler. She's not interested in clicking through hundreds of pages on the off-chance; she wants to drill down and so will ask something specific. Skimming 75 results is perfectly acceptable and she soon finds a link to a news release distributed six months earlier by our niche West Midlands practice. It's about a fairly similar case. Anne Jones successfully represented the employer at the EAT, and as part of their wider PR strategy the firm put out a release using an online distribution service. The journalist is interested and decides to call Anne to find out more.

What is of crucial significance here is how the connection was made—this journalist never saw the release when it was first distributed. Even if she had, she wouldn't have been interested as she wasn't researching the topic at that time and the story *in itself* was too parochial. Indeed, the release is unlikely to have attracted much in the way of media attention anywhere, but its existence on the web has turned it into a timeless media resource. What's more, after reading the release, the journalist will without question have gone straight to the Adams, Brown and Curtis website to check out Anne's credentials. As well as a news release archive, the site features a series of short scenario videos—including one focused on parental entitlement—and Anne has recently written a white paper exploring the widening of workplace rights for new parents. The journalist looks at the video—she already knows her facts, but it's always useful to brush up, and more importantly it gives her a feel for the ethos of the practice. Next she downloads the white paper before having a look at the senior partner's blog where she finds that a useful debate on parental rights and responsibilities is under way. By the time she lifts the phone to call Anne, not only has she a very clear picture of who she is talking to, and the type of practice Anne works for, she has also already significantly benefited from the free content on the firm's website. Is the journalist likely to use Anne again? Is she likely to also put a star against the firm's website as a particularly valuable source of well-produced information on discrimination law? You bet—and the connection will be forged all the more strongly if Anne follows up using the formula outlined in Chapter 6.

12.2   Out of the newsroom and straight to your next client

You've seen how the journalist made her way to Anne. Not only is this a radically different route from the one any journalist would have taken even a few years ago, what applies to the media now applies equally to everyone else. Instead of a journalist Googling "dismissal during pregnancy", it could quite as easily have been the director of a West Midlands SME with a staffing issue looking for somewhere to start. He could have taken exactly the same steps as the journalist—reading the release, visiting the website, watching the video, downloading the white paper, looking through the blog postings—before calling Anne. The key difference is that the cipher—the journalist—has been removed from the equation, and the news release has led a potential client directly to the firm's door. And what this perfectly illustrates is the ever-accelerating shift away from the rigid channelling of messages that Scott and others have identified—the news release that just goes to journalists, the sales pitch that goes straight to consumers. In its place we have an abundance of information presented in myriad styles and formats from myriad platforms, freely available to anyone, anywhere on the planet. And to make the most of every news release you send out, you need always to hold this thought.

12.3   Adjusting to the 'new rules' news release

As you saw in Chapter 6, when you're writing a news release for direct distribution to the media you need to focus on short, catchy headlines that will stand out from all the others in the newsdesk inbox, and tightly-written copy.

You need to modify those rules when your targets also include the general public and the search engines. Yes, you still need to make sure your release grabs and holds the reader's attention, answers the journalist's W5 questions (who?, what?, when?, where?, why?), and clears the obstacles of indifference. If it can trigger AIDA (attention, interest, desire and action) as well, so much the better. But now you also have to introduce *keywords*, in reality usually phrases rather than single words, the signposts the search engines and distribution hubs need to link the release to an inquiry, now or at some time in the far-off future. As an example, let's return to the journalist who was led to our West Midlands discrimination practice. She Googled "dismissed during pregnancy" and "dismissal during pregnancy". One—or possibly both—of these *keyword phrases* featured in the firm's news release.

To use keywords effectively in an online news release, you must put yourself in both the journalist's shoes and those of your wider audience. You must step right back and identify not only the more general terms which will return thousands of results ("discrimination" is an obvious example), but put together much more focused strings of words that sum up the essence of the story you're telling. You also need to include your firm's name and those of the key players very much more prominently than in a traditional release, along with your location. And you need to do this without completely undermining the story's flow and purpose.

Let's return to the release highlighting Adams, Brown and Curtis's abseil (see Chapter 6 for the "old rules" version). This time we've put it in the past tense, tweaked it, and formatted it for online distribution. The keywords and phrases are highlighted in bold, and the underlined words would appear as hyperlinks (formatted links to web pages).

Birmingham Lawyers Celebrate Milestone by Taking Hard Way Down for Charity

Ten solicitors from **Birmingham employment law specialists <u>Adams, Brown and Curtis</u>** *have raised £12,500 in a* **charity fundraising abseil** *for the* **<u>SunRise Birmingham Hospice for Children</u>**. *The fundraiser celebrated the law firm's tenth birthday.*

BIRMINGHAM, UK, 24 April 2009—A group of **employment lawyers** from **West Midlands** firm **<u>Adams, Brown and Curtis</u>** have abseiled down a **Birmingham** office block, raising £12,500 in a fundraising celebration of their firm's tenth birthday.

The ten solicitors from the **Birmingham specialist discrimination law practice** were joined by lawyers and clients from across the West Midlands in the charity challenge at the firm's head office in King Street on Thursday 16 April.

Senior partner John Adams said:"This was a fun way to mark the firm's milestone and our continued expansion as a boutique **West Midlands discrimination law firm**. We have raised money for the local **<u>SunRise Birmingham Hospice for Children</u>**, and well exceeded our target of £10,000—£1,000 for each of the past ten years.

Mr Adams said Anne Jones was stepping up to partner level after six years with the practice. "Anne has made an enormous contribution to our business—particularly in her specialist area, which is **defending sex discrimination claims for employers**.

"We've seen a steady rise in our workload due to the broader **scope of discrimination law**, and Anne will now get extra support from Carol Davis who also specialises in **West Midlands sex discrimination** cases and is based at our Wolverhampton office. She joined us from Coventry law firm Duggan, Edwards and French.

"We have also welcomed Bill Smith who is handling our rapidly growing portfolio of **age discrimination law** work from the Birmingham office. Bill comes to us from Gee & Harris in Stafford."

Mr Adams added: "Both Bill and Carol volunteered to join us in the abseil even though it was their first week with us—something of a baptism of fire, but they both thoroughly enjoyed the experience!" The practice has set up a donations page at www.justgiving.co.uk and there is more information about the fundraiser on their website, www.abcemploymentlaw.co.uk.

ENDS

"This was a fun way to mark the firm's milestone and our continued expansion as a boutique West Midlands discrimination law firm."

More information about the charity abseil from John Adams on 0121 111 3333. <u>Adams, Brown and Curtis</u> is a niche employment law practice specialising in defending discrimination claims for SME employers in Birmingham and the West Midlands, UK.

Compare the two versions and you will see that the online release is significantly more specific than the traditional one, and just manages to avoid becoming too repetitive or tautological. It doesn't flow as cleanly, and certainly couldn't be published without some editing, but it stands a significantly higher chance of being found by the search engines than the standard version, written solely with ease of publication in mind.

To successfully make the jump, you need to be aware of the protocols. One of the world's leading news release distributors is PRWeb (more about how this works later in this chapter), and their website offers detailed guidance on writing, preparing and formatting for maximum impact online. Let's check our release against some of PRWeb's key tips:

1. Headlines should be no more than 80 characters long, including spaces.

   ✓ Ours is 74 characters.

   It should be written with the first letter of each word capitalised (this derives from American headline styles and may over time be modified to allow the more usual UK practice of capitalising only the first word and proper nouns).

   ✓

1. The optimal length for a release is between 300 and 800 words.

   ✓ Ours is just over 400 words, so at the lower end of the scale.

3. Include a one-paragraph summary of one or two sentences. Sometimes only your headline and a summary appear on distribution points.

   ✓ Ours is two succinct sentences and includes two links.

4. Include a dateline. The date should be the day the release is distributed.

   ✓

5. Include a highlighted quote for visual impact.

   ✓ We've used one from John Adams—this would appear outside the main text.

6.   Limit the number of web page links to one for each 100 words.

     ✓✗ Ours is slightly heavy, with five, but that's because we're showing you how to do it!

     Web page links include the full URL hyperlink (as in **www.abcemploymentlaw.co.uk**), and anchor links, which appear <u>like this</u> as part of the text. (We're not going to attempt to offer any more technical information on this. Your IT team or website host will be able to help, and there's a wealth of information online.)

7.   Only use industry jargon if you include a definition everyone will understand.

     ✓There's no legalese or marketing gobbledegook in here anywhere!

8.   Reaching a milestone is a good reason to send out a release.

     ✓That's at the hub of the story, the firm's tenth anniversary.

9.   Don't include an email address in the main text. If your release is distributed via a site like PRWeb, it will be protected from "spambots" (spiders that harvest email addresses for spam mailers) with a notice to that effect overwriting the address. If you want to offer an email address, you could create a template for your releases in which you embed all your contact details. Another way around the spambots is to use the following format, although you may feel it looks unprofessional in this context: john dot adams at abcemploymentlaw dot co dot uk.

     ✓We've kept out John Adams's email address. Anyone interested can phone or reach him via the website.

Make the release available to download as both a Word file and a PDF, and because this story focuses on something that's already happened, it needs to be accompanied by some JPEG images, an audio clip, or—ideally—a short video. A charity abseil lends itself particularly well to video. This would really bring the event to life and put faces to the firm's names. Indeed, whenever you're publicising anything online, always aim to include at least one photo and ideally video. Not only is your release more likely to be opened, it will also be indexed by image search engines, increasing your general online visibility. And, of course, people buy people—the more you can humanise your message, the better. If your release is promoting, say, a new white paper or e-book, then attach that as a PDF as well. (You'll find more on writing and formatting online releases and other additional ways of giving them extra value from the sites listed in the Resources.)

12.3.1 Getting it out there

You can of course just post your release on your website. If it's properly optimised with good keyword use, it will appear somewhere on the search engines. But we strongly urge you to do more and investigate distributing all—or at least a good percentage—of your releases through one of the professional sites dedicated to getting you maximum visibility. Yes, you may have to pay, and how much depends on the service you choose. But in return you get benefits including...

- optimum formatting of your release for online recognition

- your release appearing on the distributor's website

- your release becoming part of the distributor's archive

- syndication to targeted media outlets

- direct access to potential clients through search engine results

- links back to your own website that are highly rated by the search engines.

There's a good choice of distributors now. We've already referred to

PRWeb, which has been putting out online news releases since 1997, has its headquarters in Washington State, and is one of the bigger hitters. The company—a subsidiary of Vocus Inc, of whom more shortly—now has a standalone UK service, launched in February 2009, and is working in partnership with the Press Association, the company providing a news feed to the overwhelming majority of British media. All releases issued through PRWeb's UK arm are optimised for the UK search engines (Google.co.uk, for example, rather than the US-biased Google.com), all timelines are in GMT, and currencies are shown in sterling rather than the dollar. The cost of sending out a single release starts at £46 for a very basic service. Among the useful additional features PRWeb offers are a link to your website through an embedded "iFrame" showing your site in real time and allowing direct access. (An example of a PRWeb all-bell-and-whistles release can be found here: **www.prweb.com/press_release.php**.) You can also create personalised templates, allow comments and feedback, and include links allowing readers to sign up to an RSS feed for future releases.

Also worth investigating is PRNewswire, established in 1954 and with more of a straightforward media focus than PRWeb. Like the UK PRWeb, PRNewswire distributes through the Press Association and also maintains what it claims is the world's largest database of journalists' contact details. Among PRNewswire's products is a small business service, with single release distribution starting at £220. Like PRWeb, PRNewswire includes options to monitor who opens your release and where it's used. Other distributors include UK-based RealWire and NeonDrum, both young UK companies specialising particularly in Web 2.0 online targets. (There's more information about all of these distributors in Resources.)

12.3.2 Getting others to help you get it out there

If you're going to use news releases as part of your overall online PR strategy, and we strongly suggest you do, you need—as Scott says—to ensure a reasonably regular flow. It's just not going to work if you leave months between them, in the same way that adding a new blog post once a quarter won't have any impact.

We appreciate there's a time commitment here that you may not want to make—at first, anyway—and one option is to outsource the whole release writing, distribution and monitoring process. This doesn't mean hiring a PR agency, just selecting a distributor that offers a writing service as well. Those listed above are among those who do.

At the other end of the spectrum, if you're happy to write your releases in-house but want a more hands-on way to manage distribution and monitoring, you could try a service like that offered by Vocus, PRWeb's parent company. For an annual subscription, you can use their software to build highly targeted distribution lists to journalists whose profiles you can read first. These are so detailed that you can, for example, find out whether they prefer to receive releases as email body text or as attachments! Vocus, not surprisingly, uses PRWeb for release distribution, and all its subscription models include access to a full monitoring, clippings and analysis service. (See Resources for more details.)

And just to hammer this message home: in addition to distributing a steady flow of news releases, you need to ensure your website is kept regularly updated, that you're properly archiving older material and adding new content *all the time*. Seeing your online presence as a single, constantly evolving whole needs to become something hard-wired.

Action

Rework the news release you wrote in Chapter 6 for maximum search engine visibility and online impact, following our advice and using our release as your template.

Then visit the distribution websites listed in the Resources, identify the three that look most likely to match your needs, and explore their services in depth. Use their internal search engines to look for keyword phrases, take product tours, and download whatever is on offer to broaden your understanding of the process.

Even if you're not ready to go down this route just yet, you do need to know how it works—and how it may already be working for your competitors.

13

The age of permission marketing— and beyond

Ten years ago, all that a legal website did was act as an online brochure or shop window. There'd be a bit about the firm's services, a bit about the history, a few contact details, and that was about it. It might have looked quite impressive, with various bells and whistles courtesy of a designer's love affair with Flash (the animation software unveiled by Macromedia in 1996), but it didn't actually *do* anything in marketing terms.

Now all that has changed. Lawyers across the land understand the importance of a well-designed website that does more than just give visitors "the firm was established in…", a phone number and an email address. Or do they? Not perhaps everyone, and we'll come on to that shortly. First though let's look at what they—and you—should be aiming for in the age of "permission marketing".

13.1 Who's giving permission for what?

What do we mean by "permission marketing"? At its simplest, it's this process:

1.   You're on a website, having a look around.

2.   You're offered something—a white paper, an e-book, a video, a free trial DVD, or (commonly) the option to sign up to a newsletter.

3.   You quite fancy that, so you click on the link.

4.   You're then asked for your contact details—always your name, always your email address, and sometimes more.

5.   You complete the form, click send, and then get a message thanking you and asking you to go to your inbox where you'll find a message.

6.   You go to your inbox, and there's the message. It more often than not asks you to click on a link which takes you back to the website (this is called double-opt in, and is to ensure that you do want to subscribe and have not either made a mistake or your email address has been harvested).

7.   Once back at the site, you can download whatever it is you signed up to get, or just await the arrival of the newsletter in your inbox, or the DVD through your letterbox.

This is permission marketing (more about the mechanics in Chapters 15 and 16), and by following this process you're giving your consent to be put on a database and contacted again. From being just an idle onlooker, you've been invited to begin a relationship—and you've agreed. It's these websites that are most likely to draw you further in by offering interesting content, to encourage you to look deeper, as happened with the journalist who found Anne in the last chapter. And while today's software allows designers—and their clients—to do a raft of other exciting things that were impossible even five years ago, it's this fundamental paradigm shift from the passive to the active that's the real key to your website's potential as a powerful marketing tool.

The principles of permission marketing are not new. They're tried-and-tested features in long-established practices such as direct response advertising, telemarketing and direct mail, all of which we'll look at later. However—telephone marketing apart—what makes online permission marketing so effective is the immediacy and accuracy. You know right away who wants to find out more, when they clicked on the link that launched their relationship with you, and even how they found you.

Should you, though, use permission marketing right across your website? When the journalist visited Adams, Brown and Curtis's site, would she have been prepared to fill out a form in order to download the white paper, watch the video and look through the news release archives? David Meerman Scott is among a growing number of internet marketers who cautions that you can over-do permission marketing, that the concept is now just beginning to lose its power. In his e-book, *Lose Control of Your Marketing*, he says: "... many folks create valuable and interesting information online and then do the exact wrong thing to distribute it— require visitors to provide personal information first. When you make people give an email address to get a white paper or watch a video, only a tiny fraction will do so; you will lose the vast majority of your potential audience."

Scott's premise is that *all* information should be made freely available, that the viral nature of the Web 2.0 social media platforms we have explored do the job of spreading the word for you, and there is no need to keep any tabs on your website visitors as they will return to you organically.

We suggest that you compromise. With something that inherently involves two-way traffic like a newsletter, then you clearly need your visitors to sign up. The same with podcasts—you can't receive a download unless you've provided details of where it has to go. With white papers, e-books, videos, your news releases and newsletter archives, and other information-rich content, you do however have choices, and we would recommend you make some of this freely accessible. Why not experiment? Try making one white paper, for example, instantly accessible and then attach a sign-up procedure to the next one you publish. It's not scientific, as the subject matter obviously plays a significant role, but you should get a good idea of how many downloads each attracts.

13.1.1 Do I really need to do all this?

You may still be thinking that you have no need for any of this on your website—that your practice is different, that your clients are different, and that's not what they want.

There are always exceptions that get away with bucking the trend—we'll highlight a couple of examples at the end of the chapter. Generally, though, we think that you continue to ignore the realignment towards good content and permission marketing, and your public's online expectations, at your peril.

You'll also ultimately pay a price for any of the following, in any combination:

- bad aesthetics

- poor layout

- dull, ungrammatical, feature-heavy copy

- complex navigation

- slow-loading pages

- old "news"

- out-of-date or no people details

- broken links

- poor use of testimonials

- "splash" pages—the introductory pages (often animated) where you're invited to click "enter" or "skip" to get to the real home page.

There are other factors—such as meeting accessibility standards—but we'll focus in this chapter on exploring home pages as someone making their first visit (we'll get more technical in the next chapter).

13.2 How does the profession measure up?

The rest of this chapter summarises the results of an informal survey we undertook to gauge how well and how quickly solicitor practices are responding to the arrival of permission marketing and becoming interactive. We looked at the home pages of a range of sites, chosen largely at random (in the main from Delia Venables' excellent guide to legal resources), but also including our profiled firms.

We focused particularly on sites that listed employment law as a speciality, but also looked at others to get the wider picture. We assessed them for their use of permission marketing and interactive features (particularly whether there were any "calls to action", the "here's what I want you to do next" that invites visitors to contact them, find out more, ask a question). We also checked them against the list of interest-losing features listed above.

13.2.1 Hitting home

That old cliché, "You never get a second chance to make a first impression", could not be more apposite when it comes to home pages. This is where most of your potential clients first meet you. If you turn them off here you greatly reduce the chances of them persevering to find out more. To turn our negatives into positives, what you're trying to achieve on your home page is...

- attractive aesthetics

- a logical, easy-to-follow layout

- attention-grabbing, benefit-led copy

- simple signposting and navigation

- up-to-date news

- no broken links

- careful use of testimonials

- no "splash" page.

The rest of this chapter focuses on the findings from our survey.

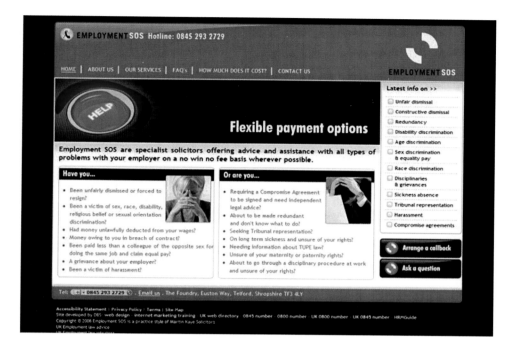

This home page has clean lines, makes good use of colour, and has benefit-led copy.

The signposting is clear, there are prominent contact details, and two calls to action: "arrange a callback", "ask a question".

The banner is an animated Flash feature which flags up other benefits, such as "covers whole of England and Wales" and "direct helpline".

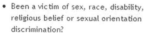

- Been unfairly dismissed or forced to resign?
- Been a victim of sex, race, disability, religious belief or sexual orientation discrimination?
- Had money unlawfully deducted from your wages?
- Money owing to you in breach of contract?
- Been paid less than a colleague of the opposite sex for doing the same job and claim equal pay?
- A grievance about your employer?
- Been a victim of harassment?

www.employeesos.co.uk
Telford, Shropshire

This home page is bright and fresh-looking. There is simple signposting and a call to action to sign up for email updates, leading to permission marketing.

There's also a link to an item highlighting an award:

latest news

Sep 2008
LAW FIRM OF THE YEAR 2008

Leading North-east law firm, Raeburn
Christie Clark & Wallace has won "Law
Firm of the Year" (over 50 fee earners)
at the Law Awards of ...

The main copy is a little jargon-heavy, but it's well-written:

a traditional firm with a modern outlook

www.raeburns.co.uk
Aberdeen

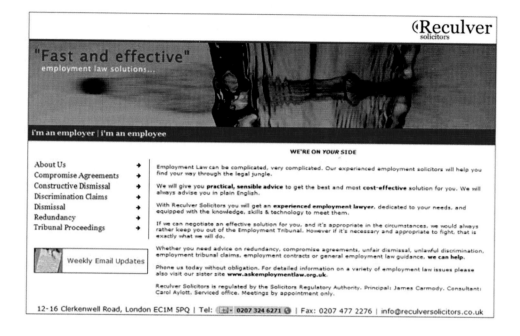

This home page has a tidy layout, although the main image is a little confusing and it's unclear why "Fast and effective" needs to be in quotes.

There's good signposting—I'm an employer, I'm an employee—and the copy is straightforward, a good proportion of it benefit-focused.

Contact details are clear, though a Contact tab would help. You have to go via About Us to find out exactly where they are.

The call to action could be made more compelling:

There are no instructions (in fact clicking just brings up your email client).

www.reculversolicitors.co.uk
London

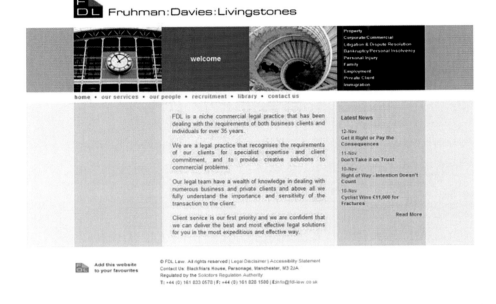

This has a very simple design and pleasing images, neat and clear signposting, and an up-to-date syndicated Latest News stream.

However, the copy is a bit clichéd:

> We are a legal practice that recognises the requirements of our clients for specialist expertise and client commitment, and to provide creative solutions to commercial problems.

And there are no calls to action.

www.fdl-law.co.uk
Manchester

A striking design, although the prominent use of an attractive young woman might grate with some visitors. And are we all supposed to have heard of Carly Stratton from *Shipwrecked*?! This is a Flash feature, so there are other testimonials and messages.

The smaller images are effective, but why is the gavel so popular with British website designers when it's not used by any of the UK judiciary? It's an American courtroom icon—nothing to do with us!

There's good signposting, and although there's no permission marketing, there's a prominent call to action, plus contact details, and tight copy that uses "you" as much as "we":

www.howardssolicitors.net/
Manchester

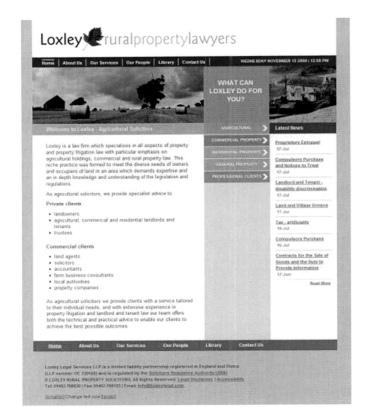

This website has a simple layout, with clear signposting and appealing, relevant images—but then rural property lends itself rather better to artistic photos than employment law!

There's no permission marketing or calls to action, however, and the copy is full of features with little in the way of benefits:

Loxley is a law firm which specialises in all aspects of property and property litigation law with particular emphasis on agricultural holdings, commercial and rural property law. This niche practice was formed to meet the diverse needs of owners and occupiers of land in an area which demands expertise and an in depth knowledge and understanding of the legislation and regulations.

When we visited the site, the Latest News was several months out of date. And perhaps a different headline might prove more engaging:

Proprietory Estoppel

17-Jul

www.loxleylegal.com
Wooton-under-Edge, Gloucestershire

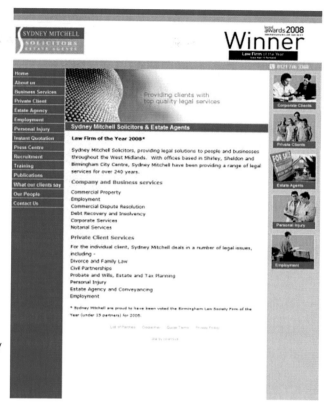

This has a minimalist, streamlined design, with great use of colour and images. The firm is justifiably flagging up a recent award, and the signposting is excellent.

There's no permission marketing, however, no calls to action, and nothing else to encourage interaction. And you have to go to the Contact Us page for contact details.

The copy could also be greatly lifted by a healthy injection of benefits:

Sydney Mitchell Solicitors, providing legal solutions to people and businesses throughout the West Midlands. With offices based in Shirley, Sheldon and Birmingham City Centre, Sydney Mitchell have been providing a range of legal services for over 240 years.

www.sydneymitchell.co.uk
Birmingham and West Midlands

A rather strange design, with a classy logo and elegant muted tones at the top of the site, and then an acre of white space with nothing in it but some text and a blue box linking to a blog:

The signposting is good. However, there are no calls to action, and the copy doesn't really tell you anything you wouldn't expect:

Capital Law is a leading provider of legal services to private and public sector clients throughout the UK, Europe and beyond. We aim to deliver more and add value wherever possible.

And the quotation adds little to our understanding of what might be on offer:

www.capitallaw.co.uk
Cardiff

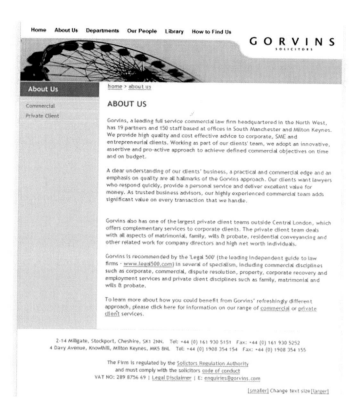

This is simple and pleasing on the eye. Perhaps a little too simple, as there are no calls to action and the contact details are tucked away at the foot of the page.

In fact, this is the About Us page, where you arrive after clicking on the pretty—but pretty pointless—actual home page:

The main problem, though, is the copy. It's almost exclusively about "us" and "we" and it really undersells this firm. Towards the end you discover that Gorvins is rated by Legal 500, but not only is this not properly exploited, the sentence flagging it up is ungrammatical and badly punctuated:

> Gorvins is recommended by the 'Legal 500' (the leading independent guide to law firms - www.legal500.com) in several of specialism, including commercial disciplines such as corporate, commercial, dispute resolution, property, corporate recovery and employment services and private client disciplines such as family, matrimonial and wills & probate.

Just to compound this, the link goes to Legal 500's home page, not to anything featuring the firm. A real shame, as this has the makings of a stylish site.

www.gorvins.com
Stockport and *Milton Keynes*

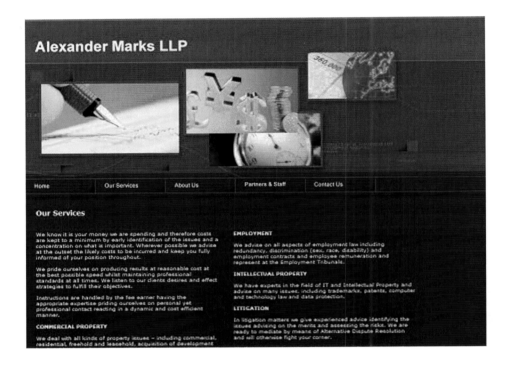

There's conflicting evidence on whether our brains are happier processing dark lettering on a light background or vice-versa, and—specific vision impairments apart—it's probably largely down to what we personally like.

What is important is that we can read the text, and this website, though aesthetically pleasing as a whole, makes it a bit of a challenge.

The text size could easily be increased by streamlining the copy, which does not get off to a good start:

> Now based in Queen Anne Street in the heart of the West End of London the firm can trace its history in this area to 1994. We aim to provide proven expertise in a personal, focused and cost-effective environment. For more reasons why you should use us, click here.

This entirely feature-led approach is maintained across the rest of the text.

There are no calls to action and no contact details.

www.amlaw.co.uk
London

What marks out this page for special mention is the use of an audio clip—an introduction to the practice from the MD:

In it he focuses on his main target client—SMEs—and highlights benefits on the site, such as the links to free legal advice. These include audio audits, which come to you by way of a permission marketing form to complete, as does general advice. There's no shortage of calls to action or interactivity here! There's also an up-to-date news feature, a search facility, and an invitation to set up an RSS feed.

This innovation isn't matched by the copy, which is a little too focused on the fact that this isn't a "typical law firm", without clearly explaining why. The text is italic punctuated with bold (which is search-engine friendly; more about this in Chapter 15), but it's not a high scorer for either accessibility or aesthetics:

Business Lawyers' *focus is on servicing individuals, entrepreneurs, businesses and business owners with clear, sensible and comprehensible legal advice provided by our company commercial law specialists.* **Our approach to service delivery is different** *from the "typical law firm"-for more information please* **click on the audio control on the right of this screen** *to hear us explain and do* **have a look at**

You also need to scroll to reach links to briefing notes, there are no prominent contact details, and the testimonial dates are from 2007.

However, overall there are the ingredients for a great marketing tool.

www.business-lawyers.org
High Wycombe, Buckinghamshire

This site is peculiar. There's endless repetition of "employment law", alone or in conjunction with "solicitor", "specialist". "advice", and so on, together with lists of English place names. We can only deduce that this is an attempt at search engine optimisation (SEO) (more about this in Chapter 15), but it's not only unlikely to work, it also makes the copy unreadable:

Our employment law specialists at The Employment Law Solicitors have extensive experience of handling matters upon behalf of both employers and employees in all areas of employment law.

The Employment Law Solicitors: Advice On All Employment Law Matters
If you require advice and assistance, then a solicitor from The Employment Law Solicitors, who can take on cases from Manchester, Cheshire, Liverpool, Lancashire, Yorkshire, Devon, Cornwall and from throughout the UK, will be able to assist you with your employment law problem.

Buried in the copy are some useful benefits, including free advice. These benefits are highlighted in eight blue boxes on the home page. If you click on one it brings up a pop-up saying exactly the same thing! Why?

There are two calls to action—a newsletter sign-up and questionnaire—and a phone number is prominent at the top of the page. Also prominent is that gavel again!

www.theemploymentlawsolicitors.co.uk
Wilmslow, Cheshire

We applied the same tests to the home pages of our eight featured businesses. They're analysed alphabetically.

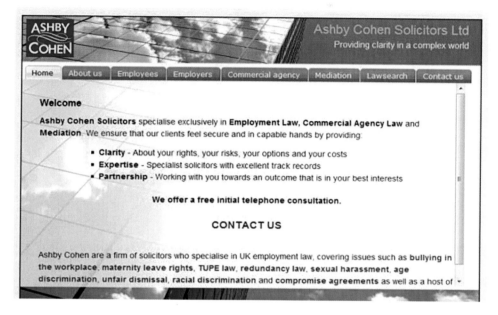

Ashby Cohen's website performs well online through the natural listings on the left of a Google results page (achieved with SEO), and as featured listings at the top or on the right (Pay Per Click).

Even so—as director Alain Cohen recognises—it could do with updating and giving visitors more to take away. As it's his firm's main business conduit, it's important that the whole site, but particularly the home page, does the job exceptionally well.

The images are fine, as are the logo and the slogan— "providing clarity in a complex world". However, there's no permission marketing, and the only calls to action are by clicking on the "contact us" button or text links to information pages on areas such as redundancy, workplace bullying, and unfair dismissal.

The copy is also a little repetitive, with the text at the top and foot of the page largely saying the same thing, doubtless for search optimisation purposes.

The internal scroll bar suggests the site was built using Frames-based software, which has now been superseded.

www.ashbycohen.co.uk
London

Colemans-ctts has chosen a stripped-down home page, which can be risky as there's a fine line between this and a splash page. The design is good, though, and you'd be a churlish visitor not to click on one of the clearly-labelled links:

Services for Business

We offer a full range of commercial and corporate support in a wide range of industry sectors serving all sizes of business through to multi-national corporations and associations.

TELL ME MORE ▶

The copy in both boxes could be lighter and less predictable, especially given the "we're people too" theme, which begins here and continues through the site.

The box at the top of the page is a Flash box. The first message says: "We may be one of the best UK law firms…"

We're not quite sure what to make of the third: too much money spent on image consultants?!

www.colemans-ctts.co.uk/
Kingston, Surrey

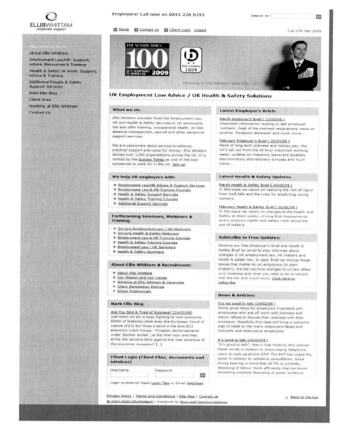

A clean and airy design, with a nice portrait of boss Mark Ellis, and smart positioning of the firm's Sunday Times 'Best Companies to Work For' award, which is referred to in the text immediately underneath.

There's a clear call to action right at the top of the page, the signposting is clear and obvious, there's a site search facility, plenty of information and a wealth of interactive links, such as these:

We help UK employers with:

→ Employment Law/HR Advice & Support Services
→ Employment Law & HR Training Courses
→ Health & Safety Support Services
→ Health & Safety Training Courses
→ Additional Support Services

These are, though, just labels and replacing some of them with benefits-led text would help lift and lighten the tone of the page.

www.elliswhittam.com
Chester

PEOPLE - REPUTATION - VALUES - PRESS - LINKS - CONTACT US

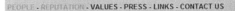

Solicitors specializing in
employment law and partnership law

*"Ronnie Fox remains one of the absolute top choices for employment
and potentially contentious partnership issues."*

The Legal 500

Fox, practising from offices in the heart of the City, has:

- the **reputation** for resolving contentious employment and partnership issues quickly, quietly and frequently without litigation.
- the **expertise** to advise on complex technical employment problems (Ronnie has been writing on employment law for over 25 years) and difficult partnership disputes (Ronnie founded the multi-disciplinary Association of Partnership Practitioners).
- the **experience** which comes from acting for both large corporate employers and senior executives, for both professional firms and individual partners (which enables us to find practical and commercial solutions).

Fox, 78 Cornhill, London EC3V 3QQ - Tel: +44 20 7618 2400

© FOX 2008 : Fox Lawyers Home : **Accessibility**

Fox Lawyers is largely built on founder Ronnie Fox's reputation, and it therefore makes absolute sense to feature *Legal 500*'s entry on the home page.

However, Fox recognises that time and technology have moved on since 2006 when this site was first designed, and that it's time to upgrade while still retaining its essential flavour.

Judged on what it sets out to do, the home page performs fine. You get a good idea of who, what, and where, the signposting is straightforward, and the contact details are clearly displayed.

www.foxlawyers.com
London

Quite unlike any other site we've featured, solicitor Dean Morris's got-the-boot.com home page is striking and straightforward. You can see what they do at the top, and the copy is generally clear and almost all benefits-led:

Have you...

- been unfairly dismissed or forced to resign and wish to claim unfair dismissal or constructive dismissal?
- been made redundant unfairly?
- been discriminated against on the grounds of sex, race, disability, age, religious belief or sexual orientation?
- had money unlawfully deducted from your wages?
- money owing to you in breach of contract?
- been paid less than a colleague of the opposite sex and claim equal pay?

There are no contact details for a reason. Enquiries are all funnelled through the site via a comprehensive form, which initiates the relationship.

The nature of the site and the business—one-off claimants—doesn't lend itself to other types of permission marketing. However, home page pointers towards something to download and take away might not go amiss, perhaps versions of some of the wide selection of guides found within the site?

The partner site, not-my-fault.com, works along the same lines, but the design is more stylish.

www.got-the-boot.com
Solihull, West Midlands

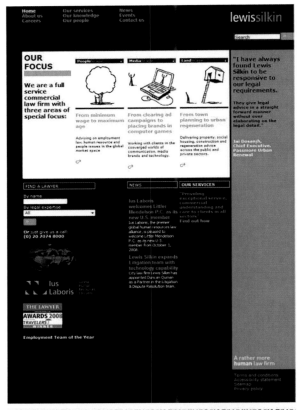

Sydney Mitchell (see page 219) made the most of their award by flagging it up on their home page. Lewis Silkin seem to place less emphasis on it and have put it right down at the bottom:

They use an unusual and striking page design. One drawback is that you have to scroll to reach a good chunk of detail, such as the award details and the firm's news. There's no permission marketing and no calls to action, but you can find a lawyer by name or expertise, and there's a site search facility.

Once you start delving into the site, the content is first-rate—one of the best websites going.

www.lewissilkin.com
London

There's a minimalist approach from our featured US firm—and one which, according to the copyright line at the bottom—hasn't been overhauled since 2006.

There's rather a lot of empty blue space, and not a lot of text. What there is doesn't tell you a great deal other than the obvious:

Experience & Innovation

Shutts & Bowen is a Florida-based law firm, representing individuals and business entities nationally and internationally.

Our goal is to provide quality legal representation, combining our commitment to client service with the latest innovations in the practice of law.

There's a useful search facility, practice area sorter, and—slightly oddly—a client feedback link, but no calls to action.

www.shutts.com
Orlando, Florida

There's plenty of interaction on Vista's stylish home page, but you need to scroll to reach most of it. Giving up so much space to the welcome headline comes at a cost.

The copy, attributed to MD Darren Maw, explains clearly who the target clients are and—a few bits of jargon and a stray apostrophe apart—is tightly presented.

There's good signposting, nice use of Flash in the banner across the top, and plenty to keep the visitor busy, with three clear links at the foot of the page, one in the middle for a newsletter sign-up, and this photo link:

This has been in place for some time, so it could do with a tweak to lose the "new" or replacing with another still from the video.

There are no contact details. You have to click on the tab.

www.vista-online.co.uk
Stockport

At the start of this chapter we argued that a functioning website was no longer an optional extra, but on our travels through legal cyberspace we found more than a few examples of home pages which, regrettably, fell rather more than a little short.

Here's a home page that goes absolutely nowhere and another two that do everything we say you shouldn't, but get away with bucking the trend!

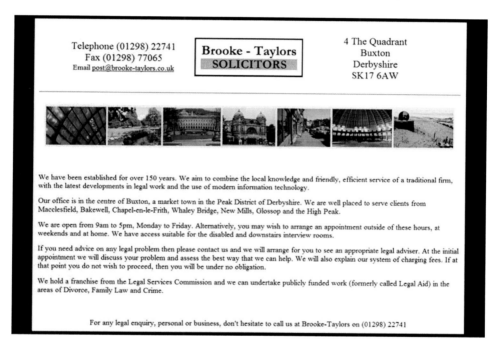

This home page was singled out because it has no links (although there are in fact other pages on the site if you delve via Google).

The copy is all about how they do business and not a lot about what they actually do for their clients.

Altogether a great shame because this is—as they say themselves—a long-established firm with a very strong local reputation that could only be further enhanced with a proper site.

www.brooke-taylors.co.uk
Buxton, Derbyshire

We've included this because it's just so counter-intuitive that it works! In fact, it's got quite a cult following and is well worth a visit. It looks as though it was thrown together by a nine-year-old with an early Amstrad, which is clearly the intention of partners Bruce Buglear and Jeremy Bate.

The Senior Partner

(Brucey)

The Junior Partner

(Batey)

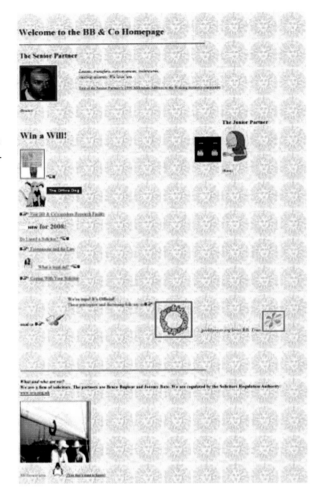

Not entirely surprisingly, if you were searching for a Woking solicitor, you wouldn't find this practice online—it's nowhere to be seen on Google. But if you stumbled on the site by chance, you might well be curious to put your head round the office door to find out more!

We wouldn't recommend it as a universal template, but we do highly recommend it for light relief from the serious job of constructing a business-building online presence, and also for some useful information, wittily written, without a single website cliché in sight.

www.buglear-bate.co.uk
Woking, Surrey

And finally…

This site has nothing interactive, no calls to action, and the copy even revels in taking a poke at some of the very elements we've been advocating. This testimonial is a finely-crafted spoof, for example:

"The service was very good especially when I hear about others who have had negative experiences with solicitors - you were very understanding and clear and informative at all times."

Ms H, Tyneside

Witty and entertaining, the copy is a breath of fresh air and it's clear everyone involved in building this website had a ball. A couple of examples:

Hello!

WELCOME to the website of CHAPPELL PASCOE SOLICITORS here in Crowborough, East Sussex.

If you're here by accident, you may want to navigate away quickly to more interesting sites, like Chappell Pianos or Dalziel & Pascoe.

We just don't touch some areas of the law, either because we think they are very boring indeed, or because we're simply no good at them.

The design mirrors the light touch of the copy but is also functional, with good signposting. You've got to be very brave to take this route, and certain of your niche, but this practice has pulled it off in spades.

www.chappellpascoe.com
Crowborough, East Sussex

There's nothing scientific about our survey, and there are undoubtedly other websites out there that do the job as well—or indeed better—than those we've singled out for praise. But the purpose was precisely to make a random selection and so avoid being led in any particular direction or risk focusing on any single website design team.

In the next chapter, we look in greater detail at the features you need (and don't need) to include on your website, and in Chapter 15 we show you how to get star billing on Google.

Action

Step back and assess your own home page against the "don't want" and "must have" points that we listed near the start of the chapter.

Then ask somebody unconnected with your practice to take a look from

Table 4 Home page check list

	✓ if used	Good? ✓	Poor? ✓	Room for improvement?
Appearance and aesthetics				
Layout				
Signposting and navigation				
Copy				
Calls to action				
Permission marketing				
News				
Links				
Testimonials				
Splash page				

a potential customer's viewpoint, again assessing the page against the checklist.

You may find it useful to complete a grid like Table 4. Feel free to add extra components—it's the process that matters rather than the tools, and arriving at an accurate picture of where you are today.

Once you've done that, identify how you will improve the three elements that work least well. If you have no calls to action and no permission marketing tools, identify ways of introducing these.

14

Making your website work

Our home page survey revealed a wide variation in how lawyers market themselves online— from the tongue-in-cheek, via the minimalist to the sophisticated and interactive. There is no single "right way" and it's not our role to try to design the perfect site because there really isn't one. As we keep stressing, what works best for one business may be less effective for another. And there's only one way to find out—first define your audience and then keep testing and measuring!

The website elements nobody can afford to ignore are...

• design and content essentials

• effective copy (we've looked at this in Chapter 5 and again in Chapter 13)

• getting seen on Google (we'll explore this in the next chapter).

14.1 It's for the visitor, not you!

As we saw in Chapter 13, user-friendly design and content is crucial for holding your visitor's attention and interest. And how easy your site is to look at and use is a great deal more important than an elegant logo, tasteful animated images, and experimental use of colour. Here, as everywhere (as we explained in Chapter 2), you need to give your visitors what they actually want, not what you *think* they want.

So start by taking a step back and, as you did in the last exercise, approach your website planning as a visitor. Then look at it from four perspectives, those of...

1.   your existing clients

2.   somebody who's reached you through a search engine (like our journalist in Chapter 12) and is looking for information

3.   somebody directed to your site

4.   somebody looking for a job.

They all arrive at your website—and most often your home page—through a mix of routes, but very few will be there as part of a general "What shall I do in my lunch hour?" session, which probably hops from eBay to Twitter by way of Facebook, your blog or someone else's, a detour to Amazon, and a check on the BBC headlines.

So let's consider what each type of visitor is most likely to be seeking.

14.1.1 'What's your number again?' Your site as a phone book

Your existing clients already know who you are, so they're going to skip what you're saying about your business. They're there for a specific reason, and it's frequently something as mundane as getting your phone number—it's often quicker just to pull up your site than dig about in their contacts folder. So make it easy for them. This is **design and content rule 1**:

•   Display your main contact details on *every page*—along the bottom is fine—and more prominently on your home page.

Yes, the downside is that they won't spend so long on your site, but they probably wouldn't have done anyway if all they want to do is call you.

An existing client may also arrive looking for something you've told them about—an important judgment, new legislation, an upcoming event, a new white paper. And they may go to your home page even if your email includes a direct link to what they're looking for. Why wouldn't they just click on that? Any number of reasons, but most likely because they've just been on another site, remembered your email, and then headed for your home page rather than delve in their inbox. So this is **design and content rule 2**:

• Whenever you put anything new on your website, include a short summary and a link to it from your home page, even if you email your main audience with a direct link.

If your website includes a case management system, your existing clients will want to be able to log in with as few clicks as possible, so include this facility on your home page or display a prominent link.

14.1.2 'I need to find out about…' Your site as resource

Your visitor has come to you because, like the journalist in Chapter 12, they're looking for information about employment law, and as we've already stressed, it's crucial that you deliver. Perhaps they want to know whether they have grounds to pursue a claim, whether it's worth their while doing so, or just how to launch a claim, or defend one. They may be ready to seek your advice at this stage; they may not.

Either way, you need to give them as many reasons as possible to stay and find out more—about what's troubling them and about who you are. This first means not only ensuring your website is rich in legal content, but that this is strongly and clearly signposted from every page on your site. You want this type of visitor to spend plenty of time exploring your service, to have a thorough look around, and to take something away with them. This is **design and content rule 3**:

• Signpost your legal information from every page—and especially from your home page.

If they find this content useful, they'll naturally want to find out about you. Indeed, among the most clicked links on any site is the one leading to Our People (or Our Team, Our Staff, or Who We Are, or Who Are We?, or however you wish to label yourselves). We'll go into detail about getting this content right below. Meanwhile, this is **design and content rule 4**:

- Signpost your Our People section clearly from every page. It needs to stand alone and not be labelled as a sub-section of About Us or Contact Us.

14.1.3 'What can they do for me anyway?' Your site as a showcase

This visitor has arrived at your site through a recommendation. Maybe they're a referral from an existing client, already interested and wanting to find out more. Or perhaps they've been forwarded an update email you put out, or seen an item on your site mentioned on somebody else's, and either followed a direct link or come looking for it via your home page. They have not got there because they're seeking general employment law information, and nor have they reached you via a search engine—somebody sent them.

Clearly our first four rules apply here too, but you also now need to add as an essential ingredient a succinct home page overview of who you are and what you can do for them. You'll expand on this at points across your site, including About Us, but here is **design and content rule 5**:

- Tell them who you are and what you can do for them on your home page with clear signposting to where they can find out more. No practice histories here, please! (Have another look at **www.employeesos.co.uk** in Chapter 13 for a helpful example.)

The essential ingredients of this are, to return to Frank Kern's summary:

1. Here's who I am.

2. Here's what I've got.

3. Here's what it'll do for you.

4. Here's what I want you to do next.

To briefly expand on these points:

1. Make it absolutely clear you are employment lawyers—and whether you're a niche practice or you also handle other work.

2. Spell out what makes you different. Do you specialise? If so, make that plain too—employers or employees? Vista (**www.vista-online.co.uk**) and **www.got-the-boot.com** are useful examples.

3. Tell your visitors how they will benefit if they choose you.

4. Include at least one call to action.

14.1.4 'Would I want to work for you?' Your site as a recruiting tool

Whether you're actively recruiting now or not, if you're on somebody's list as a potential employer, they will without question go online to check you out. This applies to qualified lawyers as much as to graduates, and it's therefore essential that you factor this in when building your site. Most larger firms do include a section—usually labelled Recruitment, Careers with Us, or Work For Us—but we recommend that all practices do this, as it's another way to showcase what makes you stand out, and is therefore also of interest to your other visitors.

Here are two ways of doing it:

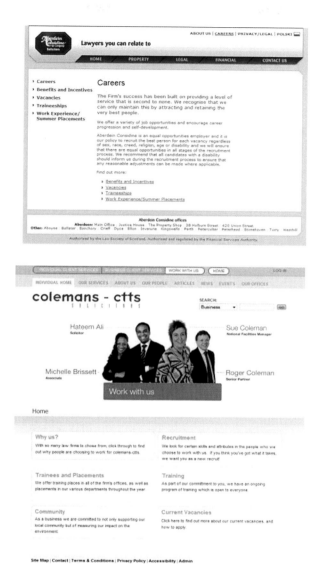

The first is a straightforward approach from Scottish firm Aberdein Considine and above is Colemans-ctts's "we're people too" branding in action.

www.acandco.com/careers/
www.colemans-ctts.co.uk/Work_With_Us/

To round off this visitor touchdown section, a few more design and content elements that you can't afford to ignore, beginning with keeping it contemporary.

14.1.5 Don't drift past your sell-by date

No matter how your visitor has travelled to your site, and no matter how well you've held their initial attention once they've arrived, few things undermine confidence more than a "Latest News" section led off by a story from two years ago, last year or even a few months back. As we said in Chapter 11, if you're going to run a home page news feature—and we strongly suggest that you do—then *you must keep it up to date!* This applies to both legal news and to your own news (the appointment of a partner, a seminar next week), and if you're not at the moment confident you have the time or resources to do this, then just include a more discreet link to another page rather than risk losing credibility. The easiest way to keep content fresh is through a content management system—more about this later.

A related, though less crucial, detail is your copyright note. One that reads "© 2005 Your Firm" suggests that your site is not regularly updated. You don't need to carry a date, but if you do, make sure it's this year's. This is **design and content rule 6**:

*   Constantly update your home page news or don't carry news at all, and put this year's date in your copyright line, or don't use a date at all. (See Resources for a quick and easy way to do this.)

Another way of instantly sowing seeds of doubt is by running home page copy which, regardless of the quality of the message, includes poor grammar, spelling or punctuation. We highlighted an example in Chapter 13 (**www.gorvins.com**). Proofreading is always absolutely essential across all your marketing materials, but in few places does it matter more than on your home page. This is **design and content rule 7**:

*   Check your home page copy. Then check it again, and then get someone else to check it!

14.1.6 Start building that relationship

As we explained in Chapter 13, you're missing an important opportunity if you don't use permission marketing on your website. Unless you have some compelling business reason to ignore it, this is **design and content rule 8**:

- Include at least one permission marketing call to action on your website—if not on your home page, then very clearly signposted from it.

Action

Following on from the exercise you did at the end of Chapter 13, look again at your home page from the perspective of the four types of visitor we've identified. How well does it perform? What could you improve? What do you need to add?

Table 4 Home page checklist 2

	Existing client	Seeking information	Referral	Potential employee
Instant contact details	✓			
Link to emailed update	✓			
Signposting to information-rich content	✓	✓	✓	✓
Signposting to Our People		✓	✓	✓
Signposting to Careers		✓	✓	✓
Brief 'who we are, what we can do for you' summary		✓	✓	✓
Up-to-date news	✓	✓	✓	✓
Permission marketing call to action		✓	✓	
Free-to-download content	✓	✓	✓	✓

14.2   The foundations of your site

The content elements your site *must* have are...

• an About Us page

• an Our People section

• a Contact Us page.

We make no apology for stating what may appear obvious. Our trawl revealed some significant shortcomings!

14.2.1   Who you are and where you've come from

We've already explained why you need to keep your practice life story off your home page (too many features, not enough benefits), but that doesn't mean you don't need to give visitors a flavour of your lineage and pedigree. And the place to do this is your About Us page, clearly signposted from your home page and following the copywriting rules from Chapter 5. Here are some examples.

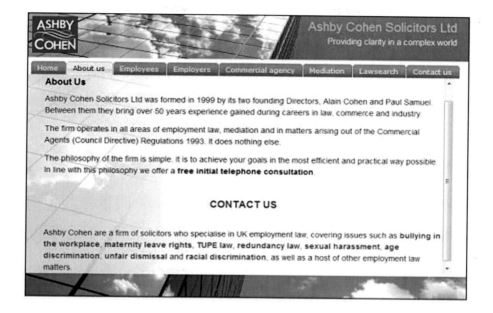

Ashby Cohen's text is succinct and tells the visitor what they need to know:

- Who founded the firm?

- What did they do previously?

- When was the firm founded?

- What does it do?

The copy also reiterates a key benefit—the free telephone consultation—and includes a link to Contact Us.

www.ashbycohen.co.uk/about.html

There's more detail here, but again there is a clear structure, so that we quickly know…

- when the firm was founded

- where it is based

- who most of its clients are

- the Capital Law *modus operandi*

- how the firm is managed.

Within the text there are links to the Our People section as well as to individual parts of it, and to its page on Consulegis. Links on the right are logical: Introduction, Recent Firm News, International, and Careers.

Bar a few bits of jargon ("our lawyers are straight-talking and proactive", and another vacuous quote at the top, "our advice is always clear, focused and expert"), this does the job well.

www.capitallaw.co.uk/site/about/aboutintro/

The Law Offices of ⸻ is committed to providing competent and legal services to UK and Foreign Clients. We pride ourselves in our informal, modern approach, providing an excellent service to our clients in plain English, free of jargons.

The Firm is comprised of 3 Partners, 3 Consultants and are in 2 offices in the UK, both in London and its Associate firm of ⸻ in ⸻. We continue to grow as a Law firm that works to develop an understanding of clients' professional needs.

⸻ is continually developing by being a pioneer in the establishment of networks with other Law Practices, both in the UK and intercontinental practices in the USA and Africa. This means, the firm not only enjoys an international dimension, but also has available access to a pool of expertise from law firms and consultants, within the UK and different countries to provide a complete service and support to both its clients with interests in the UK and those interests outside the U.K.

We help our clients navigate the complexities of the dynamic marketplace by initially working with you to develop an understanding of your professional needs, and thereafter providing a thoughtful analysis so that as a client you have all the information you need to make important decisions. We pride ourselves in keeping our clients fully informed, and are dedicated to representing our clients with integrity, yet always being considerate of the costs and uncertainties associated with issues. Our teams would work with you to achieve a solution that meets time scales.

Since our founding, through our growth into the established firm of today, ⸻ has combined its deep business knowledge and, commitment to emerging and established businesses, with its legal expertise of providing advice to multilateral organisations, including associations and local authorities, in both mature and emerging markets.

⸻ has pioneered the practice of Property, (both contentious and non-contentious) and Construction law practice, and combines this work with strong Corporate/commercial, Litigation, Immigration, Personal Injury, Oil & gas and shipping. The firm adopts a keen commercial and practical partner-led approach and builds on long-term partnerships with its clients

This, alas, is how not to do it. We've blanked the name to spare the blushes. There are acres of text, but we discover next to nothing:

The Law Offices of ⸻ is committed to providing competent and legal services to UK and Foreign Clients. We pride ourselves in our informal, modern approach, providing an excellent service to our clients in plain English, free of jargons.

… or:

We help our clients navigate the complexities of the dynamic marketplace by initially working with you to develop an understanding of your professional needs, and thereafter providing a thoughtful analysis so that as a client you have all the information you need to make important decisions.

If we persevere, we do learn that there are three partners, three consultants, two offices, and links to the US and Africa, and at the very end a list of practice areas (not shown). But extracting this is hard work as the copy is—despite its own pledges!—heavy on jargon and feather-light on content. There are also errors and inconsistencies throughout pointing to a serious proofreading failure:

and consultants, within the UK and different countries to provide a complete service and support to both its clients with interests in the UK and those interests outside the U.K.

These three examples should show clearly what works and what doesn't. You can keep it brief or you can go into some detail, but you must stay relevant. Here, as everywhere, you need to have the obstacles of indifference in the front of your mind. You don't want your visitor navigating away because what you're saying about yourself is fundamentally boring.

Action

Write the About Us text for our West Midlands practice, Adams, Brown and Curtis, using the guidelines from Chapters 4 and 13 as your sources. Tell your visitor…

- who you are

- where you are

- where you came from

- what you do

- who your clients are.

Compare it to our version in the Resources section for this chapter, and then write (or rewrite) an About Us page for your own firm.

14.2.2 Bringing your team to life

As noted earlier in this chapter, after the home page the Our People pages are generally the most visited on any website. That's not really surprising since, as we know, people buy people. Visitors want to find out who you are, who does what, and—importantly—what you look like. So getting this part of your website right is very important, and there are three elements you can't afford to miss out:

1. Photos—yes, use them.

2.   Include everyone, not just your fee earners.

3.   Keep the section regularly updated.

Let's start with photos. As we said in Chapter 9, marketing materials in general—and websites in particular—now carry people pictures as a matter of course. Do you feel OK about doing this on, say, Facebook, but uncomfortable about doing it on your own website? That it's unnecessarily intrusive? You're no doubt not alone, but why are photos considered such an important marketing tool? American legal marketer Trey Ryder says: "Your photograph is worth two thousand words. A warm, friendly, engaging picture with good eye contact can do wonders for your marketing. It helps establish a friendly, trusting relationship and increases your reader's comfort. Prospects don't really care what you look like, but they feel better when they know."

So is it all good news? In a lengthy 2008 forum debate on the US Marketing Profs website, several negatives were identified:

•   If the team were all roughly the same age, this could indicate a reluctance on the firm's part to use the skills of older or younger people—or it could just trigger knee-jerk prejudices in the website visitor: "They're too young to know what they're doing", or "They're all past it and won't be able to use email".

•   The same issue surrounds a team that's all (or predominantly) one gender or all from one community.

•   A high staff turnover could cause difficulties, first because there would be a constant need to update the Our People pages, and second because it's not very reassuring to see new faces every time you visit.

•   The potential for attracting nuisance calls and email, particularly considered an issue for young women.

However, the overwhelming majority of contributors gave staff photos the thumbs up—even if they had reservations—with one main caveat: use a professional photographer!

This is a sentiment we strongly echo. There's something uniquely toe-curling about photos little better than snapshots displayed prominently in what is supposed to be a significant business showcase. These are the pictures that look as though they've been taken by the boss on a mobile, or cropped from a scanned-in family get-together. The context, tone and resolution vary from photo to photo, and the end result screams: "Amateur! Corner-cutting!"

So get it done properly. The credibility and authority you gain will repay the cost many times over. And plain white or pastel backgrounds look *so* much better than bookshelves packed with dusty law reports. (We don't have to remind you as an employment lawyer that you obviously need consent before you use anyone's photo….)

The pictures of us on the back cover of this book (and on our respective websites) were taken by photographers who we cannot recommend highly enough: Media Wisdom in London (www.mediawisdom.co.uk) and Rory Raitt in Aberdeen (www.rawformat.co.uk).

How you want to portray your staff will depend on the overall tone of your website, but here are some pages we think work well.

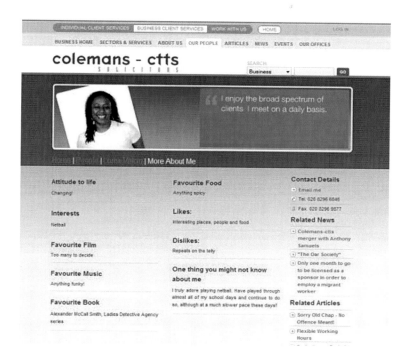

Colemans-ctts's "we're people too" branding is particularly emphasised within the Our People section. Click on the link and you reach a menu page from where you can choose by name, area of expertise or office. There's a professional page for each team member from where you can "find out more about me" and discover favourite movies, foods and pastimes. Shown here is employment lawyer Lorna Valcin's page.

Does this touchy-feely approach work? Former Coleman-ctts employment law team leader Tom Walker (now with Manches) found it helped break down barriers:

> "One barrister worked out that I went to Leeds University like him and on my profile—it was a bit tongue in cheek—it said *Joe le Taxi* is my favourite song, and my favourite film is *Starship Troopers*, which it isn't, but I enjoy watching it and it's mindless. And the barrister said, 'Oh, *Starship Troopers*—I like that as well'. Several clients have also done that— like black pudding. I do like black pudding and when that came out, several of my commercial clients sent emails. Very few thought I was being serious!"

www.colemans-ctts.co.uk/Corporate/People/
Kingston, Surrey

Pannone's People section also focuses on more than the purely professional. You're offered three ways in: A–Z, management, and "key people". Click on a name—Rodger Pannone himself is featured here—and you get to the default "expert profile", with a tab leading to "the human face of Pannone". From this we learn that he's a Leonard Cohen fan, his "guiltiest pleasure" is Cuban cigars, and he'd like to play James Bond.

www.pannone.com/people.asp
Manchester

Veale Wasbrough also takes the multichoice approach with a beautifully designed Our People main page. You can search by name, job title, sector or service—what could be more user friendly than that? And to round it off the partners and team leaders are listed alphabetically. Click on a name and you get another nicely-designed page headed "Expertise/experience". All strictly professional—no black puddings, Bond or cigars here! Like all the portraits, this one is in black and white, which does jostle slightly with the generic "people" photos used along the top of the page.

www.vwl.co.uk/site/people
Bristol

This is a straightforward, no-nonsense profile that gives you the basic information you want and the contact details you need.

We have the same reservations about the black and white portrait as aired above, but we came across enough of them to suggest that this is a clear design trend.

www.russell-co-legal.co.uk/our-people.htm
Crawley, West Sussex

Here's an unusual approach—and one which obviously only works for a small to medium-sized firm, or the page would take an age to load and stretch to Australia!

Click on the mugshots, find your person via a speciality drop-down, or choose alphabetically. The quality of the portraits is a bit inconsistent, which spoils the effect slightly, but top marks for approachability. The individual profiles are not quite as innovative and all feature a rather pointless preamble:

People

At Pagan Osborne, we believe our skills and experience are only part of the picture. Above all, we want you to enjoy working with us

That's why we have assembled a team that isn't just rich in experience and skills - but is ready to forge the lasting relationship you're looking for.

www.paganosborne.com/People/tabid/55/Default.aspx
Edinburgh

These examples show some room for improvement!

We highlighted this website in Chapter 13 when discussing the use of white text on a coloured background, and also the size of text.

Here you can see why both these factors are so important: this slab is the Partners and Staff section. No photos, no separate pages, just a very long chunk of text with a rather curious internal logic that makes locating a named individual far harder than it should be. Most of the information is there: areas of expertise, experience, interests, email addresses (though no direct dial numbers), but winkling it out is hard work.

www.amlaw.co.uk/staff.html
London

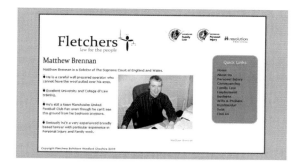

If you think the design at the top is a little wanting in the style department, have a look at what it replaced (below)! The new one's an improvement, but unless you're going deliberately retro, DIY is still generally a poor idea.

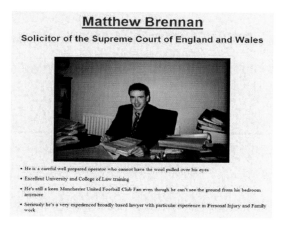

The new photo—like the page—is an improvement, but not only is it also clearly a snapshot, it's been badly cropped so we have evidence of a cluttered desk, a corner of a waste paper basket, and way too much radiator. The text (lifted straight from the page it replaced) tells us:

> ● He is a careful well prepared operator who cannot have the wool pulled over his eyes.

and

> ● Excellent University and College of Law training.

If you were a casual visitor, how confident would that make you feel? We respectfully suggest it could be time for a professional makeover.

www.fletcher96.freeserve.co.uk (Fletchers)
Winsford, Cheshire

When you're compiling your team biographies stick to a single format, even if you find you have a lot more information about some staff than others. Using a questionnaire to elicit information is one way to pull in the same basic data from everyone, and helps ensure consistency. Clearly the senior partner can be afforded more space than a member of the support team who joined three months ago, but do it by building on a single set of essentials rather than using several different formulas.

Keep this section properly maintained. As already noted, out-of-date content alienates visitors, and here more than anywhere you have to be accurate.

Action

If you already have an About Us page, how well does it work against our list of essentials? Are all your profiles up to date? Is there internal consistency, or should you consider rewriting the copy to achieve this? If you're featuring photos, are they of a high standard and taken by a professional? If not, consider fixing this as a priority.

If you don't have a people section at all, then it's definitely time you did! Study our examples, have a good Google, and decide a style that works best for you. Then draw up a questionnaire, and use the responses you get as the basis for your individual staff profiles.

14.3   How easily can visitors find you?

We've already highlighted your website's role as a phone book. Now we need to expand on that function with a good Contact Us section. This should be clearly signposted from every page, preferably more than once, and needs to contain...

1.   your full postal address or addresses

2. your main switchboard and fax numbers

3. your general email address

4. your DX number (if appropriate)

5. a map (or maps)

6. directions by road and rail, plus where to park.

We're not going to give you detailed instructions here as this is really straightforward. So here are just a few pointers:

- Either embed a map—from Google Maps, for example, or Multimap—in your page with your office clearly marked, or link to a mapping site. Either way your visitor can see where you are immediately and can then zoom out to put you in a wider context. Or combine a functioning map with a static one just showing where you are.

- With your "how to find us" directions, include…

  - details about the nearest railway/subway station
  - how long it will take to reach you from there by taxi or on foot
  - how to get to you by bus and where to get off
  - how to reach you by car from the main routes into your town or city
  - where to park, availability of spaces, and costs if you don't have your own car park.

Include the main elements in a downloadable PDF.

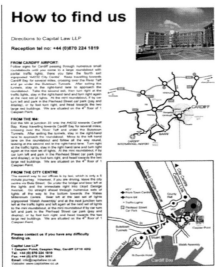

The Google map in the Employment SOS contact page is fully functional, though there's nothing in the way of actual directions.

Capital Law puts their directions in a PDF and also includes links to Google Maps from the main Contacts page.

Both, however, assume you'll be getting to them by car.

www.employeesos.co.uk/contact-us.html
www.capitallaw.co.uk/cms/document/Directions_to_Capital_Law_LLP.pdf

Here are two more well-designed pages, from Colemans-ctts and Lewis Silkin. The photos on the Colemans-ctts site are interactive and open a new page with details of the office and how to get there. There are links to maps, parking details, and to the biographies of the staff located in each office.

Lewis Silkin's design is simple, with an embedded interactive map and details of where to park.

www.colemans-ctts.co.uk/Personal/Our_Offices/
www.lewissilkin.com/contactus/Pages/default.aspx

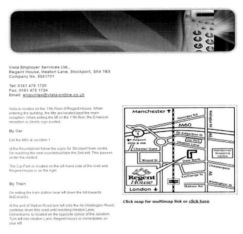

Vista brings together directions for motorists and rail passengers with a neat map which links to a full Multimap page when clicked.

Veale Wasbrough hits the jackpot with pretty much the full set: a map, directions for drivers, how to get to head office from the two main Bristol stations, parking details, and a series of PDFs with directions and maps for each of the firm's offices. All that's missing are some bus routes.

www.vista-online.co.uk/contact.htm
www.vwl.co.uk/site/contactus/

14.4 Sign up here... permission marketing nuts and bolts

In Chapter 11 we looked at the key elements that make your website content rich. Principally, these were...

- news releases

- regular updates, for example client newsletters and briefing notes

- guides

- white papers

- e-books

- video and podcasts.

To these add a straightforward enquiry form, which a visitor fills out if they want you to contact them in preference to emailing you or calling.

Of these elements, only the enquiry form, newsletters and podcasts actually require some input from your visitor—all the rest your visitors can just download. And if you really feel uncomfortable about using permission marketing, then both newsletters and podcasts can be delivered via an RSS feed (of which more in the next chapter) that doesn't involve your visitor handing over any personal data.

We will, however, proceed on the basis that if you're not already using permission marketing in any form, you're going to follow our advice and at least thoroughly check it out.

Let's start with a few examples of enquiry forms.

Pannone offer visitors a variety of ways to get in touch. This includes a straightforward enquiry form with the minimum number of fields necessary to gather the essential data— name, address, email address, telephone number, the enquiry. Because the form is simple, it's more likely to be used than one that includes a large number of fields. However, in terms of data collection, having only one field for the address means somebody has to separate out street names from postal towns from postcodes. We'd suggest being a little less casual!

Shutts & Bowen also goes for a basic contact form, which does the job, though—as with Pannone—the address field is not as finessed as it could be.

www.pannone.com/contact-pannone.asp
http://www.shutts.com/index.cfm/fa/home.contact/contact.cfm

The Aberdein Considine website has a simple contact form, and the firm commit to responding within 24 hours. This form is very much an optional extra as there are numerous other ways of reaching them.

With Employment SOS, the form is a direct link from the home page to set up a callback. The form is simple to complete, and the accompanying copy clearly flags up the free nature of the offer. A slimmed-down version of the form appears when you click on the "Ask a Question" link.

Both these examples are on clean, tidy pages.

www.acandco.com/contact/contact.html
www.employeesos.co.uk/questions.php

By far the most common use of permission marketing is for regular newsletters, normally delivered monthly or quarterly. (We'll explore in more detail how this works in Chapter 16—for now we'll just discuss how the relationship begins.) The nuts and bolts of the form your visitor needs to complete are much the same as for making inquiries, and while it's tempting in this context to have a go at harvesting as much information as you can, be mindful that the more fields the visitor has to fill in, the more likely they are to lose interest in what you're offering in return and move on.

Here are some examples of sign-up forms for newsletters and other update material.

The Pannone and Vista websites have two simple sign-up forms.

Pannone asks for a postal address and offers a hard-copy newsletter option, but otherwise the quantity of information sought is about the same, and both do the job.

www.pannone.com/newsletter-dtl.asp?nlid=112
www.topica.com/f/v.html?1700072204.1700026842

The websites for Maclay, Murray and Spens (MMS) and Pagan Osborne both provide multiple sign-up choices, an impressive number in MMS's case. The MMS form also features a large number of fields, though only the basics are obligatory.

Both are clear and easy to complete.

http://emailinfo.mms.co.uk/go.asp?/.pages.knowledge/bMMS001
www.paganosborne.com/NewsEvents/RegisterforUpdates/tabid/92/Default.aspx

Some legal websites ask you to register before you can access any of the firm's online content. This has its pros and its cons:

• On the plus side, you know exactly who is looking at what on your site, and when, and you harvest the email address of every visitor interested enough to find out more about you.

• On the minus side, a significant number of visitors—and you'll struggle to measure how many—will baulk at filling out a form just to read, say, a short briefing paper, and head elsewhere.

Here are a couple of solicitor practices that adopt this gatekeeper approach.

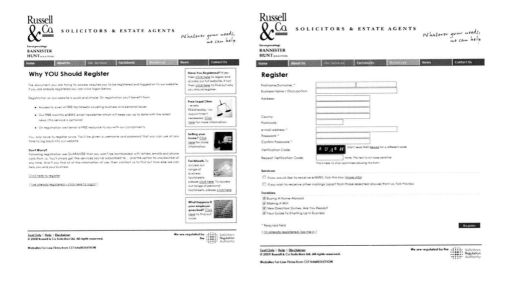

Sussex law firm Russell & Co offer a "free resource" which is emailed out once registration is complete, as well as unlimited access to online guides and a monthly newsletter. We're not sure about the "Why YOU Should Register" headline—some visitors might feel they're being somewhat harangued.

www.russell-co-legal.co.uk/ard/register_reason.asp?AID=1116&Source=

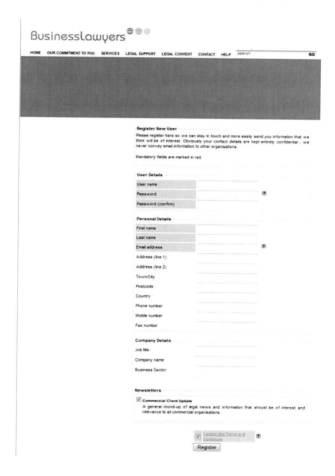

To access the information on the Business Lawyers site, you need to sign up:

Register New User

Please register here so we can stay in touch and more easily send you information that we think will be of interest. Obviously your contact details are kept entirely confidential - we never convey email information to other organisations.

You're also asked to tick a box agreeing to a 17-point set of website use terms and conditions before hitting Send. Again, we wonder whether putting such obstacles in the way of visitors is always a good idea, though you can of course be pretty confident that if they follow through they're likely to be really interested!

www.business-lawyers.org/cms/section/homepage.html

14.5 It's the way that you say it

This section provides another quick reminder about copy. You saw in Chapter 5 that well-written, accessible, benefit-led copy lies at the heart of successful marketing, and nowhere more so than on your website. We dissected several practice descriptions to demonstrate just how important this is, and we're hoping your own is now doing an excellent job!

To bring the rest of your website copy up to scratch, you need to apply exactly the same rules as you did in that exercise, using the home pages we featured in Chapter 13 as examples of good—and less good—practice:

1. Focus on what you're offering, not on how good your team is at being lawyers.
    a. Here's who I am.
    b. Here's what I've got.
    c. Here's what it'll do for you.
    d. Here's what I want you to do next.

2. Check your copy against the obstacles of indifference.
    a. Who cares?
    b. So what?
    c. What's in it for me?

3. Engage AIDA.
    a. Attention
    b. Interest
    c. Desire
    d. Action

We're not going to take a journey right through a hypothetical website because, as we keep stressing, a style and tone that works perfectly for one law firm may be entirely inappropriate for another. It's what underpins your words that matters, and we hope that by now you have a clear idea of how to make the copywriting rules work for you.

In the next chapter we'll be returning to keywords and their crucial role in getting your website seen. But before we move on, we'd like you to complete an interesting exercise.

Action

Starting with your home page copy, read out aloud everything on your website. Yes, really! Read it all aloud—and preferably to an audience of at least one. Nothing unmasks below-par writing faster than hearing the words spoken, and you'll immediately be able to identify what does work and what you need to revisit. If you're not convinced, try reading these practice descriptions (from Chapter 5) out loud first:

1. WE provide practical, straightforward legal advice which is cost efficient and client orientated. We're not too big to provide a friendly, approachable and really personal service to all our clients but not too small to provide a professional, experienced team of lawyers offering a first class service. Whilst [FIRM'S NAME] has a strong tradition, it lives in the present and plans for the future.

2. [FIRM'S NAME] combine experience with innovative approaches. We are proud of our past, but embrace modern technology and look forward to a dynamic future.

   You may contact us by e-mail should you require more information or wish to arrange an appointment.

   As you browse through the [FIRM'S NAME] website, you will find that we provide a comprehensive range of legal services. With three offices in the [AREA] we have the capacity to provide a service that is "local" in feel across a large geographical area. We value our close links, established over many years, with the communities we serve.

We've deliberately gone for a couple of examples that use the type of largely empty language found right across law firm websites—hopefully not yours!

15

Getting your website seen

You may have the most elegant website in the world, each page a design gem with an array of eye-catching images. But if the search engines can't find you—or don't like what they see when they do—it sadly counts for very little. In this chapter we look at the two ways of getting your website seen:

1. Through natural optimisation of your website.

2. By paying to advertise.

What do we mean? We mean using ethical and sensible search engine optimisation (SEO) strategies to rise up through the Google ranks, and getting there through pay per click (PPC), principally Google's AdWords. Do you need to do both? You decide—after you've read this chapter!—but you definitely can't afford not to optimise your website, so that's where we'll start. Before we do, though, a reminder that we're not website designers, professional optimisers or techie experts of any other sort. We're showing you the mechanics solely from a marketing perspective, giving you the basics of how to put them into practice, and offering some pointers towards good sources of more detailed information.

15.1 Why you need to optimise

There are two types of search tool: the crawler-based engines like Google, and those that depend on real people making the decisions. We're going to focus on the first variety as it's within Google, Yahoo!, and to a lesser extent Ask and Microsoft's Windows Live that your position matters most.

The process begins with a spider (also known as a crawler, robot or bot) "crawling" a web page on your site, assessing it, following links from it to other pages within the site, and backtracking to external sites linked to it. The spider indexes everything it finds, and will then make regular return visits to the whole website to look for changes. Whenever a page is changed, the index is also in due course changed. Note though that the crawler has to pass by first for that to happen—your update doesn't automatically update the index.

When somebody enters a query, billions of indexed pages are sifted and the search engine software ranks them so that those matching most closely appear first. So far so good, but unfortunately the search engines don't follow exactly the same rules. How Google ranks your site differs from how Yahoo! does, which is why dual searches often produce very different results. Furthermore, some will index more pages, others index more frequently, and to cap it all just when you think you've cracked the code, the engines—particularly Google—go and tweak their rules. What worked a treat yesterday can suddenly see you drop a dozen pages, and you may never find out why because Google will never tell you. Looking at the process more closely, the first time a search engine arrives at your door, you will be assessed on the basis of…

1. what you're saying about yourself, and how you say it

2. what everyone else is saying about you—who's linking to your site.

It's essential to get both right, but it's the quality of the *inbound links* to your site that matters most to the search engines. We'll show you what you should be doing to help achieve this, but unless you want to get drawn into the real nuts and bolts of SEO, you're well advised to seek some professional help as well, at least to get your website moving in the right direction. Be choosy, though. SEO is a far from exact science and you should be wary of listening to anyone who tells you they can "guarantee" you a top Google ranking!

Also very important to the search engines is the age of your website. All other things being equal, the older, the better—but as only time can influence that, we're moving quickly on!

15.1.1 Why content is always king

We saw in Chapter 11 that the principal reason to make your website *content rich* was, in addition to making it an indispensable resource, to maximise your search engine visibility. To expand on that, you need to optimise your content. Here's how you can do it:

• Have a large number of individual web pages—the higher the volume, the better and the greater the chances of the search engines directing traffic to you.

• Provide high-quality, targeted, relevant content—a good mix of the types of material we looked at in Chapter 11 is ideal.

• Update your content frequently. The more often you can refresh your pages, the better—and not just for SEO purposes—remember that old news is not news and is a turn-off for all visitors.

If you want to boost the SEO potential of your content, consider incorporating material provided by a service of the types we discussed in Chapter 11, such as those offered by Emplaw and Conscious Solutions. (See the Resources for Chapter 11 for details.) Be mindful, though, that this content will not be unique to your site.

Having a wealth of great information only takes you so far, however. You'll recall from Chapter 12 the crucial importance of incorporating keywords into news releases you write for online distribution. It's exactly the same for your website, only very significantly more so! In fact, this is possibly the most important part of the SEO code for you to crack—to optimise both your content and the inbound links to your site—and we'll look at it in some detail.

15.2 Keywords are the key

To grasp the importance of what you say on your web pages, and where you say it, get into the habit of looking at your site from the search engine's point of view—SEPOV, as it's known to SEO professionals.

The first time a spider passes by, it is assessing what it considers comprise the main *topics* of your website. On this crawl—and all subsequent crawls—it's not remotely interested in the *aesthetics* of your site, only in the text it finds there. It is therefore essential that the text says something that makes sense to the spider, from a SEPOV, as well of course as to your human visitors. And this is achieved through the intelligent use of keywords—actually, as we saw in Chapter 12, phrases of usually two to five words rather than stand-alone words.

Your goal with your website then is to write engaging, benefits-led copy that clears the obstacles of indifference and the other tests from Chapter 5, *and* includes a good proportion of relevant keywords.

When it comes to keywords, only two things matter to the spider: which ones you use and where you put them.

The keywords you choose need to match as closely as possible the words you'd expect someone looking for your services to run past Google or another search engine. So you must first think like a potential client before switching roles and assessing your choices from a SEPOV. And you need to be specific, but without being so specific that you rule out any chance of ever being found.

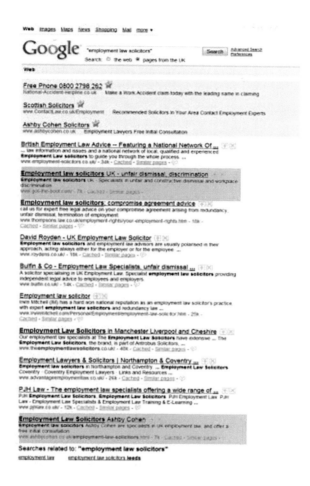

For example, if you Google "employment law" you'll get around 670,000 organic UK results and the chances of you getting on the first page are slim indeed. Emplaw generally wins top spot on this search. Incidentally, co-author Daniel Barnett's site often features on the second page—and it's normally top spot for "employment law barrister"!

Narrow it down to "employment law solicitors" and there are around 7,100 results. One of our featured businesses—Morris Legal's got-the-boot.com—consistently appears in the top five on page one, closely followed by Ashby Cohen, which is usually on the first page as well. (Ashby Cohen is also always among firms featured in the first page pay per click listings, just above or to the left of the main organic results—more about that later.)

It's no coincidence that both businesses are almost exclusively web-based. Optimisation isn't a luxury for them, it's an absolute commercial necessity.

So how did Morris Legal and Ashby Cohen manage that? In part—and only in part—through using the keywords "employment law solicitors" prominently right across their websites. In particular, both use the words, or a variation, in the "title tags" of most of their pages, and this is *the* most important location. A webpage HTML title tag tells the search engines what your site is about, and—crucially—it's what it uses as a link on the results page, in turn telling the visitor that you are what they're seeking.

Let's explore that a little more closely. You can do exactly the same with any website—no trade secrets here, just a case of knowing what you're looking for!

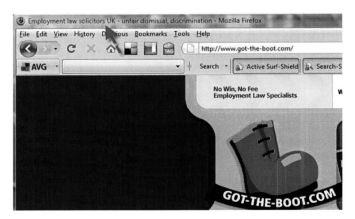

Look in the title bar—across the top of your browser—to see the words used in that page's title. Ashby Cohen went for "Employment Law Solicitors Ashby Cohen", while Morris Legal chose "Employment law solicitors UK—unfair dismissal, discrimination". Dig a little deeper and find the "page source" (exactly where will depend on your browser, but it's under Page in Internet Explorer and View in Firefox) and there you'll see how the title has been input, along with other important information stored as "meta tags" and the rest of the page's HTML code. (This is about as technical as it's going to get! We're including it because you can't leave any of this to chance.) Meta tags are not displayed and while they don't in themselves have significant influence on your page ranking, many search engines will use your meta "description" in their results, putting it under your title tag, which acts as the listing headline. Here's Morris Legal's:

```
<title>Employment law solicitors UK - unfair dismissal, discrimination</title>
<meta name="keywords" content="Employment law solicitors UK - Specialists in unfair and constructive dismissal and
<meta name="description" content="Employment law solicitors UK - Specialists in unfair and constructive dismissal .
```

From this you can see the title and the meta description which in full reads "Employment law solicitors UK—Specialists in unfair and constructive dismissal and workplace discrimination". (You can also see the meta "keywords" tag which is not as important to the spider as the title and meta description. Nonetheless the field needs completing; only include words that are very relevant to your firm and by extension to your website.) Now see how this translates into got-the-boot's Google results listing:

Now that you see how it works you'll appreciate how important it is not to write something like "Welcome to our Home Page!" in your title tag. It's astonishing how many people do—more than 2,500 on a Google search of those exact words, and if you fail to put in anything at all you'll be joining nearly 37 million other untitled documents. Also go easy on words that are ignored by search engines, such as "the", "that", "and", and so on, but keep the title readable.

For the search engines, after your title tag (and ahead of your meta description and any other meta tags) often come your web page's *header tags*, with the first (<h1>) afforded the most importance, and the rest (<h2>, <h3>, etc) proportionately less. These translate into actual headlines on your page and therefore need crafting carefully so that they work for real people as effectively as they do for the spiders. Here's how Morris Legal have brought together spider visibility and visitor accessibility.

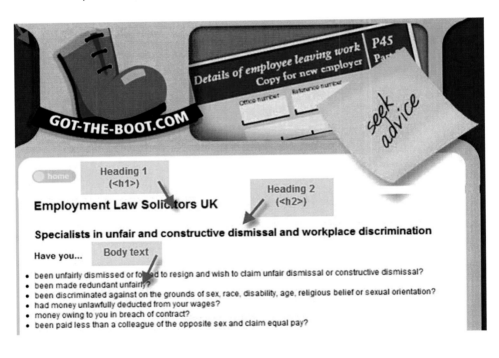

Note that the words in the title are repeated in the first headline— "Employment Law Solicitors UK"—and the powerful keywords "**unfair** and constructive **dismissal**" and "workplace **discrimination**" in the second. The first chunk of body text is then rich in a mix of the same keywords and new ones—"unfairly dismissed", "made redundant unfairly", "discriminated against", "sex", "race", "disability", "age", "religious belief" or "sexual orientation", "money unlawfully deducted", "breach of contract", "paid less than a colleague", "equal pay". Unusually, there are four one-word keywords here.

Web pages should ideally carry somewhere between 200 and 300 words of text, including keywords, and the search engines pay particular attention to any they find emphasised, in **bold** or in *italic*, for example. But be careful. Too much pandering to the spiders can make your page difficult for real people to read, as we saw with the Business Lawyers website in Chapter 13 (see page 223). Always aim to use your keywords and your formatting in ways that look natural.

How many keywords should you use on each page? If you do a Google search for "keyword density", you'll find a lot of conflicting advice. Some say you should always aim for a specific "density"—the number of keywords as a percentage of all the words on the page—and that Google looks for x% and Yahoo! for y%. This is largely a blind alley as some pages with what's thought to be the perfect density fail to cut it with the search engines, while others with a very low density come back highly placed. Of much more importance is the keywords used in the *sites that link to you*, to which we'll return shortly.

Crawling with a linear view

Search engine spiders index your page content in linear order and will afford priority to what they find nearest the top. Therefore, you must ensure that you use your most valuable keywords in headings and body text as close to the top of the page as possible—in your first heading and/or second heading and the first paragraph of the first chunk of copy. Aim to position this text above images, use of Flash animation or anything else that could dilute its importance in getting your page accurately and competitively indexed.

15.2.1 Which keywords should I use?

This, of course, is going to depend on what type of employment law service you are offering. Morris Legal works almost exclusively with claimants and this is reflected in the keywords—and indeed the website name—used in got-the-boot.com. Look now at another of our featured businesses, Ellis Whittam, and you'll see some overlap with Morris Legal, but also a significantly different set of keywords (returned on a search for "UK employment law employers"):

UK Employment Law Advice / **UK** Health & Safety Solutions ...
Ellis Whittam provides fixed fee **Employment Law**, HR and Health & Safety services to **UK employers**. We also offer training, occupational health, ...
www.elliswhittam.com/ - 24k - Cached - Similar pages -

The title tag reads in full: "UK Employment Law Advice / UK Health & Safety Solutions. Employment law solutions for UK business"; the meta description reads in full: "Employment Law and Health & Safety Solutions for UK employers. UK Employment Law Advice / UK Health & Safety Solutions. Employment lawyers, advice on case law, employment tribunals, health & safety compliance." However, note that Google has used text from the home page—to which this listing links—rather than the meta description:

Ellis Whittam provides fixed fee Employment Law,
HR and Health & Safety services to UK employers.
We also offer training, occupational health, on-line
absence management, payroll and other personnel
support services.

On the home page, the keywords view the employment relationship exclusively from the employer end: "UK employers", "HR and Health & Safety services", "absence management" and "personnel support".

Action

Using Morris Legal (**www.got-the-boot.com**) and Ellis Whittam (**www.elliswhittam.com**) as your benchmarks, search for a minimum of three other sites that specialise in claimant and respondent work and compile a list of the keywords each uses.

Then identify a further five competitor sites that most closely match your own specific area of expertise and do the same with them. If you were our West Midlands discrimination boutique practice, for example, that's the type of site you'd be most focused on. Look in particular for the most popular and the most specialised keywords and play around with them in both Google and Yahoo! to see which return the most results and which sites get the highest listings.

Explore the page source data for some of the sites you visit. It will give you a better feel for how the jigsaw is put together and you should find some useful word combinations. Try using this tool from Yellowpipe to compare the number of keywords used on different web pages: **www.yellowpipe.com/yis/tools/wordcount** (there's more information in Resources). Go through the content on your selected sites as well, to see how well keywords are being used in, for example, white papers and online guides.

Your next task is to narrow down your own niche keywords. Don't forget to include the following:

• Your location. A significant number of people will look for a service based on geography—"employment law solicitors Manchester", for example—and using it in a title tag for at least one page will increase your chances of showing up in the search results.

• Plurals—"employment tribunals claims", for example, as well as "employment tribunal claim".

• Misspellings. Never underestimate what people can do to the English language, by accident or otherwise. There is a difference of opinion among SEO specialists, with some recommending you include as keywords misspellings like "unfair dismisal", "sacked during prgnancy", or "constructavely dismised". Google will generally pick up on mistakes like these and give you the "Did you mean: .." option, but not everyone can be bothered clicking that link and will just scan the results they got on their DIY spelling. However, on the down side you will have misspelled words on your website, and they will show in the results listing. Is this the first impression you want to give visitors?

By now, you know which keywords your competitors are using most effectively, and which ones are not working so well. This, though, is not very scientific and happily there are plenty of tools to help you identify which combination of words will work best.

The easiest is your website's referral log, which will often show the keyword query a visitor used to find your site—and some of these can be quite bizarre!

Look too at the Google AdWords Keywords Tool. Its prime aim is to help you write ads, but it's just as useful for honing SEO keywords. The public-access version can be found here: **https://adwords.google.com/select/ KeywordToolExternal**. A search for "age discrimination", for example, returned a long list of keywords used in Google AdWords, accompanied by the number of searches made on each. Just the first few are shown here:

The most highly rated by SEO professionals is Wordtracker (**www.wordtracker.com**), which costs £29 a month. However, there is a free seven-day trial and even though you do have to hand over your card details to check it out, we think it's worth it. The significant benefit of Wordtracker is that there are no vested interests involved and it looks at organic results, not ads. You can evaluate the actual value of keywords— here is the result with the same term, "age discrimination":

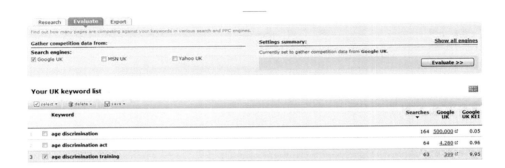

What this shows is that more than 500,000 UK web pages include the term "age discrimination" and there were 164 Google searches made in the previous 160 days. However, 63 searches were made on "age discrimination training" and there are only 4,280 pages using that keyword phrase, significantly increasing the odds of an otherwise well-optimised website achieving a good ranking. Wordtracker has automatically selected this phrase as being the most competitive. (There are details of other keyword tools in Resources.)

15.2.2 Anchoring your text

Anchor text plays a crucially important role in optimising web pages. In case you're not sure what this is, it's the visible text in an HTML link, either to another page on your site or to somebody else's. So instead of showing the full URL, for example http://www.yoursite.co.uk/ agewhitepaper, or click here, you show the link as "You'll find many more examples in our new age discrimination briefing paper".

And to double your visibility to the search engines, position the most important anchor text as high up the page as possible. Aim if you can to include a link in your first (<h1>) or second (<h2>) headlines, and definitely in the first chunk of body text. Don't, however, force it—how well and how often you can manage this is going to depend on the subject matter of the individual page, and you don't want to alienate your human visitors with text that teeters on the edge of a hard sell.

Action

Assuming you've signed up for a Wordtracker trial, make full use of the free tutorials you'll get access to, and have a go at evaluating the keyword phrase "employment law"—it's very illuminating! And whether you have or not, do try out the other free tools we've suggested.

Your research complete, your next task is to produce new copy for your home page. Refresh your memory by referring to the copywriting guidelines in Chapter 5 and then—drawing on the best website examples you found in your earlier trawl—write no more than 300 words of keyword-rich, benefits-led body text topped with at least two headlines featuring your strongest keywords.

We will turn to the next—and arguably most important—SEO element shortly. First, here's a quick look at a few other elements of your website that will affect how the search engines assess you:

- Include a site map that links from your home page, and ensure that every other page links back to your home page. This way each page is only one click away from the site map and from your home page, and this is the best way to make life easy for the spiders. They find pages by following links from pages they've already indexed, so make sure any new pages that you want indexed are always linked to the site map.

- Flash—if you're going to use it, don't make any page one large Flash file because it almost certainly won't be seen. There are similar problems associated with Frames and JavaScript. We suggest you seek professional advice if you want to use any of these.

- Don't bother formally submitting your site to the search engines. You'll see invitations to do so on all their sites, but there's no need. If your site has even a few good incoming links, their spiders will come to you. And beware of companies offering to submit you to all the search engines—completely unnecessary and a waste of time and money!

15.3 Who's linking to you?

Building inbound links to your site is *the* most important SEO element and it's a complex business. As we've already stressed, you're well advised to get professional help with this. Both our featured web-based law firms, Ashby Cohen and Morris Legal, outsource their SEO and, as you've already seen from their impressive search result listings, it's an investment well made.

That said, you need to understand the principles in order to make an informed choice—whether that's to find out more and have a go yourself or it's to employ a specialist.

What makes link-building so difficult is finding the balance between accumulating enough (and enough of a sufficiently high quality) to make your presence felt in your specialist area, and triggering the array of spam filters the search engines have put in place to stop cheats abusing the system. Let's look briefly at how this works:

- An *inbound* link is one pointing towards one of your web pages.

- An *outbound* link is a link on one of your pages pointing to somebody else's page.

- A *reciprocal* link is where each site links to the other. These do not generally score highly with the search engines unless they're between highly-rated pages. They are, however, still useful for sending traffic direct to your site, so don't be afraid of acquiring them as long as they're coming from quality, relevant sources.

- A *triangular* link is used in a bid to prevent search engines detecting reciprocal links. Three or more websites swap links without any of them being reciprocal. In reality, most search engines can spot this one a mile off!

Your options then are to accumulate a large number of links, get a few links from a handful of pages the search engines really rank, or—ideally—do both. Using the classic 80/20 equation, the sort of balance you should be looking for is...

- 80 per cent of your links from very focused and relevant sources

- 20 per cent from more marginal and unrelated sources

- 80 per cent of your links going to your home page

- 20 per cent going to other pages within your site.

Of all these, finding ways of connecting with important pages will bring you tangible rewards the fastest. A few really good links will win you more SEO brownie points than any number of links from less valuable, lowly-ranked pages.

So how do you achieve this? Start by taking a SEPOV...

15.3.1 What the spider is looking for

Search engines like to find natural-looking links to your site and will quickly become suspicious of anything with an unnatural structure.

Specifically, they will be impressed by...

- finding different <u>anchor text</u> within different inbound links

- an inbound link count that grows gradually

- outbound links to reputable, relevant sites

- a low reciprocal link count.

And they tend to take a dim view of...

- finding identical <u>anchor text</u> across all your inbound links

- a sudden increase in your inbound links

- outbound links to "link farms" (sites that do nothing but provide links of varying quality) or "web rings", large-scale triangular link arrangements

- a high number of reciprocal links.

The very best, top quality link is unrequested and comes from a highly-ranked site—a link made to your site voluntarily because of your excellent content and relevance. That, though, involves having already built up some visibility and an online reputation. It's a neat Catch 22!

Clearly you have to start somewhere, and there are numerous ethical link-building strategies that work—we recommend an excellent guide in Resources. We are, however, going to focus on just two: getting listed by directories and producing a steady stream of well-written copy.

15.3.2 Directing the traffic

Begin by submitting your site to good web directories, of which Yahoo! and DMOZ are two of the best (there's a list of some others in Resources).

How does this work? First, don't confuse the Yahoo! directory with the

Yahoo! search engine—they are separate entities. The huge advantage of a directory listing here is that all the search engines—not just Yahoo!—value it as a very sound inbound link. It's not free, and it's not easy—a non-refundable $299 to submit your site for listing, then the same again per year for commercial websites. And you have to jump a lot of hurdles to be accepted—this is not a pay-and-go arrangement. You must meet all Yahoo!'s exacting criteria (details on their website) before your site will be listed. For example, you must have your firm's name in the title tag, and in some cases they will even check that your domain name is actually registered to you before proceeding. But if you can afford it as part of your online marketing strategy, it's well worth it. Not only will you be listed in the UK-focused directory, you'll also appear in all Yahoo!'s other international directories, so you actually get half a dozen or more quality links for your fee. And you might also pick up some significant traffic from real people looking for real services, not just the spiders! (We give the relevant Yahoo! links in Resources.) Of our featured firms, Fox Lawyers, Morris Legal (as got-the-boot.com), and Shutts & Bowen all have Yahoo! directory listings.

Carrying even more kudos from a SEPOV is a listing in the entirely free DMOZ. So highly rated is this (it's also known as the Open Directory Project) that Google uses it as its directory. But getting in is arguably even harder than getting a Yahoo! listing. A DMOZ entry shows you've passed some very serious quality control tests and in SEO terms this is as good as an inbound link can get. However, getting in isn't just a question of filling in a form and sitting back because each DMOZ category is edited by real (unpaid, volunteer) humans and you have to wait for one to get around to noticing you've submitted your site and then having a look at it. Then they decide whether you're in the right category, and then you have to jump those quality control hurdles.

For all its enormous authority, the DMOZ site is, to say the least, minimalist. A results page is remarkably basic, somewhat retro in style but easy to follow.

Here's Ashby Cohen's listing. Note that it appears alphabetically:

Search | the entire directory | ▾

Top: **Regional**: **Europe**: **United Kingdom**: **Business and Economy**: **Legal Services**: **Lawyers and Law Firms**: **Business and Corporate Law**: A *(8)*

[A | B | C | D | E | F | G | H | I | J | K | L | M | N | O | P | Q | R | S | T | V | W]

- Aaron and Partners - Commercial law firm based in Chester handling litigation, commercial and property law for businesses, public authorities, charities and individuals. Features details on the expertise, services, events and training opportunities at the firm.
- Addleshaw Goddard - Corporate law firm with offices in Leeds, London and Manchester. The firm is organised around the key practice areas of commercial, corporate, employment, litigation, finance and projects, private client and real estate law. Details of services, partners, publications and recruitment matters.
- AJ Colfer Solicitors - Hampshire based business solicitors. Information on contact details and expertise of the firm.
- Allen & Overy - Offers a range of legal services for business and industry, from offices globally. Information provided on the partners, expertise, careers, news, publications and pro bono activities of the firm.
- Anderson Fyfe - Glasgow based solicitors with expertise in company and commercial law, particularly in corporate, litigation, property and security matters. The firm also provides legal services to private individuals and works for other solicitors in certain commercial and litigation matters. Information provided on the personnel and expertise of the firm.
- Archon Solicitors - London based solicitors specialising exclusively in employment law matters. Provides information on the philosophy, people, results and location of the firm.
- Ashby Cohen - Law firm specialising in employment law, commercial agency law and mediation with offices in London and Manchester. Information on contact details and expertise.

Note also that Ashby Cohen has chosen "Business and Corporate Law" as the final category sub-section to be listed in. Of our other featured firms listed here, Ellis Whittam appears in "Regional: Europe: United Kingdom: England: Cheshire: Chester: Business and Economy"; Lewis Silkin in two—"Regional: Europe: United Kingdom: England: London: Business and Economy: Legal Services" and "Regional: Europe: United Kingdom: Business and Economy: Legal Services: Lawyers and Law Firms: Business and Corporate Law"; and Shutts & Bowen in "Society: Law: Services: Lawyers and Law Firms: Business and Corporate Law: North America: United States: Florida".

Because the directory's purpose is to provide truly relevant, accurate, well-presented information to its users, you will only get in if you tick every single box. The editor assessing your site will be inclined to include you if you are adding something of real value to their category, which is another compelling reason to ensure you have plenty of good content.

Here are some pointers:

- Choose your category with care. For example, Ellis Whittam and Shutts & Bowen both chose geographical listings, which, particularly in Ellis Whittam's case, really narrows down the competition as far as the editor is concerned.

- Ensure your site is working properly before you submit it. All the links need to work, all the copy needs to be internally consistent, all the images must load.

- Fill out the submission form very carefully. The editors take a dim view of misspellings (no "Did you mean...?" here), and match your title and description to the DMOZ standard.

- If your site is rejected more than once or twice, there are no technical reasons why, and you still want that link, choose a category with no editor and volunteer! Be mindful though that DMOZ will take a dim view of you signing up if all you want to do is get your own site listed. You'll need to be able to explain *why* you want to become a category editor (you won't get paid a thing, by the way), and don't assume you'll be accepted first go.

Is it worth all the hassle? Your call, but little beats a DMOZ inbound link from a SEPOV, and being a category editor can be rewarding. If you do decide to go ahead, you need to follow the detailed instructions (to the letter) on the DMOZ website. (There's more about DMOZ in Resources.) Much easier (though not as prestigious from a SEPOV) is to simply pay for a listing in, for example, Yell.com or Thomson Local. Or get a free listing in one of the many other directories out there, being mindful that these are not highly-rated inbound links and you don't want to end up with too many. (There's a list in Resources.)

15.3.3 Get writing!

One of the most effective—and least complex—ways of building the type of quality links the search engines favour is simply to produce a steady stream of relevant, readable copy for your own site and for publication on other well-ranked sites across the web. This is largely an extension of the strategy we explored in Chapter 12 for using online news releases to funnel traffic to your site, and through it you can acquire two significant SEO benefits. These are...

- unsolicited inbound links to content on your site, the result simply of you having something useful to say

- inbound links from copy—articles, news releases, contributions to blog and forum discussions—that you get published on other people's sites without the need to reciprocate with an outbound link.

Clearly, the two are interdependent. There's no mileage in spending time and effort getting your words to a wider online audience and building inbound links if you have nothing to offer either the spiders or real people when they get to your door. So we suggest you look at this as two parts of a single whole, and as we've already looked (in Chapters 11 and 12) at how to maximise your own content and news releases, we'll focus on writing for publication elsewhere.

15.3.3.1 Using articles to build links

Writing articles for online publication is big business. There are numerous agencies—among them SEO specialists—on both sides of the Atlantic who will produce reams of copy for you. The quality will mostly be connected closely to the price you pay for it, and if you choose this route we do advise shopping around carefully to find writers with some empathy for your niche. And that accomplished, we still recommend that you generate a significant proportion of your output yourself. You know your specialist subject inside out, and what you say is always going to carry more authority than anything a commissioned writer can hope to achieve.

To make your writing stretch as far as possible we suggest that as a starting point you produce something for your own website, for example a white paper. Then...

- publish the white paper on your own website

- publish an extract on another website, or

- rewrite it (perhaps reducing it in length, or realigning the focus), and

- publish the rewrite on another website.

Using this approach means you get the maximum value from everything you write. If you hone your content and link-building copywriting strategy at the same time, you'll be able to really maximise on everything you produce—from e-books and white papers, newsletters and online guides, right down to two or three-paragraph case law updates. And the really good news is that finding somewhere to publish your articles is nowhere near as challenging as it is in the printed world!

One simple way to get started is to submit your copy to article directories, of which EzineArticles is globally the best known (**http://ezinearticles.com**). You can submit up to ten articles for free and thereafter you'll be charged a modest fee. Or maintain a high enough standard, get yourself classed as an "expert author", and carry on submitting for no charge. (All material is assessed by real people.)

If you follow our copywriting guidelines—and be careful to disengage what you're saying from your promotional message about yourself—you should achieve this without too much difficulty. Have a good look at the other material from the UK (and particularly from other lawyers) to get a feel for how to tailor your website copy for EzineArticles. What you get in return is exposure to thousands of visitors to the EzineArticles website who are looking for material, either for research purposes or to use across their own websites and newsletters. When your article gets syndicated elsewhere, the new publishers are obliged under the EzineArticles terms of service to leave the copy unedited and attribute it to you, complete with— yes, you've got it!—an inbound link to your website. There can be a cascading effect thereafter, and one article can end up appearing in myriad locations.

There is a minor downside with this. As we've already said, search engines will downgrade material they meet too often. To prevent this happening to anything on your own website, just follow our advice and put a slightly different spin on the original copy before submitting it elsewhere. Using articles for link building, and to raise your visibility in general, has yet to be seriously embraced by lawyers on this side of the Atlantic, and while you won't be the first UK employment law firm to follow this route, you'll certainly be among a minority. (There are details of other article directories in Resources.)

Another more law-focused route to follow is to use a site like Mondaq (**www.mondaq.com**), an online service providing a range of business, legal and regulatory information contributed by professionals including lawyers. Mondaq charges you to submit copy, but in return makes your articles available to a range of major mainstream and specialist media, including Reuters, Westlaw, Lexis-Nexis, Bloomberg and the *Financial Times*. Once online in these media, the listings are in turn picked up by the search engines, giving you even more exposure, and providing you with top-quality inbound links. Featured firm Ashby Cohen has been using Mondaq since autumn 2008, submitting two articles a month. Here's an example (the URL is **www.mondaq.com/article.asp?articleid=72650**).

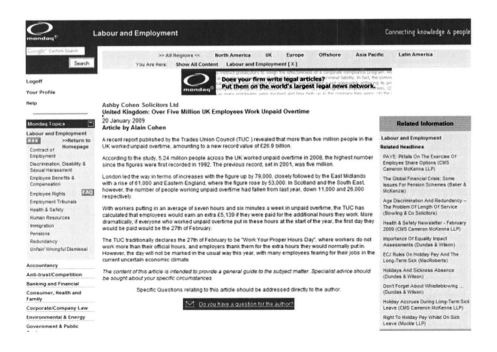

Making the most of Mondaq

Alain Cohen, of Ashby Cohen, uses SEO specialists to optimise his website, and they provide the copy for Mondaq:

> "It's the eight-thousandth most read website in the world and thirty per cent of the readership is UK-based. It sends your articles through its own systems and to other news agencies, like Reuter, *FT*, *Times*, main newspapers and other major publications in the UK, Europe and worldwide. Its readership is good—corporate companies. We don't expect them to come to us, but what we do hope we will see is the people who actually read the articles, who are executives. They may be on the move, or having problems. It's another way of marketing and spreading the name around as well as getting links."

Cohen uses the updates he receives from his Emplaw feed as raw material for a second site allied to his own, which has been set up primarily as an SEO tool. It's formatted as a blog and features regular case law and legislative updates, written by his SEO firm's copywriters. From this site, selected items are then reformatted by his SEO firm and sent on to Mondaq. "They're not legal writers, they're copywriters, but they do a reasonable job and it's meant for general consumption, it's not meant for professionals."

Wherever your articles are published, always make sure that you've used keyword-rich anchor text within them to link back to one or more relevant pages on your own site. Generally this should not just be your home page but somewhere offering further insight into the topic you're addressing. Also include your full contact details.

Action

Spend some time exploring sites that publish articles, including EzineArticles and Mondaq, and go through anything you've already written for possible material you could tweak and submit.

Look too at what other UK law firms—and particularly employment lawyers—are getting published. Is anyone already writing about your niche? If not, submit a test article and see what happens. If somebody's beaten you to it across all the main sites, consider how you could do it better, or at least very differently.

15.4 Blogging as a building block and adding RSS

As we saw in Chapter 10, a good blog has the potential to become one of your best SEO tools because it is by its very nature frequently updated. It's therefore more likely to be visited by the spiders more regularly than a static web page, and its interactive nature makes it likely to attract good one-way inbound links from relevant sites. If the blog is hosted on your own site, you're immediately boosting your rating. If it's hosted elsewhere, you're linking back to your main site from a site which can in turn demonstrate a good inbound link tally.

To give your blog an added advantage (and this is a tactic you can use elsewhere as well), make sure you set up an RSS feed in addition to offering updates by email. RSS—variously standing for Really Simple Syndication or Rich Site Summary—allows people to subscribe to your blog, to your online updates, or to any other of your website features that are subject to change. If you're not familiar with RSS, the icons generally look like these (taken from Kevin O'Keefe's site, left, and Colemans-ctts, right):

These are the key reasons why it makes sense to have an RSS feed:

*   Instead of your subscriber having to make the effort to check your blog for updates, software called a feed reader brings the new posts straight to their screen, where they can decide which ones to keep and which ones to delete.

- The process saves subscribers time and allows them to process a great deal more information than they'd be able to do by visiting many individual sites.

One interesting consequence of the quickly growing use of RSS is a predicted drop in the number of people who will routinely use search engines to actively seek information. Why would they if they can set up RSS feeds across the web to bring what they want straight to them? This significant shift will increasingly affect how you need to optimise your pages. In the not too distant future, it may well not be just about Google and Yahoo!

Action

If you haven't already done so, subscribe to RSS feeds from the blogs you were particularly drawn to in Chapter 10, and do the same with a variety of other sites (not all blogs) to get a feel for how RSS works.

Similarly, if it's not already in place, look across your website at pages carrying the type of content that lends itself to an update service, and consider incorporating an RSS subscription service.

15.5 Paying for your place

The easiest way of all to get on page one of Google is to pay your way. And it's Google AdWords that hogs the lion's share of the PPC market, taking around half of all search advertising, a share that's continuing to grow. Yahoo!'s equivalent of AdWords is Sponsored Search, and while it's less expensive to set up and arguably easier to manage, an ad here obviously won't reach as many people. Just to clarify what a Google AdWord looks like, here's one of Ashby Cohen's, on a search for "employment law London".

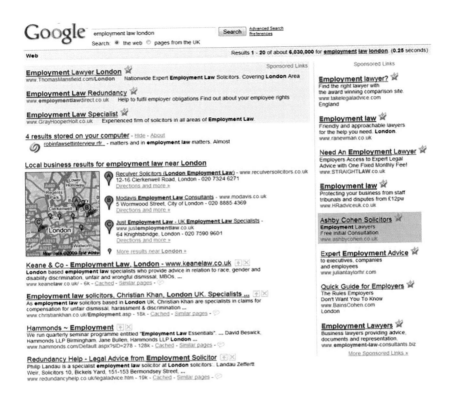

Don't be fooled by the apparent simplicity of PPC. Finessing any programme can be incredibly time-consuming and complicated, and it's all too easy to spend a great deal of money very quickly and achieve nothing. We therefore urge you, before you dip even a toe into the PPC water, to research the topic very thoroughly indeed, and don't just rely on what Google and Yahoo! tell you about their respective packages. And definitely don't just rely on this overview either!

Why is PPC so successful? Because—as American AdWords expert Perry Marshall puts it—"it combines three enormously powerful concepts: you only advertise to people who are looking for what you have *right now*; you only pay when they respond—when they click through to your site; pricing is determined by an ongoing, real-time auction based on true market values". Another huge advantage is that, unlike almost any other kind of advertising campaign, you can turn PPC on and off at will. You're not locked into any prescribed arrangement.

Google ads not only appear on their own sites, but also across subsidiary and affiliate sites including gmail, AOL, Ask and Earthlink. There are several entry points:

- AdWords Starter Edition is for the complete PPC novice, allowing you to run a single ad after specifying your budget, your keywords, and your text. It costs only $5 to activate.

- AdWords Jumpstart puts you in touch with a Google ad rep who can help you write your ads, choose your keywords, and so on. This costs $299, but it does buy you support and the payment also goes towards your advertising budget. A word of caution though—the ad reps may understand the system, but they don't necessarily understand employment law. You're well advised to arrive with your own keywords nicely honed after detailed research rather than rely on their suggestions

- Once you're confidently past the beginner stage, Google gives you the option of getting stuck in right away, for a $5 fee.

Where Google places your ad in their paid-for results (the ads that run along the top of the organic results and down the right-hand side of the page) depends on the following factors:

- **Your cost-per-click** (CPC)—what you're actually paying Google every time someone clicks on your ad. The process is exactly like an auction. Your position is determined by how much you bid on each click, and the more you pay, the higher up the pecking order you go.

- **Your quality score**, which comprises…
  - your click-through rate (CTR)—the percentage of people who actually click on your ad against the number of people who see the ad. Every time your ad is seen, that's scored as an *impression*. If you get 100 *impressions,* and one person clicks on the ad, your CTR is 1 per cent.

  - the relevance of your ad text—does it match the keyword the bid is being made on?

  - past keyword performance—has the keyword done well for past advertisers?

  - the quality of your landing page—does the page where your visitors are taken match the content of your ad and the keyword on which the bidding is being made?

The final equation is…

$$\text{your CPC} \ \times \ \text{your ad's quality score} = \text{your ad's position}$$

Of course, it's never quite as simple as that, and because Google is extremely efficient at maximising its AdWords profits, it's no longer easy to find many keywords for which the bidding comes in really low. The most popular, like "employment law", are now at a premium and you need to balance the advantages of the high-quality, targeted traffic Google offers against the disadvantages of what could become a costly and unpredictable campaign. We recommend you explore the guidance given by two AdWord experts: Perry Marshall, who we have already quoted and who has been using Google's system since it was launched in 2002, and Mark Widawer, who also focuses on optimising your landing pages, where your customers arrive. (There are full details in Resources.)

Yahoo! offers a range of paid-for services, of which Sponsored Search is just one. Ads will also appear on Windows Live, AltaVista, Excite,

G02Net, InfoSpace, and various content sites such as CNN. There's a $30 non-refundable deposit to get started, though this does cover the cost of your first click-throughs, and a minimum $20 a month spend. Yahoo! offers its own Fast Track service, but—as with Google—be cautious about taking the ad rep's advice on keywords.

Of our featured firms, only the two whose businesses are primarily driven through their websites use PPC. Ashby Cohen uses Google AdWords and Morris Legal uses Yahoo!'s Sponsored Search.

There is one final ingredient—Google AdSense, where you host other people's ads on your own website, or pay to have yours appear on somebody else's. We can see possible ethical problems with this for law firms, and you would definitely need to be very careful about the types of ad you were prepared to display—and where. There's more about AdSense on Google's website.

Action

Take a tour of both Google's AdWords and Yahoo!'s Sponsored Search PPC programmes and evaluate each.

Yahoo! over Google

Dean Morris chose Yahoo!'s Sponsored Search for his got-the-boot.com website, which he set up in 2006: "At the time, that was the one I got my head around to use. You need a degree to operate any PPC campaign, whoever you do it with, so I learned Overture [Yahoo!'s previous PPC programme], then they changed it! My decision was based on the fact that we have a reasonable organic ranking with Google anyway, and therefore if you're going to spend money on PPC, go to the other side first. That was the logic. And it's not nearly as cost prohibitive as PI—the PPC charges for PI are immense."

Visit the websites of the two PPC experts we've named (details in Resources) to get a better idea of how to really make a campaign work.

We're not going to make any recommendations here. PPC is ideal for some law firms and completely unsuitable for others.

16

Permission marketing from the inbox end

We know we don't have to introduce you to email—you're using it every day, at work and at home. We all are. And we're all increasingly choosy about what we're prepared to give inbox room, most of us routinely using software to (not always successfully) keep out the worst of the dross. Does this mean email has lost its edge as a marketing tool? Yes and no. It all depends on how you use it, and because you're not aiming to make any kind of immediate sale you stand a very greatly increased chance of being opened and read.

Let's start by stepping back. Email—electronic mail—has been around in one form or another since the early 1960s and pre-dates the internet by a couple of decades. In fact, it played a central role in the development of the internet and the two have since grown in tandem, taking us to where we are now with email woven inextricably through the fabric of our professional and personal lives. For anyone under 30, the idea of working without it is largely incomprehensible and we all benefit hugely from the way it's speeded up communications and made it easier to shunt information around the globe.

But there is of course the downside. It's hard enough just keeping up with the messages that need our immediate attention, never mind the more marginal stuff. We've become susceptible to "email fatigue" or "email bankruptcy"—that depressing feeling you get when you know there is no chance you'll ever touch even half the messages sitting in your inbox, and there's only one way to go, and that's to have a largely indiscriminate purge. If it's happening to you, it's also happening to your existing and prospective clients, so you need to ensure that anything you send them outside specific transactions…

- is something they've asked for (see box opposite for definition of spam)

- is instantly engaging—well-designed, well-written and easy to navigate

- is compelling—intrinsically worth their while to open and read

- is relevant—what you're saying has direct and lasting value for them

- works properly—that any mail merge elements are correct and the links go where they should.

We'll look in more detail at what you should send shortly, but first let's consider the mechanics of the email relationship.

16.1 The beauty of autoresponders

We're all familiar with the autoresponder (or mailbot)—it's the software that tells you the person to whom you just sent that urgent email is out of the office until Monday, or bounces the message back altogether. In marketing terms, however, it is what's made the whole concept of bulk emailing feasible and has radically changed the way we send and receive information.

If you're already using an autoresponder it will be located either on your own website server or hosted by a specialist provider who gives you remote

Labelling our inbox guests

Other than the mail over which you have direct control, the rest of what comes into our inboxes can be loosely categorised as follows:

Spam: also known as Unsolicited Bulk Email (UBE) or Unsolicited Commercial Email (UCE). This is exactly what it says on the can—email sent in vast quantities to email addresses harvested without consent from across the internet. It's named after the subject of the famous 1970 Monty Python sketch. A lot of it is unsavoury, some of it is a danger to your computer, all of it is deeply annoying, and sadly it comprises a staggering 85 per cent or more of all the emails sent. Responsibility for the first commercial spamming is laid at the door of two American immigration lawyers in 1994.

Bacn: pronounced "bacon" and in the online lexicon since 2007. The name is derived from the concept of being "better than spam, but not as good as a personal email". The comestible theme is clear, but slightly less so is the lack of a vowel, unless it's to maintain the four-letter symmetry. This is email you've signed up to receive. You may not always remember having done so, but it's entirely legitimate and has every right to arrive in your inbox unless you unsubscribe. It's been described as "email you want but not right now"— and may never quite get around to reading. It includes newsletters, alerts from social media sites like Facebook and Twitter, and RSS feed update notifications. What you send clients as part of your marketing strategy can be classed as bacn.

(See Resources for more about spam and bacn and useful links.)

access. (We're not exploring the actual mechanics here.) We mentioned in Chapter 13 the basics of how the process works, so here we're going to briefly run over some of its benefits. The key benefits are that you can track…

• who opens your messages

• who clicks on the links inside your messages

• which addresses are no longer valid.

From this you can very quickly build up a detailed picture of the type of messages that work best, the ones that work least well, and whether some types of client favour being approached in one way while others favour another. You can dig—in truly forensic detail—into the data any autoresponder program provides. How much time you devote to this will depend on how big a role you want email to play in your marketing mix.

American autoresponder service provider MailerMailer produces reports every six months analysing the metrics generated by its own clients, and while none are in the legal sector the findings are nonetheless a useful benchmark. Its November 2008 survey (covering data collected between January and June 2008) showed, for example, the following information:

- Nearly a third of messages were opened within the first two hours after receipt (this reflects the UK legal sector average of around 30 per cent), and about 75 per cent within the first 24 hours. Those who opened their messages clicked on links at a rate of just under 2.75 per cent.

- Sundays and Mondays were the best days to send marketing email (although mid-week, and around midday, may work better for some B2B clients).

- Emails sent to groups of fewer people were opened and clicked on more than those sent to a large list.

(The latest MailerMailer metrics report can be found here: www.mailermailer.com/metrics.rwp)

Note that these open rates are based on messages sent in HTML, which include an invisible image allowing the sending servers to track when it was displayed and by whom. They don't include anything sent in plain text. Open rates tracked in this way have been steadily declining since 2004 as email agents with default image-disabling have become more popular, and more people have begun accessing their inboxes from hand-held devices. This doesn't necessarily mean fewer HTML messages are being opened, just that more people are now declining to download the accompanying images.

Autoresponders also of course allow you to personalise your messages, set up as many groups (and sub-groups) of recipients as you like, run sequential mailings, and create a range of templates. But first you need your names.

> Co-author Daniel Barnett runs a 23,000-strong mailing list and makes extensive use of autoresponders: "It's not so much for promoting professional barrister services—although that's just laziness on my part—but my other businesses. These include my own-branded employment law bulletins for solicitors' firms where autoresponders send out a sequence of 'personalised' emails over the course of 12 months from an inquiry, leading to an extremely high conversion rate." (For more information see **www.emplawservices.co.uk**.)

16.1.1 Building and maintaining your list

Everyone receiving your email marketing messages has to have first given their consent, so how do you get that? We've already looked at using your website to collect consenting subscribers, and for prospective clients this is without doubt the most efficient way. Here are some other suggestions:

- Whenever you exchange business cards—at a networking event, say—follow up by sending a quick email checking in with them and asking whether they would like to join your subscriber list.

- When you're meeting a new client and gathering their details, ask whether they would like to go on your list.

- If you're hosting an event, make sure all your guests fill out a response form that includes the option of giving their consent to receive marketing emails from you. You could sub-divide this with tick boxes for information about events, your newsletter, or one-off updates.

Provided that you very clearly have someone's consent (written or electronic), you can go ahead and include them in your mailings. Consent can generally be deemed to have been given under the Privacy and Electronic Communications (EC Directive) Regulations 2003 if you've already done work for a client and have built a "business relationship", but it would nonetheless be sensible to get their specific consent before you start sending them marketing materials.

However, with every single message you send out you *must* include an unsubscribe option, and you must include a link to your privacy policy. Here's an example from Workplace Law Network's bulletin (left), and the web page you reach by clicking on "unsubscribe".

The unsubscribe process must be completed and confirmed as quickly as possible. A recent report by Return Path, an American email marketing expert, found that around 60 per cent of businesses surveyed do what Workplace Law does—they provide a link from the email to an unsubscribe web page, and most provide immediate confirmation that the request was successfully processed. Far fewer go further and offer—as Workplace Law does—unsubscribe options, which greatly increases the likelihood of subscribers deciding to remain in part opted in.

Not recommended is requiring the subscriber to send an email with "unsubscribe" in the subject line, but be mindful that even if you're offering a link-based opt-out some people may still go this route unilaterally and you must ensure your software is set up to spot any that slip through the net. And it must also be configured to remove unsubscribers' addresses immediately. The Return Path survey found that 20 per cent of its surveyed companies sent at least one more marketing email after confirming an unsubscribe, something that is actually illegal in the US under the CAN-SPAM Act. You also need to ensure that all bounced addresses get taken off your mailing list as quickly as possible to prevent internet service providers (ISPs) classifying you as a source of junk and identifying everything you send as spam.

Make it easy for subscribers to easily change their email address and other profile details. Our example includes this on the unsubscribe page, which is intelligent since that's exactly what some people may be doing—not unsubscribing as such, but just changing addresses.

Equally, ask your subscribers to make it easier for you to reach them. As the sheer volume of rubbish mail grows, so ISPs are becoming increasingly prone to arbitrarily marking perfectly legitimate messages as spam. You will undoubtedly have had this experience yourself—digging about in your ISP's spam folder for something you've been expecting that's failed to reach your inbox. Or worse, never finding it at all.

With your own outgoing messages, ask recipients to add you to their address books and put you on their "whitelist". We suggest you consider including detailed instructions on how to do this on your website at the point where a visitor is handing over their details, and include a link in your first email to them. Try this as a useful template: **www.cleanmymailbox.com/whitelist-sample.html**.

Before we leave the nuts and bolts of this, a word about privacy policies. You must have one and publish it, and we hope we don't need to explain why. It needs to address both your website and your emailed material and at the very least cover collection, use and disclosure of personal data. And if you don't already do so, include on every email you send a footer listing your registered office address, a contact email address, registered number, and country of registration. Again, if you're not already doing so consider adding a standard disclaimer saying something like: "This email is confidential and intended for the use of the intended recipient only. If you have received this email in error, please tell us immediately and then delete it. Unless it specifically states otherwise, this email does not form part of a contract."

Action

Go through the marketing emails you're already receiving and give each of them a thorough technical appraisal. How well does each work aesthetically? Do all the links go where they should? Is it easy to unsubscribe? Is the privacy policy accessible, and is the disclaimer written in plain English? How many are getting trapped by your ISP's anti-spam software?

That done, draw up a list of three ways you can build up your email list—through networking, perhaps, or simply ensuring that you ask all new clients to consent to receiving information from you.

16.2 Using email wisely to reach your clients

We saw in Chapter 13 the importance of using permission marketing across your website to begin a relationship with potential clients—asking for their email addresses in return for access to some of your site content, or in order to receive regular information from you. That's what we're focusing on here—messages you send as part of a mass mailing to those email addresses you've been given permission to use.

Primarily these are...

- newsletters, also often labelled "bulletin" or "update"

- one-off notes, usually in response to something newsworthy, to let clients know about forthcoming events, or to flag up a blog entry.

We'll look at newsletters first.

16.2.1 Newsletters that get read

You're no doubt already familiar with the format, but so that we're clear, here are a few examples.

On the top row is the UK-focused Workplace Law Network bulletin and Employment Law Weekly News. On the bottom row is the Law Marketing Newsletter and Marketing Profs Today, both from the US.

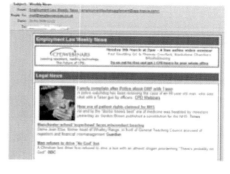

These newsletters were all created using HTML, making them visually appealing, allowing the use of branding and images, and—as discussed above—tracking. But they don't have to be. Indeed, many marketing experts will point you strongly away from intricate design in favour of straight text. British consultant Chris Cardell says: "Complex newsletters are making the customer's life complicated." He argues that we are programmed to receive personal messages from people we know: "Imagine if your best friend sent you an email in the form of a newsletter with 17 different links in it, and lots of graphics and pictures. You'd think they were crazy. Why do businesses do it?" And legal marketing communications consultant Gerald Newman says: "Bland brochure-style text is unlikely to be read, because recipients lack the time and patience. HTML and PDF formats can be made visually attractive. But recipients may opt not to open, download, print or read your HTML or PDF pages. Plain text emails, with simple punchy information and with links to detailed material on your website, may work more effectively." There's only one way to find out what works best for you and your clients, and that is through testing different designs and formats to see which produces the most—and the most positive—feedback.

What is it you want to achieve with a newsletter? As with everything else you produce, you need to be offering your clients *benefits*. Legal IT consultant Alex Heshmaty says: "An email newsletter performs two primary functions: staying in touch with clients and reminding them why they may need or want legal advice. Ensuring clients are aware of any new legislation or important case judgments *which could affect them* is one of the most powerful marketing tools at your disposal." And David Meerman Scott says in an article published on Pragmatic Marketing's website: "Email newsletters have been around as long as email, but still have tremendous value as a way to deliver a regular series of thought leadership content." So rather than just explain what a judgment means, spell out the implications, following the copywriting rules from Chapter 5 and keeping each item as tight as possible. Here are some other newsletter pointers:

- Position the most interesting item at the top—you've more chance of the recipient then reading on.

- Use short paragraphs.

- Ensure at least half the items have a link, either to a source of further information on your own website or to an external site, such as BIS or Acas.

- Ensure that the links to your website go to the right landing page.

- Include a named individual's full contact details.

If you'd prefer to delegate your newsletter production, why not investigate outsourcing to Daniel Barnett's Employment Law Services? You can choose to have a monthly or quarterly newsletter written by Barnett and delivered direct to your clients, with your own branding. Here's an extract from (a very old!) one.

There's more information at **www.emplawservices.co.uk**.

"When I was at Colemans-ctts, our own newsletters would go out every Friday. We also used Employment Law Services' excellent quarterly newsletter. Certain of our bigger commercial clients would say, 'Actually, Tom, your weekly updates—we know all that anyway because we're all CIPD members and they're a bit beneath us, but the quarterly ones are great because that gives us the details that we need'. However, with the SMEs, the quarterly ones might go over their heads and therefore it's the weekly ones they prefer. It's a fine balance." *Tom Walker, formerly with Colemans-ctts, now with Manches*

You'll note that we haven't said keep your newsletter short—just that you should write tightly, write well, and provide plenty of benefits. Veteran British direct marketer Drayton Bird says: "I cannot count how many times I've heard from this or that email expert... that emails should be short and eye-catching. Quite frankly I could never believe this to be true, probably because so many times over the odd 50 years I've been in this business I have heard similar claims about direct mail, press ads, television—you name it. And time and time again, whenever a client has been willing to test a short message, perhaps with a very eye-catching graphic, against a long, relevant and interesting message, the latter has performed better."

Bird argues that what works offline works online. His own marketing newsletter has an unsubscribe rate of under 1 per cent. As with formatting, trial and error will show you what works best for you and your clients.

How often should you send out a newsletter? David Gilroy, sales and marketing director of legal marketing firm Conscious Solutions, recommends quarterly for private clients and monthly for commercial clients. "There is enough going on each month, particularly around the area of employment law and in a business-to-business relationship for a monthly frequency." MailerMailer has found that emailing only once a quarter or just a few times a year leads to a higher "bounce" rate—and more people are likely to have forgotten who you are and will delete the message without reading it. Sending too frequently is also counter-productive, annoying people for different reasons.

Always post the entire newsletter on your website and make it downloadable as a PDF.

What do our profiled firms think about newsletters?

Tom Walker passes on some advice from a former client from his time at *Colemans-ctts*: "This was a tip given to me by a retiring HR director. He said, 'I am every week bombarded with countless updates, all clients are, and here are my tips: 1. You shouldn't have to scroll; 2. It should be user-friendly; and 3. Interesting'. And that's how I tried to make them, and the feedback I got was very, very good. I wouldn't give the legal in great detail—'this burden of proof has shifted'—because that's boring, and I'd not send out a full analysis because that's too long, and in employment law I have the luxury of picking interesting things."

Darren Maw, MD of Vista, sends out his In View newsletter in a ratio of 80 per cent to existing clients and 20 per cent to people he and his colleagues have previously worked with, "but who are not in a position to use us at the moment". He says: "Lawyers try to compete on being the first to deliver the news, but that in itself doesn't deliver value: getting there three days earlier makes no difference. There's a misunderstanding that clients attach a lot of significance to being the first to know because they don't. They attach significance to understanding what it means to their business and what they should do differently so we work hard on that. If it's an issue that's relevant to a client business—let's say a change to annual leave and you've got an organisation with lots of lorry drivers—we'll say, 'this is coming up, I think we should sit down for an hour and talk about it'."

Mark Ellis, CEO of Ellis Whittam, is committed to keeping in touch with his clients: "We recognise that with the fixed-fee, fixed-contract term model we have that it's very important that we are proactive rather than just reactive. A very easy way of building rapport is to send relevant information to clients. We send a lot of the same stuff to all because employment law applies to all of them. But equally we do personalised things, so for example if there's something that's relevant to schools and colleges, or to food and hospitality, we'll send it to that sector as far as we are able to within the constraints of the database. We do case law updates, we do briefings, we give *ad hoc* information. We cross-sell the webinars and seminars in the employers' briefs, we will also email directly in respect of them as well. It's such an easy way to reach people. We're having a debate about the best way to send out an email. Our agency would rather like us to send it out in bright colours, but our experience is that plain text, matter of fact, no nonsense, just a short, simple message with a link, works better... Obviously we try not to send attachments as they can get caught up in junk, so we just have a link to the relevant document on the website."

Florida law firm Shutts & Bowen doesn't put out newsletters, although many US practices do. Attorney Robin Fawsett says: "We don't do that, because no one bothers to read them and they take too much time. Also, other firms copy them and put their own letterhead on them! We do have an electronic database of existing clients and selected prospective clients, and what we call 'friends of the firm'. When something they need to know about happens or threatens to happen, such as the Employee Free Choice Act, we write something useful and brief and are able to send it electronically to all existing practice group clients, selected clients of others in the law firm, and others to whom we think sending something like that is appropriate."

Lewis Silkin produces a range of email information. Senior marketing executive Mirella Sikorski says: "Examples of our e-news series include e-news Employment and e-news TUPE. These are available online, and are more in-depth, more dry, but still aimed at HR people. We've got a section called the Human Zoo with humorous stories from all over the world which is proving popular. Our e-news goes out every eight weeks, but we're trying to make them more regular. We don't send out general emailings to clients, not blanket ones. Everything is always tailored to the specific client. I've never done blanket emailings anywhere I've worked. We don't use autoresponders on the website. Instead we ask visitors to email us and we'll personally get back to them. It works fine and we don't need to use autoresponders. This is not a high volume business, and we like to keep it personal."

16.2.2 What else can you say?

Away from the structure and routine of a newsletter, email is ideal when you want your clients to know about something in a hurry. Whether you send individual messages or harness your autoresponder, organising a round robin is the easiest way to disseminate information quickly. Obvious subject matter examples are important judgments and the announcement of new legislation and, like newsletters, you ideally need to include a "further information" link to a website, preferably your own. Events (seminars, lectures, webinars, anything at all that you're involved in) are another key contender for an email alert—and ideally suited for setting up a series of emails sent at intervals. Again, always include a link to a specific landing page on your website where clients can find out more and—crucially—sign up.

And don't forget news about members of your team. Remember people buy people. If one of them is going on maternity or paternity leave, let clients know, and let them know when the baby arrives! This serves two purposes: giving clients practical information and making them feel part of your wider loop. Don't of course force it—and don't do it too often or you'll devalue a very useful currency. Always personalise this type of one-off email, addressing the recipient directly: "Dear John..." The vast majority of people know intellectually that it's just the autoresponder, but at an emotional level seeing our own name is very effective in breaking down barriers.

> Not everyone grasps the autoresponder concept first go. In 2007, Daniel Barnett sent out a 'personalised' email bulletin to the solicitors on his mailing list: "I was promoting my own-branded employment law bulletins service, and the email started off: 'Dear [firstname]' and continued to say, 'Would you like to know a tried-and-tested way of obtaining new clients around [town] for [firm name]?'. This triggered about 30 responses from solicitors expressing concern that I had sent the name of their firm out to thousands of people. These were people who were unfamiliar with autoresponders and had no concept of how they worked. Hopefully, they are now in a very small minority!"

Action

If you're not already producing a newsletter, draw up a list of the pros and cons of doing so for your business and your clients. Do you have the time and resources to do it well? Is it worth considering outsourcing? Would ad hoc updates work best for you?

If you already distribute a newsletter—and/or updates—how well do they match up? Look at them from the recipient's perspective. Do they grab and hold your attention? Do they overcome the obstacles of indifference? List three improvements you could make and then set yourself deadlines for achieving them.

16.3 Successful emails start with attention to detail

Here's a quick rundown on avoiding a few of the more common email pitfalls, starting where we just left off, with mail merge. How many messages have you received addressed to "Dear [xxxx]" or to somebody who is definitely not you? If you're using mail merge—and as we've noted, it's a valuable device—you must check and double-check that it's done the job before your message leaves your server. Send a copy to yourself first to make sure, and print it out and read it right through while you're at it. In the same vein, check all names, dates, phone numbers and email addresses are correct and that all your links work properly, and if you're using images that they load correctly.

And before you do any of that, finesse your subject line very thoroughly. Drayton Bird refers to research carried out by online technologies company Sun. They found that the subject field was critical. "No wonder: it is the first thing people see, like the headline. It [the research] explained that benefits are important and that you should use plain language—no puns, humour or playing with words. You should be careful about teasers—busy people dislike surprises." And people really dislike carelessness and will delete your message—or worse, your sloppy subject line can be forwarded as an object of ridicule, hugely undermining your relationship with clients and your image further afield.

The Retail Email Blog publishes an annual "Oopsy Hall of Fame", which highlights mistakes made by major American retailers. And if they can cock up, so can you! Here are a few examples from the 2008 Hall of Fame, with comments from blog owner Chad White, research director at US email marketing strategy and creative services agency Smith-Harmon.

Target—subject line
The subject line slip crown goes to this "Target" subject line.

Oriental Trading—Create the ultimate Halloween haunt & get fee shipping
If you leave the "r" out of "free", you get the exact opposite of what you intended to offer.

CompUSA—Memoiral Day Only – Acer 22" LCD $219 – Lenovo Dual-Core Laptop $499 & More

Misspelled "Memorial".

Bluefly—Its Time To Think About Cashmere...

It's time to think about spelling "it's" correctly in subject lines.

Road Runner Sports—What are you waiting for Runner? FREE SHIPPING ends today!

Plenty of retailers mess up greetings. There should be a comma after "for".

Spiegel—The NEW Take on Tweeds Spiegel Shows You How To Make the Look Your Own + 20% OFF

Missing punctuation after "Tweeds".

J. Crew—As seen in the the New York Times...

Repeated "the".

Ross-SimonsEstate Jewelry: 100's of NEW items – on Sale TODAY! (FREE Shipping included) Sears—1000's of Tools on Sale + Big Savings on Electronics

The apostrophes after "100" and "1000" are unnecessary. Proper spelling is "100s" and "1000s".

Road Runner Sports—You want it.. you got it! FREE Shipping on NEW Arrivals!

One dot is a period. Three dots is an ellipsis. Two dots is nothing.

There are more of these—and other emailing gaffes—at **www.retailemailblog.com/2009/01/oopsy-hall-of-fame-2008-inductees.html**

Action

Choose a random set of 20 marketing emails you've received and analyse the subject lines. Look for poor grammar and spelling and other signs of inattention to detail. Then check the last 20 emails you sent out to clients. Is there any room for improvement yourself?

Finally, reward yourself by watching the *Monty Python* spam sketch at **www.youtube.com/watch?v=anwy2MPT5RE&feature=related**

17

Knowledge as a marketing tool: seminars, webinars and other events

Playing host and sharing what you know about something of relevance to your audience is a tried and tested way of building client loyalty and attracting new custom. And the internet (in particular Web 2.0) has done nothing to diminish the power of this marketing tool. Indeed, it's strengthened it by opening up new ways of communicating.

We're going to explore three ways of connecting with existing clients and prospects—some in more detail than others:

• seminars

• webinars and teleseminars

• mock tribunals.

What they all have in common is putting you centre stage and giving you an unrivalled opportunity to demonstrate your role as an employment law authority and a thought leader in your specialist field.

17.1 Face to face with your clients

You'll undoubtedly be familiar with the seminar concept, even if you've never hosted one yourself. Unlike the more formal lecture—where the traffic is largely one way and you do all the talking—seminars are generally for fewer people and are designed to accommodate contributions from participants.

Let's return to our West Midlands discrimination law niche practice. They're getting a steady stream of inquiries from employers anxious about running foul of age regulations if they include a preponderance of older staff in their redundancy pools. So the partners decide to put together a half-day training package that spans both the discrimination and redundancy basics. Let's look at their options in the form of a grid.

Table 5   Which event works best?

Best for...	Lecture	Seminar
Small groups		✓
Large groups	✓	
Single venue	✓	✓
Multiple venues (including clients' premises)		✓
Audience involvement		✓
Audience feedback		✓

From this we can see that generally seminars are more useful and more flexible. Where a lecture does score is when you have a "star speaker", someone whose reputation is such that you know you can fill a large space with a large number of people, winning enormous kudos in the process. In reality, though, few legal practices outside the Magic Circle are going to have the resources or appropriate client base for this, so we'll focus on seminars.

Let's use the journalist's W5 checklist (who?, what?, when?, where?, why?) for this exercise, and use the discrimination in redundancy idea as the topic:

- *Who?* Clients—or clients and prospective clients.

- *What?* A half-day seminar—and make it free. This is not a money-making exercise. Charging £20+VAT towards "refreshments" sends the message that your firm is tight-fisted and will try to eke every penny it can out of its clients!

- *When?* Within the next six to eight weeks.

- *Where?* The seminar format gives you choices, which broadly are...
  - at your office
  - at your clients' premises
  - somewhere else (a local hotel or a seminar room in a conference centre, for example).

- *Why?* To build relationships with clients and prospects, by guiding them through making employees redundant without breaching unfair dismissal or discrimination law (particularly the age regulations).

Breaking this down further, you need to make the following decisions:

- Is this seminar for your existing clients alone or do you want to extend the invitation? If you focus on existing clients, you can make the event more specific; if you broaden it out, you will need to be more generic.

- You've got the basic format—a half-day seminar. Now you need to decide who's going to deliver it.
  - Will it be just you? Or you and another member of your team? Do you want to involve anyone from outside your firm?
  - Are you going to be fairly formal—using a PowerPoint presentation, for example, with a classic speaker–audience chair arrangement and a single Q&A session at the end? Or

would you prefer a more hands-on approach, with perhaps just a simple hand-out as a prompt, sitting around a conference table, perhaps, and encouraging everyone there to contribute throughout the session?

- You need to find a balance between giving your potential audience enough notice for them to accommodate the date in their diary, but not so much that they forget about it! For a seminar like this one there is also a degree of urgency attached—setting the date for nine months' hence would strike the wrong chord. For something linked to, say, new legislation, you can plan further ahead; the same would hold true were our West Midlands firm to host an annual discrimination law update.

- There are advantages and disadvantages wherever you host a seminar:
  - You're on home territory if you host the event at your office, with the resources you need at hand, tried and tested technology, and so on. You and your fellow speakers may feel more comfortable here and you can show off your facilities. The downside is that unless you have a lot of space you're likely to be limited numbers-wise.
  - Moving outside your comfort zone and into your client's office does bring advantages. In particular, more of their staff may be able to attend, they will anyway make sure that you get a good turn-out, you can very accurately tailor your content, and if you only visit irregularly it's a great opportunity for you to pick up on this client's workplace "buzz". The downside is that you may have to rely on their technology unless you're going the informal, round-the-table route, and you're only addressing one client at a time.
  - Hosting the event on neutral territory in a central location means you can invite a larger number of clients, allowing them (and you!) to use it as a networking event as well as a source of

information. It's a good option for attracting potential clients who might feel joining a seminar at your offices puts them under an obligation, and a chance too for them to assess the calibre of your existing clients. The technology should work fine, and someone else is making the teas and coffees. This option is also best suited for involving other professionals in a joint venture. On the downside, it's obviously going to cost you more and it's less intimate than the other two options.

- Always approach hosting any event as a giving process. Your underlying motivation might be to build client loyalty and attract new custom, but it's important to park this and focus instead on what you can do for your client, and how your advice and guidance can throw light on a complex issue—on the day and thereafter. We return, yet again, to making benefits your priority and distancing yourself from anything resembling a sales pitch.

Once you have all these pieces in place, you need to decide who to invite and how. If you've decided that your presentation will work best in your client's workplace, then by far the easiest way of setting this up is just to lift the phone and discuss the logistics with your main contact. Take the lead from them, on both the number of people they want involved and the type of presentation they'd like. For example, if it's just senior management they might prefer you to sit around the table; if there's a mix of management and employees, a more formal presentation might work better.

Staying for now with Adams, Brown and Curtis, they have decided to host their seminar at a nearby hotel so that they can also use the event for networking and to attract potential as well as existing clients. What next? First—and this may be stating the obvious—decide who's going to do what. If you've never hosted an event like this before, you must put in place a system. Most obviously, who's going to make the presentation? (NB: a useful option if you're stuck for a good speaker is to phone up a set of Chambers you use and ask the clerks if one of the barristers will speak for free, but make sure you get someone experienced.) Who's going to liaise with the venue? Who's going to organise invitations and monitor responses?

The Adams, Brown and Curtis team have done this before, so they already know that senior partner John Adams is going to lead the presentation, with support from age discrimination specialist Bill Smith. One member of the admin team will deal with the hotel; another with the invitations. They next need to decide who to invite, drawing up a list of their own clients and sourcing the names of other non-client business contacts who may be interested (including names harvested from the website). Phoning apart, these are the three principal ways of doing the actual inviting:

- *Email*—works best for all your clients (including the ones you phone) and anyone else who has given you permission to contact them (through your website, for example).

- *Through your website*—works for all your clients and prospective clients. Feature the event on your home page and link to a dedicated landing page—the same page your email recipients will reach from your message. Ideally make it possible for people to register here.

- *Direct mail*—may work well for your clients and is ideal for prospective customers with whom you have no permission marketing relationship.

We'll consider just the email and direct mail. For both you must of course focus on the seminar's benefits as well as including all the essential information, and ideally write separate emails for your existing clients and prospects. With direct mail it might not be worth your while producing two versions, so you may need to phrase your message to work for both.

17.1.1 Inviting by email

We've brought together the copywriting basics from Chapter 5 and the essentials from Chapter 16 to help you put together an email for your clients. Here's a quick reminder—you need to write with all these elements in mind, starting with internet marketer Frank Kern's succinct summary:

1. *Here's who I am* (Adams, Brown and Curtis).

2. *Here's what I've got* (a free seminar).

3. *Here's what it'll do for you* (guide you through the redundancy process).

4. *Here's what I want you to do next* (register online or ask for more information).

Next you need to remember AIDA:

*   *Attention* (all SMEs—the firm's target audience— are worried about redundancies)

*   *Interest* (flag up the potential risks of doing nothing)

*   *Desire* (flag up the *benefits* of attending the free seminar)

*   *Action* (numbers are limited, register now ...).

And then overcome the three obstacles of indifference:

1. *Who cares?* (A significant proportion of this firm's clients will.)

2. *So what?* (A significant proportion will grasp the relevance to them.)

3. *What's in it for me?* (Something free that's of direct use.)

So you'd want to write something like this:

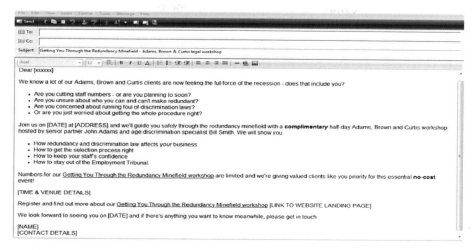

You'll note that we haven't used the word "free". That's because it's a spam trigger word and there's a risk of your message not getting through—attempts to get around it such as "f.ree" or "fre*" just look unprofessional. We agree completely that "complimentary" and "no-cost" are not as good! There are no design bells and whistles here, and you really don't need them for a simple invitation like this. This would act as your launch email, and you'd want to follow up at weekly intervals with reminders. They need to say much the same. Here's an example for the week before the event:

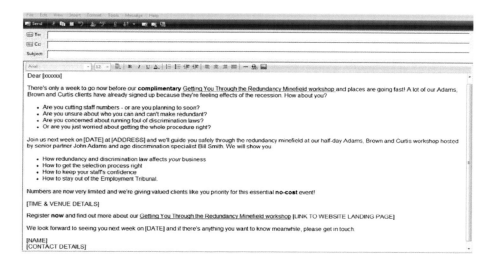

17.1.2 Inviting by direct mail

Before email, direct mail is how you'd have done it. If you were organising an event, you'd put your invitations in the post and wait for a response. And let's be very clear, direct mail still plays an important role (see Chapter 19), but arguably nowhere near as big a role as it did, and not in this context. Where its role is clearly undiminished is when you have a list of prospective clients who have not given their permission for you to contact them by email. Do you change your message from the one sent by email? In terms of the general tone, not really. But you will need to say more. You must assume that if you're going cold calling, your recipients may never have heard of you. Everyone you contact by email, by default, has.

We'd therefore suggest including with the information about the seminar some or all of the following (most of it is detail that we'd also urge you to include on your dedicated website landing page):

• Your practice description (you may want to change this slightly from the version used elsewhere on the site, but assume some visitors are reading it for the first time).

• Biographies of your speakers, with photos (link to the website versions from the landing page).

• Full contact details, including—and frequently—your website address and that of the dedicated landing page (keep this simple: **www.yoursite.co.uk/events09**, for example).

• A map of the venue, and contact details.

• A response tear-off section, but making it clear that registering online is easier!

Because this is largely addressed to non-clients, we'd suggesting pitching your letter like this:

Dear [xxxxxx]

We know a lot of our Adams, Brown and Curtis clients are now feeling the full force of the recession. What about you?

- Are you cutting staff numbers—or are you planning to soon?
- Are you unsure about who you can and can't make redundant?
- Are you concerned about running foul of discrimination laws?
- Or are you just worried about getting the whole procedure right?

We'll guide you safely through the redundancy minefield. Just join us at a **free** half-day workshop on [DATE] at [ADDRESS] hosted by our senior partner John Adams and age discrimination specialist Bill Smith. We will show you...

- how redundancy and discrimination law affects *your* business
- how to get the selection process right
- how to keep your staff's confidence
- how to stay out of the Employment Tribunal.

Numbers for our *Getting You Through the Redundancy Minefield* workshop are limited and we urge you to sign up now for this **free** event.

[TIME & VENUE DETAILS]

To register, visit our website at [WEB PAGE ADDRESS] or complete and return the enclosed [OR ATTACHED] registration form.

We look forward to seeing you on [DATE] and if there's anything you want to know meanwhile, please get in touch.

[NAME]
[CONTACT DETAILS]

You must identify the right person to send the invitation to. If you're in any doubt, phone the firm and check. Should you follow up? We suggest you play this one by ear. If you get a quick and enthusiastic response to all your forms of invitation, then you won't need to. If the response is slower, then you could phone the named recipient to check that they've received the invite. You may not get a commitment—either to attend or a definite no—but by crossing their radar you've raised their awareness of you and your practice.

How do our profiled firms feel about seminars?

Tom Walker put seminars at the heart of his relationship with his *Colemans-ctts* clients. "I just like seminars, because they're more intimate. I'm not a great fan of PowerPoint; I prefer the handout and just talking. And it's also educational for me, because it's very easy for me to say, 'right, this is what you do', and the line manager might say, 'that's not possible'. There was no cap on numbers. If someone said, 'there's only ten people, is it worth your while?', I'd say, 'yeah, we'll do it in a couple of hours'. And if someone said, 'I've got four shifts of line management, 30 people at a time, can we do it over two days?', yes we can."

Ellis Whittam sees hosting events as integral. "We've been running a series of executive briefings, seminars for directors and owners on dealing with employment issues in the current economic climate. We've run that in about 25 venues across the UK and they've been promoted to both clients and to prospects. So while we've invited clients, we've also invited prospects. We've asked the prospects to indicate whether they're interested. Did it work? Yes. We had a successful series, a good turnout across the UK. Each attendee is followed up and we have a high proportion that

turn into prospect meetings. We would probably send around 5,000 mailings for each venue, and hope to get between 25 and 60 attending each seminar, and we would hope that getting on for 50 per cent would want to see us afterwards, and convert one in three. It's very competitive—everyone does seminars these days and the key is providing a good seminar that's not an obvious sales pitch. We're genuinely trying to educate, trying to provide education, and using the seminar as a demonstration of the quality of service we provide rather than as a sales pitch. We provide training as part of our fixed package. It's not cost-effective to do it on clients' premises, so a number of clients are invited to a hotel, a central base, or we train by way of webinar."
Mark Ellis, CEO, Ellis Whittam

"Our seminars are offered as added value for our clients—key clients don't pay. We host discussion forums and networking groups for specialist areas, for example media. We use these events to showcase our specialist lawyers' expertise. We have around 12 guests per event, with a maximum of 25. Networking events like this definitely bring in new business."
Mirella Sikorski, senior marketing executive, Lewis Silkin

Ronnie Fox doesn't host seminars or other events as part of his marketing mix. "I have done a lot of it and I've just not found it cost-effective. Partly the type of client and partly there are a lot of people who get invitations from law firms, go along, and never have the slightest intention of instructing anybody. They're there to learn. We did a very intensive programme of such things at Fox Williams and I asked them pointed questions about the benefits. And the trouble is people invest in these things, emotionally as well as financially, and they don't like 'but it hasn't actually produced anything'."

17.2 Webinars and teleseminars—doing it the 21st century way

One of the key ways Web 2.0 has changed how we communicate is through the webinar and teleseminar. The webinar in particular has revolutionised how we can share knowledge and put low-cost, flexible, high quality training within the reach of businesses of all sizes. If you're not sure what a webinar is, Wikipedia defines it as "a specific type of web conference ... that can be collaborative and include polling and question and answer sessions to allow full participation between the audience and the presenter. Webinars may provide hidden or anonymous participant functionality, enabling participants to be unaware of other participants in the same meeting".

Co-author Daniel Barnett was one of the first UK lawyers to recognise the potential of this format, and CPD Webinars, of which he is a director, has been a leading provider of professional legal training (specialising in employment and PI law) since 2006. Now an increasing number of law firms are hosting webinars as a cost-effective way of delivering legal updates to both existing and potential clients. They also have other advantages:

• Webinars can be used for multiple audiences—first for those taking part in the live event, and thereafter for those watching a streamed or downloaded recording.

• You can use recorded webinars to add very valuable content to your website.

• Webinars are highly measurable. You can see who registers, who participates on the day, who asks what questions, who watches the recordings, and from that refine how you communicate with individual clients and prospects.

As a report from business consultants Warrillow says in a 2008 briefing paper: "Marketing has always been considered 'part art, part science'.

Webinars reflect the new reality of marketing in a Web 2.0 world in that they help bridge the gap between the 'art' of engaging an online audience and the 'science' of analysing and predicting behaviour."

We're not going into the technicalities—we're not techies, etc—and there is a wealth of information about the nuts and bolts of the process available online from the main service providers, including free trials. The quickest way to understand how webinars work is just to sign up for one. Essentially, however, a mix of dedicated software and basic hardware allows you to communicate by streaming via your own PC with a— usually capped—number of viewer PCs. A good provider for basic webinars is **www.gotowebinar.com**, which can put on a decent webinar very cheaply. Undertaking a full video webinar from a TV studio, including hiring of studio, cameras and the streaming technology (as CPD Webinars does) can cost up to £10,000. To this you can add interactive features such as giving participants online text or telephone access. And as you stream, you can record and then offer "on-demand" webinars.

For employment lawyers, there's never a shortage of good material, but as Bob Hanson, president of US lead generation and conversion consultancy Quantum Leap Marketing, says, the content itself "will be the biggest factor in the success of your webinar". It should therefore be "newsworthy, informative, educational, timely and/or valuable to the target audience— ideally all of these". He recommends "narrowcasting" rather than "broadcasting", focusing on a niche, rather than a larger but less clearly defined audience. Going beyond the live event, Hanson identifies some of the key benefits of on-demand webinars as...

- *intimacy*—you're reaching your audience at their own desk

- *availability*—your audience can access an on-demand webinar around the clock and download the file as they would a music recording, for as long as you want to keep it online

- *high value*—once the webinar is hosted and recorded, there are few further costs involved.

Hanson says: "Companies can get tens, hundreds, or even thousands of people to view their webinar recordings with little or no incremental creation or delivery cost. Also, firms can keep unique content such as niche topics or popular outside speakers available to their target audiences without repeating live sessions." One highly effective way of creating good content for both a live and on-demand webinar would be through surveying your clients. Identify their top three concerns and then produce three webinars specifically addressing these. Adams, Brown and Curtis could, for example, easily repackage their half-day redundancy seminar into either one or two webinars.

Add to this being able to send a copy to everyone who registered for the live webinar, or to those who registered but did not take part, promoting it as valuable website content, and using it as a tool for internal training.

How do our profiled firms feel about webinars?

Lewis Silkin has been hosting webinars for about two years. "One thing we started doing that now everyone else is doing is hosting webinars. Our first was in March 2007 and we were the first firm of solicitors to host these regularly. We see ourselves as quite leading edge, unstuffy, and we like to come across as laid-back, real people. The content of our webinars is therefore quite innovative and interactive. It's not just people talking—it's people having discussions, asking questions. We don't have talking heads. We target existing clients, potential clients and colleagues in the profession— basically everyone on our contact list. Webinars offer added value for clients—we ask everyone to pay £80 per organisation, but that's just to cover costs. They are definitely a marketing tool rather than money-maker and we always hold them at lunchtime to make it easier for people to take

part. For prospective clients, it's to show them what we're doing, more of a profile-raiser. We also invite non-competitors from other law firms and our Ius Laboris clients so that they can learn about what we're doing and more about UK law."
Senior marketing executive, Mirella Sikorski, Lewis Silkin

"We run webinars monthly. Some are just for clients; some are opened up to prospects as well, in the same way as the seminars. We've been doing it less than a year, with members of the team delivering the training. It's new technology for us, but it's certainly a good tool."
Mark Ellis, Ellis Whittam

A teleseminar is the webinar's close relation. It can take place entirely over the phone (hence the name) or through a mix of phone and online interaction. What it lacks is the streaming video element of the webinar, but this can make it more flexible, easier and less expensive to set up, and certainly easier to organise at short notice.

Teleseminars can be recorded and made available in the same way as webinars—to participants, people who registered but failed to take part, and prospective clients. They can also be added to your website as valuable content for both visitors and the search engines.

One of the acknowledged masters of the teleseminar is American online marketer Alex Mandossian—we highly recommend you spend some time exploring his websites (there are details in Resources). He says: "Everyone knows the telephone can help increase productivity. Why reach only one person at a time when you can reach hundreds or thousands? I've just improved on the model—going from 'one-on-one' on the telephone to 'one-on-many.' A teleseminar is a phone call via a bridge line where hundreds, even thousands of people, can listen to the training and interact with the instructor."

17.3 A taste of reality

The last training event we're considering is the mock employment tribunal, something you may well not have encountered since you were learning the ropes yourself! The point of the exercise is, of course, to show clients what to expect should they find themselves facing a claim that's going all the way. A significant minority of larger law firms host mock tribunals—often in partnership with professional bodies like the EEF or CIPD—as do legal training providers, and public organisations including Acas. How useful a tool this is for your practice will depend on your client base. Clearly it's of little value where the principal clients are claimants, but greatly more so for firms with a largely commercial clientele.

Our featured firms were divided on the issue of mock tribunals, with none of those who specialise in claimant work—Ashby Cohen, Fox Lawyers and Morris Legal—viewing them as relevant.

"Mock tribunals are a waste of money, brains and time. I think they're brilliant for teaching students but I'm not in the business of teaching students."
Ronnie Fox

The response from businesses dealing largely with respondents was mixed.

Vista managing director *Darren Maw* hosts both seminars and mock employment tribunals for his clients. "We do so with a lot of restraint and we never offer open invitations or advertise. We do run seminars and mock tribunals for people we know, often a mix of clients and non-clients, usually to showcase a piece of work we're doing, some innovative training programme or online material. People leave understanding more about what Vista is doing."

"Mock tribunals are not really part of the mix. It is something we might look at, but there's only so much you can do in the day."
Mark Ellis, Ellis Whittam

17.4 After the event...

There's not much point hosting an event if you don't follow up afterwards, particularly where you're focusing on attracting new clients. So you need to put in place a process for doing this, and seeking feedback is one of the most effective ways. For both live seminars, webinars and teleseminars always ask each participant to complete a questionnaire at the end, and seek their consent for you to use their email address in future. You in particular want to know...

- whether your event was of use to them

- whether they'd be interested in taking part in anything else you organise

- how well it was presented

- how they think you could improve your format

- any other ideas they might have.

Where somebody is downloading your on-demand webinar or teleseminar from your website, make sure they provide their email address as part of the access process and that they give permission for you to contact them in future. If you're going to include a questionnaire, stress strongly that it's optional. This is a very different context from a live event and not everyone will warm to being asked to take part in your market research!

When you have received your feedback you should have a clear idea of who liked what, who thought there was room for improvement where, and which of your speakers performed best. You can use this data to very quickly improve your presentations. You should now also have a longer list of prospective clients you can contact using email to help you build new relationships.

Action

Identify a topic from your specialist area. Then design and organise the following:

- A half-day seminar—consider in particular content, speakers, venue, numbers.

- A one-hour webinar—research the service providers, watch their free trials, explore how the different software options work.

- A one-hour teleseminar—as with webinars, research the service providers, listen to free trials and find out how the software works.

- An invitation strategy—how are you going to attract your clients' attention? Write an email inviting existing clients to your seminar, and a direct mailing inviting prospective clients.

- A follow-up strategy—how are you going to make sure you know what your audience thinks? Devise a questionnaire for those attending your seminar, and an online questionnaire for webinar participants. Write a follow-up email to existing clients who took part in the seminar, and a second email to the prospects who joined your teleseminar.

To move from theory to practice—and if you want to test any of these training tools—ask a sample of your clients to nominate their three main areas of concern, then seek their feedback on offering training in your favoured format. Then do it all for real!

PART THREE
Advertising and other tried and tested tools

18

A new role for advertising in the Web 2.0 era

You may be puzzled about why we're discussing advertising so near the end of this book. It's an essential marketing tool, isn't it? Doesn't everyone do it, in one form or another? No, they don't, and we question whether those who do are still getting as much out as they put in.

Consider this. American writer, journalist and "new rules" pioneer David Meerman Scott tells the story on his blog of the day in December 2008 that the latest Yellow Pages were delivered to his Boston office. "As a wired sort of guy, I don't recall having used the yellow pages in years. Google is my first place when I need to find something, so I put my copy on the table in the office hallway expecting that maybe someone could use an extra." However, the following morning there was a pile of directories on the table. "In my office building are several small law firms, an accountant, an architectural firm, several psychologists, and an executive recruiter. From the looks of the stack of Yellow Books, nobody wanted their copy. What a waste of resources to print and distribute tens of millions of these things that go unused! But worst of all, what a shame for the companies still paying to be listed in a directory that very few people use."

His entry produced a large number of responses, all supporting his observations, with one contributor noting: "The only thing I've used my phone books for in the last ten years is to prop up my monitor because I'm tall and need to have the screen ergonomically correct."

Yes, that's the US and not the UK, but stop and think. When did *you* last use Yellow Pages to look for anything? Don't you usually Google when you need to find a professional service? We're prepared to bet you do. Which begs the more important question—how many of your prospective clients do you suppose start searching for an employment lawyer by flicking through a book? And if you're still advertising in Yellow Pages (or another physical directory), do you know why? Further, if you're advertising in any kind of published media—newspapers, magazines, trade press—can you quantify whether it's achieving anything? British marketing consultant Chris Cardell says: "It sounds obvious, but here's what often happens: people run advertising because they feel they ought to. They're not really sure if it's working but they are hesitant to stop it because it may be one of their main forms of marketing. There seems to be a cultural myth that to run a successful business, you must advertise." Sound familiar? If it does, we strongly urge you to put what you're doing on hold—not necessarily to stop altogether long term, but to first carefully appraise what you're doing before you invest any more time or money in advertising.

18.1   Brand advertising v direct response

Many volumes have been written about advertising: its pros and cons, how to do it effectively, where to do it and so on. But the fact remains that there is an intrinsic weak link in any form of conventional advertising. Your message is only going to be of value to people who need what you're offering at the *exact moment* they read, see or hear your message. If they don't, they may remember you, but unless you are Tesco or Ford, they more likely won't. And herein lies the appeal—and what helps explain the phenomenal success—of online pay per click advertising. As we saw in Chapter 15, your ad is seen at precisely the right time by somebody who has specifically gone looking for exactly what you're offering.

Traditional advertising falls into two main categories:

1.   *Brand advertising*—what you see on TV, in magazines, on

billboards. It's aimed at getting you to remember the advertiser's name. Think Coke, McDonald's, Audi and L'Oreal....

2.   *Direct response advertising*—anything that produces a response you can test and measure.

Brand advertising is premised almost exclusively on what Scott calls "one-way interruption marketing". He says: "You're watching your favourite TV show, so the advertiser's job is to craft a commercial to get you to pay attention, when you'd really rather be doing something else, like quickly grabbing some ice cream before the show resumes. You're reading an interesting article in a magazine, so the ads need to jolt you into reading the ad instead of the article."

And although ad agencies around the world are paid megabucks to get their clients noticed in this way, they are finding it more and more difficult. Scott says: "Forced to compete with new marketing on the web that is centred on interaction, information, education, and choice, advertisers can no longer break through with dumbed-down broadcasts about their wonderful products. We turn it off in our minds, if we notice it at all." And because you can't measure—in terms of widgets sold, services bought—how effective brand advertising is, it's a poor investment all round for any but those (usually global) enterprises able to throw huge resources at it. If you're tempted to go there, we would strongly urge you not to.

Direct response works entirely differently, and if you're going to spend on advertising this is where to do it. Here you are inviting a prospective client to take some action which leads them to your door. And, unsurprisingly, as you have no widgets to sell upfront the best type of direct response advertising for lawyers mirrors what we've urged you to do online—offer something for free to start the relationship.

Our West Midlands practice could, for example, advertise the free half-day redundancy seminar in the local paper, or repackage the key content and advertise that as a free report. The ad could either direct readers to a dedicated phone number (ideally an 0800 number) and/or to a specific landing page on the Adams, Brown and Curtis website. Either way, the means are in place to measure the response and gather the names of some new prospective clients, and the firm has also achieved a little profile-raising. And it'll quickly become obvious whether it was worth the effort.

18.2 The right medium for the message

Let's look now at how you can get the maximum possible from anything you do spend on advertising. As we saw in Chapter 6 when we looked at PR, this is dictated by the type of practice you have, but generally speaking for all but the biggest, multicentre commercial law firms, your principal advertising targets are likely to be...

*   *local media*—primarily print, but possibly radio (TV is generally not cost-effective: producing an ad of high enough quality to do you more good than harm is unlikely to be within most law firms' budgets)

*   *trade press*—advertise in the publications your clients read (and also check out their website ad rates)

*   *directories*—of which Yellow Pages is the best-known in book form, but consider also the online versions which all the evidence suggests are a great deal more likely to be read.

We'll start with print media. Through his website, Cardell offers lots of useful advertising tips, including what he calls the "3 Ps": page, position and price. These apply equally to your local paper and specialist media:

*   *Page*—go for an early or late page in the publication, though this may cost you more. People read from the front or from the back; they never start in the middle. Go for a right-hand page in preference to one on the left.

- *Position*—haggle over where exactly your ad will appear. The best position is top right-hand; the worst is top left-hand. A half-page generally generates 80 per cent of the response of a full page, so think before you commit to any extra expense.

- *Price*—always, always negotiate. Rate cards are not set in stone, and the current economic climate puts you in an excellent position to get an exceptionally good price. The closer you are to the paper's deadline, the better a deal you'll get, and never book a series upfront!

Cardell also warns against listening to any sales spiel, along the lines of "if 100 people buy a copy of the paper, 400 will read it". He says: "Respond by saying, 'that sounds great and I am prepared to advertise forever provided you run the ad as a test first for free. When it brings in the results you say it will, I'll advertise forever'."

There is one further—and very effective—way of using print media, and that's through the use of editorial. There are two routes:

- *Running an ad in the same issue as a story appears.* This is copy written by one of the publication's journalists and is not advertising copy *per se* but a piece highlighting something your firm wants to publicise off the back of a news "hook" (as discussed in Chapter 6). The deal is that the publication gets a good story, and you get a double whammy of publicity. You don't pay for the space the story fills, just for the ad. There's a very fine line between this type of editorial copy and the next variety.

- *Advertorial*—unashamed advertising copy, dressed up to look like a news story or feature. You usually do pay for the space it fills and you either supply the words yourself or delegate the task to one of the publication's editorial team. However, plummeting advertising rates means you may well be able to negotiate a very favourable advertorial deal, and while most readers recognise this type of arrangement for what it is, you do get more space to attract the attention of anyone who is actively looking for your services. Remember to maintain the direct response elements: dedicated phone number, dedicated website landing page for all follow-up contacts.

Direct response advertising on radio is a challenge because it's very difficult to relay contact details and hope that somebody's going to be in the right place at the right time with a pen handy to make a note. However, you can get good deals—particularly now—and radio is a very personal medium that gives you the opportunity to test a little brand advertising. We still though urge you to take the PR route with radio and TV. You'll make much more impact.

As we saw at the beginning of the chapter, traditional directory advertising is becoming less and less of a useful marketing tool, particularly for the type of specialised and professional service you are offering. While a significant number of people might arguably still seek out a plumber or glazier in the Yellow Pages left on their doorstep, how likely is it that they will come looking for you that way when they can much more easily Google any number of variations on "employment law"?

So if you do want a Yellow Pages or Thomson Local presence, we urge you to explore advertising in the online version—which also offers pay per click—rather than going the traditional route. And don't forget paid-for legal directories (for example Delia Venables), and all the free directories out there, which also boost your search engine visibility.

18.3 Essential ad ingredients

Once again, you need to return to the copywriting basics. How much you write is going to depend on how much space you've paid for, but we would urge you to do it yourself rather than delegate to somebody's advertising department. And what you say is going to depend on what it is you're promoting, which could be…

- a general overview of your firm and your services—best for use in contexts with a long shelf-life

- copy focusing on something new or an event—best for a one-off ad or a short series.

We're going to look at the second type, not least because this type of ad is easier to fit into the direct response format and so more likely to bring measurable results. Let's return to the Adams, Brown and Curtis redundancy seminar. Here is a quarter page ad for the local weekly tabloid, drawing heavily from the copy used for the invitation by direct mail.

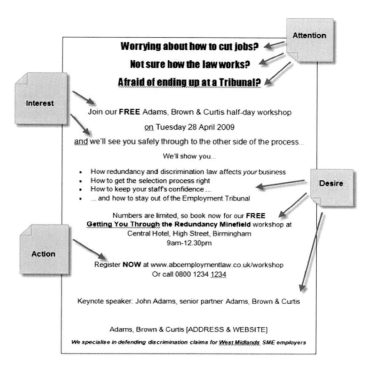

This passes all the following tests:

- W5

- AIDA (as shown)

- the obstacles of indifference.

From this exercise you can, we hope, see that once you've applied the rules to one piece of copy—as we did in the last chapter—it's easy to use that as your source for others on the same subject. This, for example, would also give a news release its basic framework. (To really hone your ad writing, we suggest you explore the websites of the leading American copywriters we discussed in Chapter 5. There are details in Resources.)

Action

Carry out some (admittedly unscientific) research among your colleagues, family and friends. Find out how many have used a delivered local directory in the past 12 months to find a business offering a professional service. Explore the online versions and check out other free and paid-for directories.

Then follow these steps:

1. Contact three local media outlets and ask what advertising deals they can offer you.

2. Pick the one that's most competitive and will give you the best exposure. Don't forget to negotiate over price, page and position.

3. Book a single insertion.

4. Write a direct response ad following the copywriting rules and ensuring you can accurately measure how it works. You must include a dedicated phone number or a reference callers will be asked to give, and a dedicated website landing page.

5. Run the ad and see what happens!

How do our profiled firms use advertising?

"We do advertise, on a very limited basis, for very specific marketing to niche sectors, in the specialist trade press. My problem with advertising is that you can spend a small fortune and there are more effective ways for us to get new clients on board. My view on advertising is that it doesn't make the phone ring. We see advertising as a support for other sales and marketing efforts. With the British Dental Practice Managers Association, while we were advertising we were also working with them closely, running seminars for their members, and doing direct mail to their members as well. We measure success ultimately by the number of businesses we get in that sector."
Mark Ellis, Ellis Whittam

"The question is not 'Why don't you advertise?', it's 'Why would you?' I can't find an answer to the first, so that answers the second. How many employers—and our target market is 1,500 employees—would pick up a leaflet and say: 'Oooh, that might be a good way to servicing our HR strategy. I'll give them a ring.' The reason people do it, in my view, is to create some brand presence."
Darren Maw, Vista

Dean Morris of *Morris Legal* has tried advertising inside a local Citizens Advice Bureau (CAB). "They have a display unit on the wall at the CAB and each speciality gets a slot where they put your name and they have a business card holder. What they don't tell you, which I found out afterwards, is that the CAB office I happened to be put in—having been approached by the advertising company—deal with all their own employment work and don't give anything to anybody. I felt I'd been done! Paid out £1,000 for absolutely nothing." If he had a magic wand, he would raise got-the-boot.com's profile "by a concerted television advertising campaign to get the name into the wider public domain as synonymous with being dismissed". He meanwhile uses online pay per click advertising to drive traffic to his website.

"To me, lawyer advertising is abhorrent. It is done in the US mainly by the lower end of lawyers. Clients are simply not qualified to judge the qualifications of lawyers based on advertising. The fact that the Florida Bar requires lawyers who advertise to put a qualifier in their advertisements is simply politically correct window dressing. The typical client isn't qualified to judge the competence of a lawyer. I think lawyers should be selected more by word of mouth, and not on the basis of advertising, self-promotion and hype. Commercial law firms like Shutts & Bowen do very little advertising. We ourselves do none."
Robin Fawsett, co-chair of employment and labour law, Shutts & Bowen, Orlando

"We use print advertising only rarely. Our buyers are sophisticated and they're not going to make a decision on the basis of an ad."
Mirella Sikorski, senior marketing executive, Lewis Silkin

Alain Cohen of *Ashby Cohen* has used newspaper and billboard advertising in the past.

"If I started billboard advertising again, it probably would be effective for a short time. It's relatively expensive, but it could be done."

19

The marketing workhorses— direct mail and telemarketing

Do direct mail and telemarketing still have a role, given everything we've said about the paradigm shift away from traditional approaches to marketing? Yes, in certain circumstances, and especially for certain business models. Indeed, as we shall see, for featured firm Ellis Whittam telemarketing is responsible for over half of all new custom and CEO Mark Ellis also considers direct mail a cornerstone marketing tool.

As with all methods, you need to identify exactly what you want to achieve before deciding whether either of these approaches is right for you.

19.1 It's not junk mail if you're in the right place at the right time

How many days do you *not* receive unsolicited mail? Unless you've registered with the Mailing Preference Service (**www.mpsonline.org.uk**), at least one piece will pop through your office or home letterbox—and very probably both—on most days.

Park any personal response to dismiss it as junk and, like the rest of us, put almost all of it straight in the recycling bin. There are good reasons why such an array of organisations—including more or less every type of business and charity—use direct mail to reach both existing and prospective customers. And that's because although we do indeed put almost all of it in the bin, we nonetheless also open and read some of it, and follow through, claiming our free gift, attending the free event, or pledging our charitable donation. Top American copywriters like John Carlton and Clayton Makepeace continue to spend a high proportion of their time producing direct mail (for more about them see the Resources for Chapter 5). Would they do this if it didn't work—for their clients and in turn for them?

There are two distinct direct mail audiences: your existing clients and your prospects.

For the first, the principal uses are to...

• send updates and newsletters (the printed equivalent of your email versions)

• send invitations to events (as we explored in Chapter 17).

For the second audience, your prospects, the strategy is to use the same permission marketing tactics you do online to start building a relationship, by offering something in return for consent to contact them again. The most obvious and most used for lawyers are...

• inviting recipients to a free event

• offering a free initial consultation.

For both audiences, these are the features that make direct mail so powerful:

• You can be very precise about who you target.

• It's the easiest way to get into a person's office or home.

• You can send a wide mix of materials—brochures, leaflets,

postcards, CDs and DVDs (though these are less appealing now that Web 2.0 allows such easy online access to video), and gifts (pens and key rings are, as you'll have noticed, popular).

- It's statistically predictable. If 1,000 mailings bring 10 responses, then 5,000 mailings will bring 50 responses.

- Above all, it's so easy to test—you can gauge response by sending out a few hundred mailings, or by sending out two versions of the same message at the same time to see which performs better.

On the downside, direct mail cannot be done on the cheap or in a hurry: do either and you risk wasting money and losing credibility. By all means write your own copy (we'd certainly encourage you to, and at the very least to split-test your own words against those of a professional), but don't skimp on design. When in doubt, just put yourself in the recipient's shoes. Would you bother to look twice at something thrown together on your office PC using ClipArt? No, and neither would your clients or prospects.

These are other points of good practice:

- Personalise your message. This usually increases response rates, and including a personalised letter increases them even more.

- Make your offer instantly compelling—include a response deadline for your offer.

- Include testimonials.

- Ensure that everything you send out points recipients towards your website—and specifically towards dedicated landing pages—and that any email addresses and phone numbers you use are directly linked to that mailing, so that you can very accurately measure traffic.

- Write long copy, but write it well. Veteran UK copywriter and direct sales marketer Drayton Bird says: "Because long copy almost always outpulls short, bad writers often write far too much. All you have to do is give *every* sensible reason why your prospects would want to act and overcome *every* reasonable objection to acting. Never use a single word more than required."

- Follow up with a phone call—you can greatly increase your response rate.

There are no cast-iron rates for conversions. As UK marketing consultant Chris Cardell says, if you're selling yachts, a 1 per cent response on 1,000 mailings is something to celebrate; if you're selling ballpoint pens it definitely isn't. "If you send out 2,000 letters and get 20 responses, you can predict with some certainty that if you send out 4,000 letters to the same group, you will get something in the region of 40 responses. Equally, if you send out 2,000 letters, get one response and lose money on the mailing, it is highly unlikely that if you send out 4,000 letters you will have a profitable mailing. When it's done well, direct mail can make your profits soar. When it's done badly, it can eat up your marketing budget instantly."

His advice? Always—as we've said above—test your mailing on a small scale first: "It needs to be small enough to be an amount of money you can afford to lose if it doesn't work out, but large enough to be able to hopefully generate at least seven or eight responses. For a typical business, that's going to be somewhere between 500 and 2,500."

19.1.1 What's in a name?

If you're considering using direct mail to cold call prospective clients, you need names—lots of names. Where you find them is going to depend on your type of practice and who your ideal client is (the one you identified in Chapter 4). You can look for them yourself, of course, especially if your target is narrow or local, or you can pay for access to somebody else's list.

There are numerous specialists whose business it is to maintain and sell or rent lists—and very finely-tuned lists.

To return to our West Midlands niche practice, they could for example pinpoint a list comprising SMEs that...

- employ between 150 and 5,000 employees

- are located within a 50-mile radius of either of their offices

- have been in business for less than five years.

Google "direct mail list" and you'll get the names of all the major UK B2B and B2C list providers, a significant proportion of which can also run your entire direct mail campaign.

Action

Direct mail can be as simple or as complex as you make it. If you want to go down this route, first thoroughly research all the elements we've outlined here. Then draw up a theoretical campaign focusing on an event for your existing clients, looking in detail at how you'd do it, what materials you'd use, who would write the copy, what they'd say, and how much you estimate it would cost.

That done, you can decide whether to proceed, testing the direct mail water with your existing clients before taking the cold calling route.

Here's a selection of views about direct mail from some of our profiled firms.

Tom Walker occasionally used direct mail while with Colemans-ctts. "When we were doing a seminar, we'd use it to invite everyone and send our brochure out with it."

"We do quite a lot of direct mail. We use it not to elicit a direct response to use our service but for example to build brand awareness by providing information, updates and by inviting people to seminars, webinars, etc. We send to both existing and prospective clients. You've no second chance to get your message right with direct mail—if you get it just a little bit wrong, you're wasting your money. But we repeatedly find direct mail more effective than email marketing—so many people now are getting junk email that's very easy and quick to delete, whereas if you send out a good direct mail exercise, it doesn't look like a direct mail exercise. I think there's more chance the target will take ten seconds to read it and make a decision on it."
Mark Ellis, Ellis Whittam

"We use direct mail occasionally. As an example, we used it to promote a retailing workshop. We wanted to expand our retailer contact list so we did a cold mailing inviting prospects to a free workshop. Our prospects were High Street retailers and we got a 25 per cent response, which is very good. We chose the right topic—immigration law—and were very focused on what retailers would want to find out. We wrote the direct mail letter in-house and compiled our own list, using an HR directory to phone and check names. We also followed up with phone calls to everyone on the mailing list."
Mirella Sikorski, senior marketing executive, Lewis Silkin

Between 1965 and 2001, the names and addresses of both parties were routinely published in the Register of Employment Tribunal Applications held at Bury St Edmunds, Suffolk. The practice was stopped in 2004 in response to government consultation, but in late 2008 the Information Commissioner's Office ordered BERR to re-open the register and publish respondent names after an ET1 has been lodged. This leaves the way clear for law firms to once again contact both claimants and respondents ahead of hearings.

> *Alain Cohen of Ashby Cohen* did this pre-2004. "We had people down there who would harvest names and we would send out about 200 letters a week, mainly to claimants, and pick up business from there. Out of 200 letters, 20 would phone, and we would get one out of that. They stopped it, but they're about to reintroduce it for the employers. Interestingly enough, occasionally we used to stop writing to the claimants and write just to the employers. So, for example, I'd have nine months just doing employees and we would get the response rate I've already indicated, and then I'd say, 'Right, we'll go for the employers'. For the next month, or six weeks, we'd go for the employers. Same number of letters, no response. It's a lot harder to get the employers. A lot already have representation, and as an employer you're used to a lot of junk mail."

> Before launching got-the-boot.com, *Dean Morris, of Morris Legal*, also used to monitor the list. "We had somebody in Bury St Edmunds go through it daily, and then target them. A complete waste of time. I think I had probably two clients out of 12 months' work. It was a ridiculous market—if we were doing it, so was everybody else. You could imagine that people would get the first few come through, then the following 20 would just go straight in the bin. We're not going that route again—it's going to be no different, except that there will be more people targeting the information."

19.2 Lifting the phone—the hardest call?

"We do lots of telemarketing. We do it in-house. Does it work? Yes, it does. It's a numbers game and it's increasingly difficult and it's a very hard job to do. It does work and our business development executives are successful every week getting new appointments for our business managers. A very high proportion of our new business comes through telemarketing—in excess of 50 per cent."
Mark Ellis, Ellis Whittam

As Drayton Bird says: "This medium arouses such strong feelings that in some countries unsolicited telephone calls have been banned." But it is, he says, "extraordinarily potent", adding: "It has the value of immediacy, with all that that implies in terms of reading results fast. It is *interactive*: apart from face to face selling, it's the only medium where objections can be stated—and overcome."

As we can see, for Ellis Whittam telemarketing is indeed "extraordinarily potent", accounting for more than 50 per cent of new business. But that's because it's an intrinsic part of CEO Mark Ellis's business model, and what works for him may well not work for you. So once again we're back to you first defining what you want to achieve. As with direct mail, telemarketing (also known in the UK as telesales) can be used for both existing and prospective clients, though it is with the latter that we have most of our more negative associations (think Tenerife timeshares, kitchen makeovers and double glazing).

Breaking this down, for your current clients you can use the phone without any hard selling at all to...

- tell them about anything that's happening—new services, events, team changes

- make them a special offer—a best practice audit, for example

- just check in—find out what's worrying them and explore how you can help.

This is all telemarketing, and you may already be doing it—it's just that you have not labelled it that way. If you want to finesse your approach, Chris Cardell suggests the following:

- Always ask for permission to talk before saying anything.

- Ask lots of questions.

- Match their speaking pace—don't gabble or talk too slowly.

- Don't use a script—make up a bullet point list.

- Practise before making the call, just as you did with your elevator pitch!

Cold calling is, by definition, harder and this is why businesses either employ their own dedicated telesales team—like Ellis Whittam—or outsource to specialist providers. The main benefits of outsourcing to a good firm are that it's relatively hassle-free, doesn't tie up your own team, and becomes particularly cost-effective if you have a good list and something strong to offer. On the downside, it will cost you significantly more than running a telemarketing campaign in-house and you need to be very choosy about your provider. Whichever route you take, your overarching aim here is to start a relationship and specifically to arrange an initial meeting. To help you get there, Cardell suggests offering to…

- email something immediately—a white paper, or an e-book

- put something in the post—a slower burn than email, but nine out of ten people are likely to say "yes" if what you're offering is intrinsically interesting.

As with direct mail, aim to tie in telemarketing with everything else you're doing. For example, follow up by email and include a link to a dedicated landing page offering more information on the subject of the call. And telemarketing can complete the circle you begin with direct mail if you make a follow-up call.

Note that, like email communications, telemarketing is covered by the Privacy and Electronic Communications (EC Directive) Regulations 2003.

Action

Follow the process you used for direct mail, putting together a telemarketing campaign focused on an offer you could make. Explore the costs and logistics of running it in-house versus outsourcing.

Google "telemarketing" and you will find a large number of companies providing basic and more sophisticated services.

20

Tendering for success—joining the beauty parade

Tendering for business through the beauty parade process can lead to lucrative and rewarding work. Or it can lead to nothing. And either way the process can be time-consuming, nerve-wracking and frustrating. We're not going to offer a blueprint for success because there isn't one and we can't. So much depends on your size and type of practice, on what you're tendering for, and the expectations of the client.

One man who has made it his business to study tendering in forensic detail is Peter Rush, a consultant, journalist and a former advisor to Pannone LLP. He trades—and writes for *Legal Marketing*—as The Pitch Doctor. Tongue in cheek, he says the tendering process is identified in four ways:

1. It is apparently competitive, either by public advertisement or private invitation, against a deadline.

2. A small group of people will normally choose the winner, and this will usually be somebody they already know, have done business with "or have come to like, want or need during the tender process".

3. The tender document will be written "in the most turgid and inscrutable English and its structure will be labyrinthine". Unfortunately you will need to deconstruct it and find out what it means.

4. Taking part in the process will cost you thousands of pounds.

Rush cautions that the decision-makers do what we all do in such situations—choose people like ourselves. Accordingly, "we need to select tender targets that match the people and products we have and targets who we need, want or would love to do business with". And there are, he says, four proven tactics underpinning a good tendering pitch:

1. Truthfulness—what "separates the chancers from the real deal. We are hard-wired to detect the false note, the over-reaching claim, so use the truth".

2. Structure. "In the opening moments, I need to know where you are taking me, why you are doing things this way, and how I will benefit from this approach."

3. Language. Understand the jargon of your would-be client and become familiar "with the special words that show you really are connected to my culture and goals". Use plain English, free of clichés and embellishments.

4. Stand out from the opposition, and seek out business only "in markets you want to be in with people you want to be with. Your people and their motivation and achievements are what sets you apart, so focus on them".

Rush says that in the current economic climate, "qualifying your opportunities becomes even more important and keeping your pitch-to-win rate high is essential". All potential clients are examining budgets. "Services need to be pitched with this new reality in mind. It is actually good for business development as we should really be able to show how we make a difference to the messages we deliver on pitches and in tenders. I like playing the 'in a nutshell' game where you use one sentence to complete a statement: 'You should choose us because...', for example. Try it and then draft four 'nutshells', choosing one of these to be your 'clincher'. Then build your pitch around that by evidencing why those statements are true."

How you present your message is of course crucial. Rush cautions that PowerPoint is becoming something of a weapon of torture. We agree. You don't need an array of slides, each carrying so many bullet-pointed words the font size has been shrunk down to nothing, and you definitely don't need to read out those words, because your audience is already well ahead of you and either bored or irritated, or both. Nor do you need to use cartoons, funny noises, or clever entrance and exit effects. Rush recommends five slides:

- **Slide one**—your branding "with snappy title and the cast beautifully fonted".

- **Slide two**—concept, context and structure: "why you are doing it this way, your credibility and competence in spades, a few words and a stunning image".

- **Slide three**—"what success looks like", plus a picture or a quote to underwrite it.

- **Slide four**—the money shot—the slide you linger on with "all your key points in 12 words or fewer", plus a stylish visual.

- **Slide five**—the financial detail.

And everything else that was on the 40-plus slide set? Put it in a handout. "If you want your audience to get to your intended destination, show them pictures. Let the words come out of your mouth, not the screen."

What do our profiled firms think of the beauty parade process?

"Beauty parades don't play a big role, but an increasingly important role. And we do see them playing a more

significant part as we seek to win bigger business. We recently did one for a business with about 60 outlets around the country and 1,600 employees. We ended up competing with three others and won that one. So it seems to be a way to win business at the slightly higher end of the marketplace, perhaps. It's always going to be a reasonably small percentage of our income because of the set-up with our business management team. Less than 5 per cent in numbers but 10 per cent to15 per cent in value."
Mark Ellis, Ellis Whittam

"We rarely take part in beauty parades. We're not often asked, and we're too easily beaten on price by provincial firms."
Ronnie Fox, Fox Lawyers

"We take part in as many beauty parades as possible. We begin with desk research on the client, and involve our library. We ask colleagues for any inside information they may have, and look at any international connections through Ius Laboris. We aim to gather in as much information as possible from all angles with a specific planning team headed by a lead partner. We will focus on what the client is looking for and our selling points. We succeed with about 90 per cent of the pitches we make, and this is definitely to do with how we present, which is creative and different but I'm not going to say exactly how!"
Mirella Sikorski, senior marketing executive, Lewis Silkin

"In the US it's called a request for proposals (RFP). Those are typically done by clients that don't understand that you get what you pay for. Choosing a lawyer to do what I do is a little bit like choosing a surgeon. If you were going to have your heart operated on you would not send it out to the

lowest bidder. The same thing is true of good legal services. You have to get a surgeon or an attorney that you trust, that you trust not to over-charge you, that you trust not to spend more time than required on a matter. A sophisticated client knows that somebody like me can answer many questions in ten minutes that would take somebody else all day to research, and then they wouldn't really have a feel for the area. There are lawyers, and then there are lawyers. All too often, corporations and public entities that issue requests for proposals simply don't understand that they're going to get the low end. We don't typically respond to them unless we think there's a pretty good chance we're going to get it and can make a reasonable profit doing it. There's nothing wrong, whether you're an American corporation, a law firm or a doctor, with making a reasonable profit: that's what built this country. Some years ago, Palm Beach County issued a RFP for labour law services and their criteria were they wanted to pay $100 an hour for first-year associate, $110 for second-year associate, $120 for third-year associate, $175 for partner—that's just totally unrealistic. A sophisticated client hires the right person and then the right person assigns the work to the right people without over-assigning and over-billing the file. Very seldom, if ever, do I participate in an RFP, and the firm doesn't do much of it either."
Robin Fawsett, Shutts & Bowen, Orlando

"We do tender for work—not usually for core work but for training work. We've rejected most of the invitations to tender for core work because we think they're asking the wrong questions—for us, not for them in the sense that they already have a very clearly defined structure."
Darren Maw, Vista

21

Drawing the threads together— and testing them to destruction

You now have a thorough overview of the many and varied means at your disposal to market a 21st century UK law firm. Only five years ago some of the ideas we've been exploring did not even exist—Twitter, for example—and we can be confident that the Web 2.0 revolution is far from over. Who knows how we'll all be marketing another five years down the line?

Throughout the book, we have stressed that…

- what works for one business may not work for another, as borne out by the very different experiences and marketing approaches of our featured firms

- before you know what will work for you, you have to do a lot of testing …

- … and then you have to do a whole lot more.

And what we are very definitely not urging you to do is try everything at once, because you can't. As American legal marketer Patrick McEvoy points out on his Rainmaker Best Practices site, you could find yourself trying to juggle nearly a hundred different strategies, a route that will lead to both failure and lunacy.

He has produced a stunning graphic on the topic:

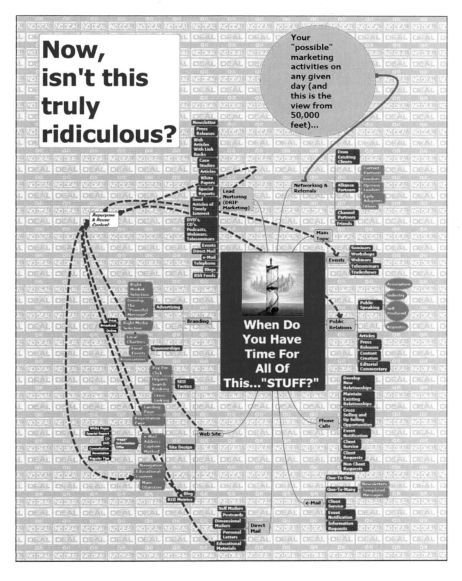

(You can download the printable PDF from his website. There are details in Resources.)

So our suggestion is that you complete all the **Action** exercises in the book.

This will give you a clear understanding of what's involved in each of the topics we've covered, and enable you to identify the advantages and disadvantages when applied to your own business.

Then, and before you go any further, make sure that everyone on your team is up to speed with the principles and themes we have discussed throughout the book:

- Know who your target client is.

- Know what your USP is.

- Understand the principles of:
  - Here's who I am.
  - Here's what I've got.
  - Here's what it'll do for you.
  - Here's what I want you to do next.

- Understand the importance of *benefits* against *features*.

- Understand and use all the copywriting and PR rules:
  - AIDA.
  - Overcoming the three obstacles of indifference:
    - Who cares?
    - So what?
    - What's in it for me?
  - W5 (Who?, What?, When?, Where?, Why?).
  - Plain English, with no jargon or clichés.

We cannot stress too strongly that the most ingenious marketing plan on the planet will fail if you don't accurately identify who you are and who it is you are addressing, and you don't speak to them using language that carries style, grace, intelligence, good humour and—above all—empathy. Next you need to consider which of the traditional marketing tools (some of which you are no doubt already using, and indeed using successfully), and which of the newer ideas, are going to fit best into your overall strategy. Let's just sum up what you've been exploring by working through this book:

- Working with existing clients to bring in new work, feedback, referrals and testimonials.

- Using the "old" and "new" PR rules to build relationships with the media, and direct with prospective clients.

- Networking face-to-face and online to find people you might otherwise never meet.

- Exploring Web 2.0 technology to give width and breadth to your online presence.

- Exploiting quality content and design to make your website a magnet for visitors and search engines.

- Using permission marketing to reach prospective clients.

- Fitting advertising into the jigsaw.

- Considering how direct mail and telemarketing could work for you.

- Making the tendering process more productive.

We can't make the mix for you because it's your business not ours, but we would stress the importance of ensuring that what you're already using is actually working before moving onto anything new. And if it isn't working, is that because you can now see that it's intrinsically wrong for your business model or because you need to rethink how you're doing it? Either way, make your existing strategies your priority and subject them to thorough scrutiny. Get testing. Anything that involves copywriting is particularly easy to measure—just try two versions and see which performs better. The trick then is to write more copy that outperforms the winner, and so on. (This incidentally is how the copywriting megastars make their money—by writing copy that can only rarely be outstripped.) In particular, test the copy you use for emailing and direct mail, for any advertising you do (pay per click ads are perfect candidates), and on your website.

Look at how you get feedback, referrals and testimonials. How could you streamline your system? Are there techniques you could add and test against those already in place? If you're advertising, have you got any way of measuring the response rate? If you don't, what technique appeals most for making that possible? With few exceptions, everything we have covered has scope for testing and measuring, and you must build this into the structure of every marketing move you make. You'll find sources of detailed information about the specifics in the relevant Resources sections.

Good luck—and have fun.